A
Citizen's Guide
to the
Social
Sciences

A
Citizen's Guide
to the
Social
Sciences

Bernard Mausner

Nelson-Hall nh Chicago

Library of Congress Cataloging in Publication Data

Mausner, Bernard, 1920—
   A citizen's guide to the social sciences.

   Bibliography: p.
   Includes index.
   1. Social sciences. I. Title.
   H51.M38   300   78-16626
   ISBN 0-88229-401-6 (cloth)
   ISBN 0-88229-650-7 (paper)

Manufactured in the United States of America

10   9   8   7   6   5   4   3   2   1

Dedicated to the
memory of
Fanny K. Singer

Contents

Preface

As the third century of the American experiment in democracy begins, the world presents a picture of bewildering complexity. This book is designed to help introduce the reader to one possible source of understanding that might aid in making sense of that complexity: the organized body of knowledge and theory called the social sciences. It is a cliché to say that the human race has made enormous progress in controlling nature but very little in understanding itself. This cliché is, nevertheless, true. We do have a heritage of ideas about the nature of man from philosophers, poets, and prophets. But the morass into which the race is sinking hardly argues for the usefulness of this traditional wisdom. In the past hundred and fifty years, attempts have been made to apply the scientific method to the study of man; the success of the natural sciences in conquering nature has provided encouragement for this enterprise. The social sciences are far from universally welcomed; many traditionalists find the scientific approach to man threatening to fundamental values. But even if one is prepared to be hostile, the social sciences should be understood and their usefulness as a guide to social action evaluated. I hope that this book will be a first step in this process.

This book is a primer. It is not intended as a substitute for systematic treatment of each of the fields within the social sciences. It should, however, give the reader a sense for the fundamental ideas that join these fields and the possible application of these ideas in the real world. Like the New England Horn Book, a primer designed to teach children to read so that they could then read the Bible, this book is written to encourage further exploration into the social sciences.

The book has three major aspects. One is a description of some of the studies, experiments, and surveys on which social scientists base their ideas. A second is a presentation of these ideas formulated as concepts or theories. The third is application to specific problems of the kind the reader or his community might face.

Two activities would be useful to supplement the book. The first is additional reading. One source would be some of the paperbacks suggested in the section called "On Your Own" at the end of each chapter. I have tried to select books that are usually available in paperback-book stores and that are addressed to the general public. I would also urge the reader to form the habit of reading a really good newspaper regularly and analytically. The columns of the *New York Times,* the *Washington Post,* and the *St. Louis Post-Dispatch* contain much raw material for analysis based on the concepts presented in this book. One final note on reading: several national publications— the *Sunday Times Magazine, Time, Scientific American,* and *Harper's,* among others—frequently publish articles on current developments in the social sciences. In addition, there are two magazines that deal almost exclusively with these developments. One, fairly widely circulated, is *Psychology Today.* The other, sociological in orientation and a bit harder to find, is *Transaction: Social Science and Modern Society.*

The second supplementary activity, also included in the sections headed "On Your Own," consists of exercises that I hope will be thought-provoking. These exercises might enable a reader to work through the ideas presented in the previous chapter and, more importantly, provide a bridge between the content of the social sciences and the reader's own experiences.

The text does not include the normal scholarly apparatus of footnotes and specific references. However, I do recognize the responsibility of making my sources available and so have appended to each chapter a list of the relevant materials from the professional literature of the social sciences. It should be fairly easy to identify the particular source for any discussion in the body of the chapter.

About the Book

It is an act of chutzpah for one person to attempt a book covering all the social sciences. The obvious solution to the problem of writing such a book is to assemble a committee of experts in each of the four or five disciplines to be included. The drawbacks of such a procedure are obvious. The experts would have to spend years learning to talk to one another. Or else they would turn out a set of disconnected pieces under one cover, no one section of which would satisfy anyone but the writer. I have taken the bold tack of disregarding my lack of credentials in every field but my own. And this book is the result.

There is no possibility that a short book like this could do justice to all of the disciplines. Therefore I make no pretense at completeness. I have chosen the areas that seem to me to have the greatest promise for the fulfillment of two goals. The first is to present readers with as unified a view of social science as I can achieve, one that emphasizes continuities among the disciplines rather than the unique character of each. The second goal is to generate a sense of connection between the reader's own life and the body of knowledge called social science. This means that lively, central areas in many of the fields have had to be omitted or treated sketchily. I am sure that many of the omissions will bother experts in each of the disciplines.

The book begins with general method, then focuses on individuals, moves to analysis of interaction and group process, and lastly discusses the community as a whole. The last section is intended both to give readers a sense for differences among different kinds of communities and to lead them to an application of social science to their lives as citizens.

In general, I have made no effort to be up-do-date. Where a twenty-year-old study or theoretical formulation seemed appropriate, I did not hesitate to use it in preference to more recent material. I hope that the book is not dated, in the sense that it dwells on issues that are no longer lively. But I also hope that it presents the general reader with a view of modern social science that is based on data and concepts that have withstood the test of time. Lastly, rather than cite many studies and theoretical systems, I have tried to give enough detail about each piece of work presented so that the reader can really develop a sense of familiarity with its approach.

It would be hard to list all of the people whose help I must acknowledge. First would come the teachers I had as an undergraduate and a graduate student many years ago, who tried to give me a feeling for man in society. They include Otto Klineberg, Gardner Murphy, Ralph Linton, Abram Kardiner, and Louis Hacker. I was exposed to the ecological point of view during my brief stay at the Graduate School of Public Health in the University of Pittsburgh, especially when I participated in a most exciting pedagogical venture, the course in Man and Environment. My interactions with colleagues in other disciplines there, notably Ted Hatch, Moshe Shapiro, David Landy, Peter New, Robert Olsen, Sidney Cobb, taught me to think in a way that I hope is reflected in this book. Lastly, my wife, Judith S. Mausner, has kept her discipline of epidemiology before me constantly; the emphasis on the interrelation of biological, social, and physical environment with man as actor required by the epidemiological model has been a vital intellectual influence. I am grateful to the Department of Social Psychology at the London School of Economics and to its head, Professor Hilda Himmelweit, for giving me hospitality during a wonderful sunny summer, in 1971. It was in that friendly environment that the book began to take shape.

Many colleagues at Beaver College and elsewhere have read portions of the manuscript and given me the benefit of their comments. Without their help, I would not have dared carry out this project. Samuel Cameron read Chapters 1, 2, and 4. Edgar Schuster reacted to Chapters 1 and 2, both as a scholar in American Literature and as a writer. William Carr lent his expertise in ethology to Chapter 3. Bette E. Landman evaluated Chapters 5 and 6 from the viewpoint of a cultural anthropologist. A. John Berrigan reacted to Chapters 9 and 10 as a political scientist. Judith Matasar read the first eight chapters. The final section is based largely on the work of an Honors Colloquium at Beaver College which focused on the design of a good society.

I should like to acknowledge the assistance of the Center for the Study of Federalism in the College of Liberal Arts of Temple University, its director, Dr. Daniel Elazar, and Ms. Bernadette Stevens, in making available files of material on the history of the interstate highway system. Mr. David Tornquist and Dr. Eirik G. Furubotn were helpful in suggesting sources on contemporary Yugoslavia.

Pat Read, editor of the *Beaver News*, read Chapter 7 and told me that it really could have happened that way. Beth Marasco, a former student at Beaver, read the entire manuscript and helped me to achieve greater lucidity by combing out some fancy language. As typist, Sandy Leotta struggled with my undecipherable handwriting.

Sarah Mausner's sense of style and training in scholarship as well as her critical intelligence were invaluable aids; she read and criticized the entire book in its last draft. Judith Mausner also examined the final draft with a merciless eye for ambiguity and cliché. Ms. Carol Gorski, who edited the book, brought to her work remarkable care and an enormous fund of knowledge. I am grateful for the polish her work provided.

I hope you enjoy reading this book as much as I enjoyed writing it. The release it gave me from the confines of my own discipline was a source of fun as well as intellectual stimulation.

1

The Nature of Social Science

Most of us are intensely curious about why people do the things they do. We try to unravel the motives of our friends, our families; often enough our own behavior needs explanation. The daily papers are filled with mysteries, with unexplained violence in the streets and between countries, with odd acts by obscure citizens and great leaders.

Some of the things that people do can be understood without much difficulty. They sleep when they are tired, eat when they are hungry, seem to enjoy beautiful things and good company. But there are so many paradoxes. Why do fathers and sons so rarely understand each other? Why do great men cheat, lie, compete for petty advantage? Why is it that the same person can be gentle and helpful at one time, cruel and destructive at another?

People turn to many sources for solutions to these puzzles. For some, the solutions come from the great religious systems. Religion often derives motives from warring spirits of good and evil. It is the devil who is responsible for human wickedness, God who leads us to doing good. For others, the answers may be found in the writings of humanists and philosophers. For yet others, the answers may be found in literature. As they read the works of Plato or Shakespeare, they find ideas that help them to understand the human condition, to predict and perhaps even control human behavior.

The social sciences represent yet another attempt to solve the puzzles inherent in the situation of man in society. This book is an attempt to present some of the basic ideas of the social sciences and the sources of these ideas. At no point do I want to pretend that the social sciences offer wisdom superior to that of so-called humanistic thinking found in literature, religion, philosophy, or the visual and musical arts. Let us say that there are many roads to human understanding, and the social scientist has chosen one of these roads.

In order to explore the differences between the humanistic and the scientific approach to the human condition, it might be worthwhile to examine a particular work of art, discuss the ideas about the nature of man presented by that work, and contrast these ideas with the results that would be obtained from tackling similar problems within the framework of the social sciences. I have chosen a great play by Eugene O'Neill, *Mourning Becomes Electra,* for this comparison. The play is a good one for this purpose because it not only provides an extremely vivid representation of a story set in a particular time and place, but also represents a retelling of an ancient legend in modern terms. It was intended to be a broad reflection on humanity and so gives a clear illustration of the scope of ideas and generalizations about human behavior that can be derived from the thoughts of a great writer.

O'Neill set his play in a small town in New England at the close of the Civil War. The action takes place in the mansion of the Mannon family, a great house of the kind you may still see in old sections of New England towns. It has broad lawns and gardens, a fine porch with Greek pillars. The rooms in the interior are large, hung with ancestral portraits, dark and richly furnished.

As the play opens, Christine Mannon and her daughter Lavinia are awaiting the return of Christine's husband, General Mannon, and her son Orin from the Civil War. The audience learns from conversation among some town people that the Mannons are a wealthy family of ship owners who have lived in the town and dominated it for several hundred years. General Mannon is not only a military leader, he has also been mayor of the town and the owner of its main industry. It becomes obvious that Christine is deeply disaffected, hates her husband, and has betrayed him with a sea captain, Captain Brant, a relative of the Mannons. Brant is the son of General Mannon's uncle and a beautiful French-Canadian maid. Many years before, Captain Brant's father had seduced the maid, then married her. But General

Mannon's father, who had himself been attracted toward the exotic maid, had expelled the couple from the household.

Lavinia accuses her mother of adultery with Brant and threatens to inform her father unless the adulterous relationship is broken. It is clear from much of this discussion that Lavinia is deeply attached to her father and hates her mother with intensity. It is also made apparent that Orin, her brother, is a dependent young man, very much attached to his mother, who went off to war reluctantly under pressure from his sister and father.

Captain Brant appears and tries to mask his affair with Christine by seeming to pay court to Lavinia. She is clearly both attracted and repelled by him. Much is made of the fact that Captain Brant looks like a Mannon and may remind Lavinia of her father. When Christine and Captain Brant meet alone, they plot to kill General Mannon.

General Mannon returns home. He has been touched by his experience of death in the war. He describes himself as having been unhappy because he felt rejected by his wife. He had turned to public affairs and to business *because* he felt unloved; he now wants to reestablish a loving relation with his wife. She is still repelled by him. Her reactions of disgust are never completely explained, although it is suggested they arise from revulsion over the physical aspects of sex during the first weeks of their marriage.

After a night of joyless lovemaking, General Mannon has an attack of angina; he has had warnings of heart disease. Christine gives her husband poison instead of medicine. Lavinia is attracted into the room by her father's cries and hears him denounce her mother before he dies. She discovers the poison.

Orin, who has been wounded in the war, now returns. We watch him revert to the intensely dependent relation he had with his mother. But when Lavinia informs him of Christine's liaison with Captain Brant, he explodes with fury. Orin and Lavinia trick their mother into going to the captain's ship. They overhear Christine confess to Brant that she has murdered their father. After she leaves, Lavinia and Orin murder Captain Brant. Orin tells about a fantasy he had during the war: he imagined, as he killed one man after another, that he was killing himself and his father. And then he sees the resemblance between Captain Brant and his father. It is almost as if he had actually killed his father.

When Christine is informed of Captain Brant's death, she commits suicide. Orin and Lavinia go for a long voyage to the South Seas and to China. Captain Brant had told both Lavinia and Christine about the joyous life of the natives in the South Seas. He had described the islands as a kind of paradise in which man can live free of a sense of guilt and enjoy the pleasures of love. When Orin and Lavinia return from their voyage, they are both transformed. Lavinia, who had been sexless and sticklike, now has become seductive—almost as if she had taken on her mother's character. She had worn black; now she wears bright colors. Orin, on the other hand, is no longer an engaging and impulsive boy. Instead, he is still and brooding, almost as if he had become his father. Orin feels haunted by the murder of Captain Brant and by the responsibility for his mother's suicide. He first tries to confess these deeds to two childhood friends, a brother and sister to whom Orin and Lavinia had been engaged. Confession does not dispel Orin's self-hatred. Consumed by his need for expiation of guilt, he commits suicide. As the play ends, Lavinia rejects life and goes into the great house. She closes the shutters behind her and prepares to live out her days in the dark, in perpetual confrontation with the sin and guilt of her parents' deaths.

A Humanistic Analysis

The play is about a single family, but it is also about all of mankind. O'Neill's message is that all of us live in a state of sin and consequent guilt. The sin and guilt arise from the relationship between father and daughter, mother and son. But the Mannons are cursed with a guilt that is greater than usual. They suffer from a strange combination of greed, lust, and pride of position in society. These forces lead to an inescapable descent into self-destruction. The sense of sin and guilt is contrasted with the free life of the South Sea islanders. These islands are referred to constantly in the play as a paradise of guiltless hedonism. But this is not only an external paradise. The islands also stand for that part of all of us that possesses the potential of living for love without the constraints of traditional morality. It is only because she has this potential within her that Lavinia could blossom as she does in her year in the islands. In that sense, the experience of life in the islands sharpens the internal conflicts that make life for the Mannons in Puritan New England so much of a hell.

O'Neill's work parallels the ancient Greek plays from which he drew the story. As you may have recognized, the story of the Mannons is based on that of Agamemnon and Clytemnestra, the ancient Greek king and queen, their son Orestes and their daughter Electra. Agamemnon was away from home at the siege of Troy for many years. His wife, angered over Agamemnon's sacrifice of their daughter Iphigenia to gain favorable winds on the voyage to Troy, has betrayed him with Aegisthus. The guilty lovers murder Agamemnon when he returns. Electra and Orestes kill their mother and her lover. Orestes is doomed to a life of guilty wandering haunted by avenging gods called the Furies.

The Greek plays, although they do deal with universal themes, are intensified because their characters are kings and queens, princes and heroes. In O'Neill as in the Greeks, it is the pride the Greeks called *hubris*, the defiance of the gods, that leads to the downfall of tragic heroes. The fact that the Mannons live on an exalted plane makes their relationships much more intense, their sin and guilt more unbearable, and their final tragedy so terrible. Still, despite the heroic size of the characters, one does have the feeling that General Mannon is, to some degree, a representative of all fathers, just as the tragedy of Orin is shared by all sons. And all mothers, like Christine, love their sons a little bit too much and feel rivalry toward their daughters.

It seems fairly certain that O'Neill's goals go beyond the telling of this particular story. He is trying to make the audience identify with the characters. He tries to impart an intuitive understanding of the conflicts among all fathers and sons, mothers and daughters, brothers and sisters as he draws his audience into the tragedy of the Mannons. In so doing, he achieves that purging through pity and terror, identified by Aristotle as the goal of drama, through which a work of theater reaches the universality of all great works of art.

The Theme of *Mourning Becomes Electra* Illuminated by the Social Sciences

The next few pages are devoted to a preliminary look at the way some of the questions raised by the play would be approached by social scientists. We examine particular studies and approaches drawn from psychoanalysis, social psychology, anthropology, sociology, political science, and economics. While the overlap among these areas is considerable, each has a core of its own. The next section tries to use the themes of the play for a first look at the orientations of these fields.

A Psychoanalytic (Freudian) Perspective

Why the intense emotion released by the relation of Orin to his father, Lavinia to her mother, each to the parent of the opposite sex? Is this a peculiar quirk of the Mannon family or a kind of feeling shared by many people? The ideas of *psychoanalysis,* developed by Sigmund Freud during the last part of the nineteenth and early part of the twentieth century, are ideally suited to a discussion of such a question. Besides, it is very likely that O'Neill was quite familiar with Freud. We discuss Freud in a systematic way in Chapter 4, but a brief review of some of the basic concepts of psychoanalytic theory directly relevant to *Mourning Becomes Electra* might be a good way to start our survey.

Central to Freud's system is his picture of the emotional development of children. He based this picture on recollections, dreams, and free associations given him by his patients as they underwent analysis of their psychological problems. Freud proposed that when children are three or four they first begin to feel sexual attraction to others. The persons to whom sexual feelings are most frequently directed are the parents of the opposite sex. Thus, sons are drawn to their mothers, daughters to their fathers. A concomitant of love for the parent of the opposite sex is a feeling of rivalry and jealousy towards the parent of the same sex. The Greek legend of Oedipus, who killed his father and married his mother, was used by Freud to symbolize a supposedly universal pattern. The story of Electra, the source of O'Neill's play, describes the parallel pattern among girls.

The tensions of this period of development, the period of Oedipal conflicts, must be resolved before a child can go through successful emotional development. To Freud, the resolution occurs when the child, unable to possess his or her parent of the opposite sex and dispose of the rival, achieves a symbolic conquest by becoming as much like the parent of the same sex as possible. This process is called *identification*. There are two kinds of identification. The first is based on events that are almost inevitable in any child's life. Parents are usually warm and accepting towards their children. But sometimes a parent is distracted, feels ill or out of sorts, and then acts cold and rejecting. The child then feels under great pressure to regain the parents' love; after all, a three-year-old can hardly know that the change in atmosphere is purely temporary. One way to recapture love is by showing that you are worthy to be loved, that you are really a copy of the one you love. Thus the origins of one kind of identification.

The second kind of identification, according to Freud, occurs only among boys. As I said earlier, Freud really felt that little boys respond to their mothers with a very sexual, biological kind of feeling. Fathers are rivals; a boy's reaction to his father is a mixture of jealousy, fear that he will be punished (by being castrated) for his rivalry, and worship of a remote and authoritative figure. One way of reducing fear of being punished for rivalry with father is to become like him. This kind of identification is a defense against fear.

O'Neill's play lends itself to a Freudian analysis almost too easily. Lavinia tells about her feeling of having lost her mother's love. Her first reaction is hatred. After her mother's death, Lavinia clearly identifies with Christine, even to dressing like her. Orin fears his father's anger, has fantasies of killing him, and finally does kill a father-like figure, his mother's lover, Captain Brant. Orin, too, in the later scenes is shown carrying himself like his father, wearing similar clothes.

The contrast between O'Neill and Freud lies not only in the latter's systematic exploitation of enormous amounts of clinical experience, but also in Freud's explicit statements of general ideas about humanity. With O'Neill, the artist, we have to make our own generalizations on the basis of the implications of his work. We can see the process of identification vividly in the persons of Lavinia and Orin, but it takes a Freud to name the process and define its origins and consequences in terms applicable to all of us.

An Experimental Approach to Identification

Freud's ideas about parents and children are interesting, and they certainly help us in understanding the play. But the evidence for Freud's formulation is shaky. It is confined to the analysis of individual reports of childhood experiences from adults who came to Freud to be treated for emotional problems. Contemporary psychologists, characteristically, try to develop relatively simple experiments that they can carry out in the laboratory. In these experiments, they try to sort out the factors related to a phenomenon like identification and nail down the relations among them. Typical of this is the work of American psychologist Albert Bandura. He has been studying a process he calls *modeling,* the way in which children learn to imitate the behavior of others.

One kind of modeling that has been examined in Bandura's laboratory is the imitation of aggression. Bandura found that children imitated a model whose aggression was followed by reward more often than a model whose aggression was not followed by reward. However, when the child was placed in a situation in which his or her own aggression was rewarded, even those children who had observed an unrewarded aggressive model showed that they had learned how to express aggression. Bandura's work and that of other psychologists has been especially important because they have found that children imitate aggressive behavior, not only from live models, but also from films of live or even cartoon figures. The notion that the aggression in children's programs on television is harmless is placed in real question by the results of this research.

Bandura describes the process of identification as consisting of several components. First you have to watch what the model is doing. Then you have to make a kind of verbal code for the model's acts. So, for example, when a child watches a cartoon figure or an adult hit out against an animal, he might say to himself, "Gee, he's hitting the animal." This might be followed by his thinking, "Hitting animals must be okay." When the child is placed in a situation in which he can hit out against an animal, the fact that he has seen an adult model carry out the aggression is recalled and, especially if he can put the experience into words, he may act in a way similar to the model.

If Bandura is right, parents are not the only source of identification. Children obviously can model other children, especially older brothers and sisters. They can also model persons seen on TV, teachers, and other significant figures. Bandura's work also suggests that Freud was wrong in saying that the model necessarily has to be a source of support or warmth first, although the quality of the relationship obviously does have an effect. Note that Bandura uses *modeling* to denote single acts of imitation, *identification* a general tendency to imitate.

What does this kind of experimentation and theorizing tell us about *Mourning Becomes Electra?* It really does not add too much to the intuitive understanding we get from O'Neill about the way Orin and Lavinia model themselves on their parents. But it does suggest the history of rewards and punishments that shaped the young Mannons into adults. Even more important, it extends the pattern of development from the particular characters in the play to people in general. As we said before, this is also one of the roles of the artist. But the artist relies on each reader's or viewer's emotional reaction; the social scientist uses the force of objective evidence. Both tell us something about parents and children.

An Anthropologist Examines the Legend

We said before that one of the things that make O'Neill's play especially interesting is the fact that the theme occurs in legends from many parts of the world. To Freud, the legend and the family pattern it describes represent a reflection of a universal family constellation. However, as social scientists have studied societies other than our own, it has become apparent that this pattern is far from universal.

One of the first social scientists to discover this was the Polish-born English anthropologist Bronislav Malinowski. During the early twenties, he studied a group of people living on a South Sea island very much like the paradise described in O'Neill's play. Malinowski's people, the Trobrianders, have a family pattern completely different from that found in most Western societies. The Trobriander family revolves around the mother rather than the father; the society is therefore called *matriarchal* (from the Latin *mater,* for "mother"). In this society, family authority lies in the mother's brothers and father rather than in the man who is husband and father. Although a mother and father live in the father's village, the children are not under the father's discipline. The father is a kind of chum who gives the children presents and helps them learn how to hunt and fish and play games. But he is not an idealized figure, and, even more importantly, he has no control over the children.

If guilt over sexuality is a product of the conflict between a growing child and his father, who is hated and feared because he prevents consummation of the boy's love for his mother, then the Trobrianders' family arrangements may be responsible for their lack of a sense of sin over sex. They engage in sexual games before they reach puberty and indulge in intercourse quite regularly afterwards. There is, however, a clear transition from the fun and games of adolescence to the serious business of adulthood, marriage, and the rearing of children.

Since there is no sense of sin or guilt over sexuality, and since the child's father is not a source of authority, the Oedipal and Electra complexes described by both O'Neill and Freud are not known in Trobrianders. That is, boys do not feel rivalry with their biological fathers, nor are girls sexually attracted towards their fathers. There must be a strong, if unlawful, attraction between brothers and sisters, because the rules of this group forbid sexual relations between them; it is the Trobrianders' most powerful taboo.

One of Freud's supports for the notion that boys love (literally) their mothers and view their fathers as rivals is his report of a common dream in which a boy experiences his father's death and goes to his funeral. Trobrianders, according to Malinowski, never dream of their *father's* death but do occasionally see their mother's brother die in their dreams. And they do not seem to have dreams about their mother; rather, they report dreams of a sexual kind about their sisters.

Anthropologists like Malinowski broaden our perspectives. If we had thought that O'Neill's plot described a universal human problem, the study of other societies would correct this idea. The Trobrianders would write the story differently. They do not have tyrannical, hated, and loved fathers or seductive and possessive mothers. Of course, there are authority figures and mothering figures, but the force of emotion cannot but be thinned when it has to be spread among a number of uncles and grandfathers, aunts and elder sisters.

Clearly, in order to understand the human condition, we will have to look at people, not only in one particular society, but in a variety of societies. We will explore this further in Chapter 5.

An Analysis of Social Setting

Even within one society such as our own, there are great differences in the way people live. To understand a family like the

Mannons, we have to place them in a particular time and a particular social level. The play does that for us. It sets the time at the end of the Civil War. The Mannons are a prosperous family who dominate the life of their town. They have enormous pride, not only in their present social position, but, even more, in the traditions of their family. The play demands a social system in which people have maintained such traditions for generations. It would be hard to imagine the tragedy of the Mannons played against the shifting social scene of a suburb of Los Angeles.

Again, social scientists are able to provide us with hard evidence on which to base a picture of the social structure of a town. As it happens, there is a well-known classic of the social sciences that describes a town very much like the community in which O'Neill set his play. This is the study of "Yankee City" by a team headed by W. Lloyd Warner. Warner's work was carried out almost eighty years after the time period of the play. But New England towns change slowly. And so, Warner's intimate picture of his town is not only useful as an illustration of the techniques and theory of social science, but it also provides invaluable background for an understanding of the complex human problems presented in O'Neill's play.

Warner's method of studying his town was very different from the intuitive procedures of a novelist or playwright. Warner's investigators talked to a great many people living in various parts of the town. They tried to find out who worked with whom, who visited with whom, who belonged to the same clubs, who participated with whom in various kinds of social activities. From this careful investigation, a picture of the social structure of the town slowly emerged. Warner described a class system in which the descendents of ship owners and shipbuilders like the Mannons formed an upper class. Everyone in Yankee City was aware both of the superior position of this upper class and of the layers beneath composed of professionals and businessmen, white-collar workers, blue-collar workers, and, finally, "the people on the wrong side of the tracks." We describe this scheme in detail in Chapter 6.

In O'Neill's play, the tragedy of the Mannons seems to arise inevitably from their position in the community. The Mannons have a set of ideas about themselves and about what is "right" for a Mannon to do that leads to an explosive clash between human desires and social customs. The original expulsion of Captain Brant's father and mother from the tight world of the Mannons came about because Captain Brant's father had stepped over class lines in choosing a mate. The wild desire for revenge that Captain Brant brought back with him arose from his fury over the elder Mannon's treatment of his mother. He tells how his mother had asked for help from General Mannon and had been refused, even though General Mannon was very wealthy and Captain Brant's mother was ill and destitute. In many societies, it would have been unthinkable that a member of a family be refused assistance under these circumstances. Only an upper-upper-class New England family with a powerful sense of pride in its social position could have been so heedlessly cruel.

The Mannons would fit beautifully into the upper-upper class of Yankee City as it was described by Warner. In the 1930s and probably also today, as in the 1860s of O'Neill's play, life in the class of great merchants and ship owners was dominated by family tradition. The ultimate sanction is, "What would grandmother have said?" Of course, the tragedy of father and son, mother and daughter transcends the particulars of class and position. And yet, the details of this tragedy are worked out in a way peculiar to the circumstances of the time and place.

The contrast between the social scientist Warner and the playwright is not primarily in the outcome of their work. When you read Warner's account of life in his New England town, you get much the same sense of a rigid, class-haunted community that you do from the play. The difference is in method and language. Warner engages in systematic surveys of the community; O'Neill writes on the basis of his intuition and his own experiences. Warner uses a rigorous system of theoretical labels; O'Neill uses poetic language. To understand fully the strange story of the Mannons, it would be desirable to have the kind of experiences that O'Neill brought to the writing of the play. But, if you do not, the systematic observations and theoretical discussions of the social scientist provide something of a substitute. Chapter 6 will deal in detail with this kind of data and theory.

Power and Politics

O'Neill's story derives some of its scope and grandeur from the wealth and power of the Mannon family. The townspeople form a kind of chorus, commenting on the action. Their comments place the

Mannons in the social system. Their reactions give vivid evidence of the Mannons' influence. In telling the story of the play I noted that General Mannon is not only a military leader. He has been the mayor and owns one of the major sources of livelihood in the town. To understand the complex interweaving of the Mannons' story with the life of the town, one must be able to describe the political and economic system in which they exercised power.

The study of power is a central theme in many of the social sciences, but it is especially important in political science. In fact, some political scientists have defined their field as an examination of the sources of power and of the way in which power is exercised in the community. Political scientists use two empirical approaches to study power. The first is an analysis of social organization, and, more particularly, of forms of government. The second is a survey technique in which questionnaires are administered to samples of the population who are asked for their opinions about issues of political importance.

A political scientist named Robert A. Dahl has done an intensive study of a small New England city not very different from the one in which the Mannons lived. His study, reported in a book entitled *Who Governs,* looks at the way in which the city of New Haven, Connecticut, is run today but also includes some background historical material relevant to our examination of O'Neill's play. Dahl discovered that, in the New Haven of the mid-nineteenth century, the governing figures were very much like the Mannons. That is, they were people who had acquired great wealth through shipbuilding and other industry or the ownership of fleets of ships. They undertook a role in government as a result of a feeling that they owed it to the community to give it leadership. An unstated motive, perhaps not quite so praiseworthy, might have been a desire to maintain control of the community and to profit from their position of leadership. A man from this "aristocratic" group could move easily from his office in the shipbuilding companies into the mayor's offices and from those into command posts in the army. He would be used to wielding authority in a manner that would permit little questioning. The unofficial rules, if not the legal formalities, permitted this authoritarian system to operate; the New England town maintained the outward appearance but not the substance of democracy.

Certainly General Mannon fits this mold. He expects the un-questioning obedience of the townspeople, of the members of his family—especially his son—and of the common soldiers serving under his command. If tyranny invites revolt, then such organization of power both in the community and in the family invites the kind of rebellion shown by members of General Mannon's family, especially his wife. And the barely concealed hostility that the son feels towards the father and expresses indirectly by murdering Captain Brant may also flow from that power structure of the family, and, more remotely, the community.

Much of this is suggested rather than directly stated in O'Neill's description of the Mannons' story. The playwright sketches General Mannon's role as lawyer, judge, mayor, general by means of a few vivid comments by the characters in the play. From these you learn something about the exercise of power in mid-nineteenth-century New England. Dahl's study is more precise but less moving. He lists mayors, tabulates their occupations and social origins. He digs out documents that demonstrate the forces that determined the character of public life. From these he draws general conclusions about the exercise of power.

Economic Organization

It might seem that economics is pretty remote from the Man-nons' story. But economic factors do play a critical role. If the Man-nons had not become very wealthy through their shipbuilding and trading, they would not have been able to exercise the power that is the source of their tragedy. And they would not have had the freedom to take political office.

There are all sorts of ways in which economic power is crucial to the play. Orin and Lavinia are sufficiently prosperous to take a year to travel around the world. The Mannons' wealth and, even more, their economic power as ship owners allow Lavinia to threaten her mother and Captain Brant with the loss of his present job as a ship's master and with disbarment from the possibility of ever getting a new place. We are never allowed to forget the wealth and power of the Mannons; the haunting mansion with its great halls and ancestral portraits, its gardens, its pillared porch are an ever-present reminder.

But the Mannons, whose wealth was based on a living industry in the first part of the nineteenth century, represent a way of life that was dying at the time of the play's action. O'Neill tells us this in a vivid incident in which a sailor comes stumbling drunkenly into the scene just before Captain Brant meets with Christine. The sailor is a chanteyman; his job was to sing the rhythmic songs that paced the work of men on the clipper ships. However, he cannot find work now because sail is being replaced by steam, and he tells a sad, if drunken, story of the squat, ugly steamers whose coming foretells a new way of life in which he will have no place.

The Mannons also cannot adjust to the new world of factories, railroads, and steamships. In a way, Lavinia's withdrawal into her sunless mansion is a symbol, not only of the death of family tradition, but also of a retreat from the nasty, brawling, but explosively productive economic world of post–Civil War America. To be able to contrast the world the Mannons dominated and the world of today, you have to be able to describe the ways people work, exchange the products of their labor, and use money as a vehicle for these exchanges. It may seem farfetched, but one could argue that a study of the economics of nineteenth-century New England is essential for a grasp of the significance of the particular events of *Mourning Becomes Electra*. But it works the other way too. Reading the play could certainly enrich one's appreciation of the impact of economics on life.

Summary

In this first chapter, I have tried to sketch some general ideas about the ways in which social scientists approach human problems. We started with a special set of problems suggested by a great play and then contrasted the methods of the playwright with those of various kinds of social scientists. As we go on in the book, you will see how the analysis of dreams in the Freudian tradition, the laboratory studies of the psychologist or sociologist, the questionnaires, the reports from exotic places and peoples, the statistical breakdowns, the analysis of documents all contribute to a picture of humanity.

Before we go on to the substance of the social sciences, we must clarify some basic issues in their methods. The most important issues arise from the ways most social scientists organize their ideas into systematic sets of concepts called theories. In addition to defining what social scientists mean by theory, we should examine the relation between theory and the empirical investigation that is the major enterprise of every science. Lastly, we should look at some of the specific problems that make the work of the social scientist difficult. Among these are the difficulties that come from the relation of ethical and social values, the search for ways of handling the individuality of particular men and women in a scientific system, and the questions posed by interrelations among the various fields within social science.

On Your Own

1. Readable paperback treatments of the individual social sciences are scarce, but you might try some of the following basic books: Aronson, Eliot, *The Social Animal.* Bates, Alan P., *Sociological Enterprise.* Broom L. and Selznick P., *Essentials of Sociology* 5th ed. (a paperback condensation of a widely used standard text). Dahl, Robert A., *Who Governs.* Elms, Alan C., *Social Psychology and Social Relevance.* Fried, Morton, *Explorations in Anthropology.* Hall, Calvin S., *A Primer of Freudian Psychology.* Richards, Cara E., *Man in Perspective.* Snider, Delbert A., *Economic Myth and Reality.*

2. Analyze a play, story, or novel revolving around family relations, using the ideas discussed in the various analyses of *Mourning Becomes Electra.* That is, apply the concepts presented in the sections on the various social sciences to gain an understanding of the behavior of a character like Hamlet, Huckleberry Finn, or the hero of J. D. Salinger's *Catcher in the Rye.*

3. What kinds of questions would a humanist ask about Watergate? A social scientist? What kind of evidence would each require for answers?

4. In thinking about the plot of *Mourning Becomes Electra,* did you find yourself taking sides in the conflict between Lavinia and her mother? Should a social scientist react this way?

2
On Scientific Method

Before we go any further in our inquiry into social science, it is necessary to trace the thought process that enables scientists to go from observations of the real world (for example, the liquid in the test tube turned red; the boy is smiling at the woman) to systematic ideas about the world summarized in such conceptual terms as "acid" or "family."

Man, in his attempts to make sense of the universe, has always had ideas that might be parallel to what we now call science. Take the phenomenon of the rising and setting of the sun. Every people, no matter how primitive, has developed a picture of the universe in which the progress of the sun over the heaven has been explained; the Greeks, for example, believed that the sun god Phoebus Apollo rode his fiery chariot from dawn to dusk. This picture assumes the idea of a flat and stationary earth over which the sun travels. As astronomical and other observations progressed, however, the notion of a flat earth with a god riding a chariot over it became increasingly hard to believe. It was not compatible, for example, with eclipses of the moon or with the gradual sinking of vessels below the horizon as they sailed off to sea. Eventually, the idea of a flat earth and a chariot god gave way to that of a round earth traveling in orbit about a great, blindingly brilliant star.

You can easily show someone how the rising and setting of the sun can be explained by the idea of a stationary sun and a revolving earth. Take an orange, a grapefruit, and a lamp. The lamp is the sun,

17

the grapefruit the earth, the orange the moon. If you had enough arms (or helpers), you could duplicate most of the phenomena of day and night, perhaps even of eclipses, with the lamp and the two pieces of fruit. The setup that duplicates the essential elements of the earth-sun-moon system is called a *model*. By extension, the ideas back of the grapefruit-lamp-orange arrangement would also be called a model.

It is worth examining the picture we drew of the relations of sun and earth to illustrate the components of a scientific system. First, there is the *observation* that the sun rises and sets. Second is the set of rules or ideas used to explain what is going on. We might call this a *concept* or *theory*. Third, there is a 'test of deductions' or *predictions* showing how new phenomena can be predicted from the theory. Neither the behavior of ships at sea nor the occurrence of eclipses could be made compatible with the model of the flat earth and the fiery chariot (although eclipses *could* be put into the system if you added the new element of a dragon that eats the sun and then disgorges it). But the model that calls for a round earth traveling around the sun *can* be used to make many predictions. And so, by the process of *induction,* observations are made the basis for a new theory that is compatible with everything already known and can in turn be used to propose *deductions,* to be tested through new observations. Induction is the development of a new idea from observation; deduction is the prediction of a probable event from the implications of a theory.

The alternation of inductive and deductive approaches is characteristic of the history of development of all knowledge. Since this pattern of alternation is so important, let me propose another example. People have noticed similarities among different kinds of plants and animals ever since man came out of the Stone Age, if not before. As observations of similarities mounted up, sets of words for classes of animals and plants came into use. Virtually all languages have such words. The step from noticing similarities among objects to the development of ideas about classes is an *inductive* step. The next move is to act on the basis of the observations of similarity. If you have an idea that all plants that fit a certain class are edible, or that all animals that fit another are forbidden or taboo, you can proceed to accept or reject a particular plant or animal on the basis of your classification.

One of the best-known systems of dietary taboos is that now followed by Orthodox Jews and based on the Old Testament. The ancient Israelites developed an exact set of classificatory categories for permitted and tabooed animals. Although most bony fish were permitted, eels, which are a bony fish, were taboo. The forbidden category must be amended to read "fish without scales." Cows were permitted, pigs were not. Permitted animals had cloven hooves and chewed their cud; all mammals that did not meet these criteria were taboo. All birds except those which eat carrion were permitted. When someone who followed this religious system examined a new source of possible food, for example, the turkey, he placed it into a forbidden or permitted category, and then, in a kind of deduction, used the classification as a basis for a decision to eat or not to eat. Any visitor to contemporary Israel is aware of the legitimacy of the turkey cutlet.

The Nature of Theory

The preceding paragraph described three sequential activities that are analogous to the components of any scientific system. These were observation (Does the fish have scales?), utilization of theory (Is it in the forbidden or allowed category?), and decision (Should I eat it?). The implication of the decision is that a person would be punished for the sin if he were to test the theory of forbidden foods by eating the tabooed animal. To use the system we must understand each of these stages; the key is in the concept of theory. And so we have to turn to an analysis of the use of theory and of the ways in which theory is related to observation.

When you observe something, you are actually engaged in a kind of measurement. The apple is red, not green; the pebble is round, not oval; the maple is taller than the oak; the lake is fifteen feet deep. All of these statements involve two components. One is a set of standards, an *idea* of redness, roundness, tallness, depth. The other is application of that idea. This particular apple fits my idea of redness. In order to carry out this operation you must have some rules to describe the differences between red and other colors. The scientist's word for such a set of rules is "theory."

Rules of measurement arose originally from specific needs of farming, commerce, or warfare. People wanted to know how much grain to exchange for a particular amount of salt or how far one could travel in a certain amount of time. The ancient Egyptians needed to apportion the precious land that was flooded annually by the Nile and so required measures of area. Ritual needs were met through still other measures; priests needed precise indicators of periods of time so that recurrent festivals could be carried out.

The measurements of the scientist are no different from those of early man, but they involve more elaborate sets of ideas. Let us illustrate by describing the historical development of the idea of temperature. Every human being can tell through the use of his own sense organs that one object feels hotter or cooler than another. Early in the history of European science, it was discovered that one could obtain exact and repeatable measures of "hotness" by putting a liquid, such as the metal mercury, in a tube and noting how the liquid rose and fell in the tube. The higher the level of liquid, i.e., the more it expanded, the hotter the surrounding liquid or gas. Thus was born the thermometer. The next step was a set of ideas about what led to the expansion and contraction of the mercury or other liquid. A scientific "explanation" of temperature says that the small particles of which the mercury is composed move around faster as they get hotter and so tend to fill more space. This, too, is a useful idea and represents a kind of theory, just as the earlier operation involved an idea of hotness. Lastly, a mathematician can now write equations that describe exactly how something he calls heat travels through a body of mercury and leads to its expansion.

To many nonscientists, the word *theory* has negative implications. Think of the cliché, "That would be fine in theory, but it wouldn't work out." Or, "He is too theoretical, he has his head in the clouds."

This disdain for theory has deep historical roots. Scholars have long been perceived as people so preoccupied with their speculations that they ignore the practicalities of everyday life. Like Socrates in Aristophanes' play *The Clouds,* they become figures of comedy. Actually, as the great psychologist Kurt Lewin is supposed to have said, "There is nothing more practical than a good theory." There are at least three ways in which a theory is useful. The first is that it gives an observer a way of organizing what he or she sees in order to make sense of it. The second is that it gives the observer a reliable language with which to communicate the results of his observation. The third is that it provides a basis for prediction. The theoretical scheme helps you formulate the predictions and also assists in setting up tests that can determine whether or not the predictions are confirmed.

The construction of a theoretical system requires a high level of creativity; in many ways it is similar to the acts of imagination that characterize the work of the artist. The concepts of the theoretical scheme are, actually, products of the scientist's creative imagination. Of course, the scientist uses the results of his conceptualizing differently from the artist. The biologist who watches a pond is exposed to the same stimuli as a painter. But to the biologist, every element gives evidences of the workings of a complex ecological system. He classifies the plants and animals he sees, and the act of classification helps him order them in his mind, helps him visualize the place of each organism in the complex play of life and death for which the pond is the seemingly placid theater. Similarly, the physicist looking at a chair "sees" the spinning of incredible tiny particles in an orderly procession. The biologist and the physicist are imagining and generalizing just as if they were poets.

If you go back to the discussion of the measurement of temperature, you can see that at least three different kinds of theories surfaced at different stages of development in scientific thinking. These three types are (1) classification, (2) conceptual model building, and (3) mathematical modeling. The three next sections describe these three types of theory. As you read, try to fit the theoretical ideas described in the various analyses of *Mourning Becomes Electra* into these types.

Theory Type 1: Classification

The first kind of theorizing is classification. Classification is characteristic of the beginning stages of a science, although classificatory schemes are necessary at any point in its development. The history of chemistry during the late eighteenth and nineteenth centuries, for example, was one of the discovery of a variety of new elements. As each element was discovered, the behaviors of chemically pure samples of the element were described in such a way that it was possible for a chemist to say without hesitation after a series of tests that a particular substance was or was not a sample of the particular element.

Classification is inherent in all languages; it probably goes back to the very beginnings of human thought. Primitive peoples categorize animals, substances that occur naturally, manufactured objects, nations and races of man, phenomena of weather, by means of their most obvious characteristics. However, early in the history of human thought, classificatory schemes were developed that went beyond sorting on the basis of superficial appearance or function. Thus, the ancient Greeks were responsible for the notion that all objects in the universe could be classified in terms of varying proportions of four basic elements: fire, earth, air, and water.

Another example of subtle classifications is found in ideas about family relations or, to use a somewhat more technical term, *kinship.* These concepts are used to define degrees of relationship so that each person in a group can identify his position relative to all others (e.g., John is my father's brother, therefore my uncle). Note the use of terms like father, brother, uncle, cousin, clan, and the picture of relationships that these describe. Knowing the way the terms are used is important. For example, in our society, the same term, uncle, is used for father's brother and mother's brother. This argues that we do not make much of a distinction among the kinds of ties that bind a person to the mother's or father's family. In societies in which a person is clearly a member of his father's family grouping but only marginally close to his mother's, one often finds different terms used for the uncle who is father's brother and the one who is mother's brother. Even today, when the actual distinction in a person's affiliation to mother's or father's family is weak, many languages, for example, Serbo-Croatian, still maintain this linguistic difference which stems from a previous era when the patriarchal family groups were tight and large and extended families lived in a contiguous group of dwellings under the direction of a ruling grandfather.

The last section proposed that classifications are useful for prediction. This point can be illustrated even better by the development of knowledge about the chemical elements mentioned earlier in this section. As more and more elements were discovered during the nineteenth century, it became obvious that their order was meaningful rather than purely random. A Russian scientist named

Mendeleev saw the implications of this and developed what he called a *periodic table*.

You probably can visualize the periodic table as you saw it hanging on the wall in your high school science classes. This table illustrates the most sophisticated use of a classificatory scheme. As the elements are listed by atomic weight—i.e., a determination of the presumed weight of a single atom—a characteristic of the list called *periodicity* emerges. Beyond the first two elements, for the first part of the list, every eighth element resembles other elements in that position in the series. Thus, there is a set of substances (argon, krypton, neon, etc.) that are totally inert gases. The next element to each of these is a chemically active metal (lithium, potassium, sodium, strontium) with similar chemical properties. The most productive application of the periodic character of the table was derived from gaps in a series. These gaps enabled nineteenth- and early-twentieth-century chemists to predict both the atomic weight and the chemical properties of the hitherto unknown elements that would fill the gaps.

A serious problem in constructing a classificatory scheme is the need for exactness in defining terms. Scientists sometimes yield to the temptation to create new technical language where dictionary English might handle the problem of terminology. To someone who is not involved in the working out of a taxonomy (a technical term for a classificatory scheme), the new language may seem absurd. That absurdity can create a sense of distance between scientist and nonscientist. Of course, most people, in their awe of the natural sciences, are willing to acknowledge the need for new terminology in chemistry and physics. Even the whimsical language of subatomic particles creates little confusion; readers of the *New York Times* hardly blink an eyelid as they follow the adventures of "charmed particles" or of "quarks." But the social scientist courts disfavor with many when he tries to label what seems obvious with esoteric language. I remember my own dismay at first being required to talk about the way people get along with each other as "interpersonal relations." The pejorative term *jargon* is only too easy to use in instances like that. But someone who calls a new terminology jargon should be able to demonstrate that it is possible to classify more simply or to use words from the dictionary according to their standard usage rather than to invent new and esoteric terms. When new words such as Freud's id, ego, and superego are needed to permit precise answers to precise questions, then calling that language jargon is pointless. The crux of the issue is the payoff for the new terms!

Theory Type II: Conceptual Model Building and Constructs

A second level of theorizing is characterized by the use of models or constructs like our grapefruit-lamp-orange picture of the earth and the sun. The notion that the solar system consists of a sun surrounded by planets was imagined or "constructed" by the philosopher-scientist Copernicus on the basis of data made available by the newly discovered telescope. Similar constructs are the notion of the electron, of democracy as a form of government, of intelligence. Each of these represents an act of imagination. The construct sits in the center of a network of observations and testable predictions.

I once had to illustrate the character of constructs for a group of high school teachers attending a summer institute at my college. In order to develop the network of observations and behaviors surrounding the idea of love, I asked them to write down all they knew about this concept. They were instructed to include folk wisdom, their private notions, anything that the word made them think of. Here is a selection of some of the things they said.

1. *Love makes you care about another person as much as you care about yourself.*
2. *Without experiencing love first, hate can never be realized.*
3. *To love and to feel loved make you aware of feelings that were previously unknown to you.*
4. *Love means security.*
5. *Love means compassion, empathy, trust.*
6. *Love means companionship, friendship, belonging.*
7. *Love means "never having to say you're sorry."*
8. *A family life that is supportive, accepting, permissive and in which parents are affectionate provides a basis for healthy (i.e., nonmasochistic, nonsadistic) understanding of love.*
9. *One can only love another if he in turn has been loved (by parent or significant other).*
10. *The universal sedative.*
11. *Receiving a heart-shaped box of chocolate candy when it isn't Valentine's Day.*
12. *Love does not equal sex.*
13. *Love and marriage go together like a horse and carriage.*

14. *Having full awareness of yourself and your potential and willingly and unselfishly offering it to another.*
15. *Feeling of deep emotion two people have for each other (love between boyfriend and girlfriend or husband and wife).*
16. *Love parents have for their children and vice versa.*
17. *Wanting to share things (love is sharing the little nothings that are everything) with some particular person.*
18. *To some, love might be a sexual relationship, to others it might be spiritual.*
19. *Those you love the most have the power to hurt you the most.*
20. *Love is a good feeling inside that makes you glow with joy and warm all over.*
21. *Love is a kind word or action that one shows to someone who is in trouble.*
22. *Love can be pain, sorrow, and heartache. Hours of anxiety over a child you love. He almost died.*
23. *You never forget those you have loved, not even after a million years. They will always be there.*
24. *Serving chicken soup is a sign of love.*
25. *Food is love—the way to a man's heart is through his stomach.*
26. *Heterosexual love is "better" than homosexual love.*
27. *Love means that siblings or relatives, though they are at odds, always have some underlying affection that will "out" in the end.*
28. *Love is instinctive between parents and children.*

There are a number of different kinds of material in these sentences. The first has to do with factors that tend to create love, the relation between parents and children, between boys and girls, friendship and closeness. The determinants of love even include such material things as food. Then there is a series of terms that seem to refer to ideas related to love. These terms include affection, warmth, compassion, empathy, trust. Lastly, there are descriptions of the observable acts that tell you that love is present. Thus, people talk about sharing, about sexual behavior, about helping or hurting, about saying kind words, about not forgetting.

One way of organizing all of this material is to try to set up a kind of three-part diagram in which the factors that create love are placed on the left, the ideas associated with love in the center, and the observable behaviors on the right (see Figure 2.1). Both kinds of theory, classification and construct, are illustrated.

For example, in dealing with love, we use words like sharing or helping in order to summarize a wide variety of acts that we classify as altruistic behavior. The second kind of term deals with inferences about the "machinery" inside the person that accounts for his or her acts. If you see a person being affectionate with someone else, then you may attribute this to something hard to define called "love." Of

26

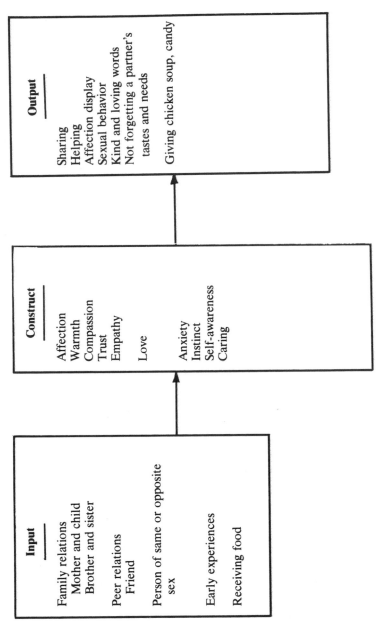

Fig. 2:1. An anatomy of love

Input	Construct	Output
Family relations Mother and child Brother and sister	Affection Warmth Compassion Trust Empathy	Sharing Helping Affection display Sexual behavior Kind and loving words Not forgetting a partner's tastes and needs
Peer relations Friend	Love	
Person of same or opposite sex	Anxiety Instinct Self-awareness Caring	Giving chicken soup, candy
Early experiences		
Receiving food		

course, it is perfectly possible that the single act of affection may mean something entirely different. It could be a mask for a desire to manipulate, to gain advantage, or to look good. However, if you watch a person over some period of time, see a number of affectionate acts, and can make sense of the sorts of relationships that lead to these affectionate acts (if, for example, you are dealing with a mother and child) then the behavior can be considered a good example of the idea of love.

The term *love* becomes a word that summarizes a guess that you make, an act of imagination, what the scientists call an inference about what is going on inside the head of the person whom you see acting affectionately. Figure 2.1 lists a number of terms that seem to be associated with each other. Most scientific systems include a number of such terms, each of which is tied to different kinds of outputs and causes. The totality makes up a system.

As you go through the book, you will encounter various terms used in the social sciences, and you may want to analyze these terms with the same sort of exercise that we just carried out for the term *love*. In fact, you might go back to the discussion of *Mourning Becomes Electra* and take a look at some of the other theoretical terms that we presented without definition. Could you write a diagram for terms like *culture, social class, identification,* and *power?* If so, you are beginning to carry out the kinds of activities that make up the heart of social science.

Fact and Theory. When we were talking about the first level of classificatory theory, the question of the truthfulness, or validity, of the theory seemed relatively simple. For each item in the classificatory system, the scientist *chooses* a set of characteristics, and then the only question is whether any given object fits. Similarly, the scientist decides which aspects of the objects being classified are linked and on that basis sets up orders of classification. You know you are looking at a dog if the animal has certain kinds of teeth, digestive system, fur, and so on. Dogs are classified as mammals because, like all the other creatures in that larger grouping, they are warm blooded and bear their young live. Biologists have decided that normal habitat (i.e., water, air, or land) is a poor basis for classification and so do not include whales with fish or bats with birds.

With the second level of theorizing, the definition of fact becomes harder to handle. Is the result of feeding chicken soup really love or is it something else? How could one know? Is this, in fact, a meaningful question? Here we can do two sorts of things. First, we can see whether there really is an association between the kinds of items on the left and on the right of our diagram. Second, we can clarify the relationships among the things we can *observe,* i.e., the items on the left and the right of the table, to the *ideas* in the center, which are not directly observable. The former operation deals with fact, the latter does not, since the relation of what we observe to our ideas is a matter for us to decide, as scientists, rather than a matter of fact. What, then, do we call a fact when we are operating at the level of concept or idea, what I have called second-level theorizing? Facts in this kind of system are the relations that tie the right and left-hand sides of the diagram.

Take the comment "Food is the way to a man's heart." We have suggested that this implies that if you feed a man chicken soup, he will show you affection. We call the chicken soup *input* (quite literally), using a term from engineering. The outward signs of affection are *output.* One would have to make a great many controlled observations to demonstrate that the old piece of folk wisdom about the way to a man's heart is really reliable. If we can demonstrate that, then we have acted like a scientist in his hunt for the tie between inputs and outputs. Borrowing a term from mathematics, scientists call such a tie a *functional relation,* implying that affectionate behavior is a function of, that is, dependent on, an input of good food.

Functional relations can be described in sentences which have the general form

"If A then B"

where A is some kind of input and B is output. Some examples, perhaps a bit better established than our thesis about chicken soup and affectionate behavior, are:

If you heat water to 100° C (A), it boils (B).

If you dissolve salt in the water (A), it boils at a temperature higher than 100° C (B).

If you increase the amount of time a mother spends talking and playing with a child (A), the child's scores on an intelligence test improve (B).

Theory is involved in the establishment of functional relations in two ways. First-level theory is needed to provide the definitions of A's and B's. Theory of all kinds may provide predictions of possible relations among A's and B's, and experimentation or other kinds of investigation may furnish evidence that a given A-B relation actually holds. As our discussion of social science progresses, I shall come back again and again to the difficult problem of specifying the inputs and outputs that form the basis of a theoretical construct.

It should be clear from the preceding discussion that a construct represents an act of imagination that, as with all acts of imagination, does not have to correspond with "reality." You cannot say whether love is "real" or not; you can merely specify what kind of inputs lead to affectionate behavior. In fact, scientists are rarely concerned about the "real" nature of their constructs. They are primarily interested in using the construct as a way of organizing observation. This need have very little to do with common sense. A physicist is easily able to use the idea of an elementary particle that may behave at times like a little hard ball and at other times like a wave in a nonexistent medium that is indivisible and yet consists of even smaller particles. If you don't believe that physicists talk such apparent nonsense, ask one. All of this seeming contradiction of common sense is required in order to create a theoretical scheme consistent with the complex data of contemporary physics.

The Payoff: Testing Predictions. The test of predictions is the most important indicator of the adequacy and usefulness of a construct or model. If a model, no matter how absurd, leads to predictions that are confirmed in test, then the model is a useful one. If the model, no matter how elegant, does not produce predictions that are confirmed, then it must be either modified or rejected. There is no such thing as a "true" theory. Theories either lead to testable predictions or do not. I might make this point clearer by exploring the analogy between a theory and a road map. Some years ago, I moved to the city of Pittsburgh, in Pennsylvania. Before I arrived I obtained a map of Pennsylvania which included what I thought was a detailed picture of Pittsburgh's city streets. On one of my first days in our new home, I started out on an errand, using a route that required that I travel down a certain street to its intersection with a boulevard. I rode confidently to the point of the intersection, only to discover that the boulevard was indeed at the intersection but at the bottom of a thirty-five-foot cliff.

The two-dimensional map was obviously a poor model for use as a guide to driving since it led to the incorrect prediction that it would be possible to drive from one street to the other. The map had to be modified in order to become a workable model, i.e., yield predictions that would be fulfilled. This does not necessarily mean that the map was "false" rather than "true." For some purposes, i.e., measuring aerial distances between points, it might have been perfectly adequate.

The test of predictions from a theory can be crude or precise. Obviously, the more exactly the theoretical system is stated, the more precise the prediction. In the last analysis, the usefulness of any theoretical system is based on its ability to generate predictions that can be tested. Of course, there are times a prediction is made on the basis of a theory and it turns out to be wrong. There are two possible explanations for the failure of a prediction to be confirmed. The first is that the measurements or the observations on which the test of the prediction is based are deficient in some way. No matter how accurate the map, a test conducted in an automobile with a faulty mileage indicator will correspond poorly with the prediction.

Secondly, a failure to confirm predictions may mean that something is wrong with the theory. For example, a map may simply be misdrawn. The history of science is full of instances where concepts about the nature of the universe have been tested, found wanting, and discarded. However, the conservatism of science is such that a limited number of disconfirmations usually does not mean that the theoretical system on which predictions were based is immediately thrown away. Most scientists prefer to wait before reassessing the value of widely held theoretical schemes, even in the face of a small number of failures. What usually happens is that a theoretical system is rejected, not when one or two predictions fail to be confirmed, but when a new integration, a new insight into the possible nature of the universe, is presented as an alternative. The great men of science— Newton, Darwin, Einstein—made their mark in precisely this manner.

Unhappily, many scientists become attached to their theoretical systems. Because they get emotionally involved in their theoretical notions, they become willing to overlook many tests in which their theories do not work. For example, Joseph Priestley, the English chemist who discovered oxygen, refused till his dying day to accept the notion that oxygen is important in combustion because he was attached to the absurd but beautiful concept of *phlogiston*.[1] According to eighteenth-century scientists, phlogiston, a substance with negative weight, was inherent in all combustible matter and was given off in flames. He persisted in referring to oxygen as "dephlogisticated air."

Theory Type III: Mathematical Models

The theoretical systems discussed in the previous section consisted of ideas about "machinery" that cannot be directly observed but whose character is imagined in order to account for observations. The concept of love was typical. You can't see love; it is an idea about what is going on in the head of a person who is acting affectionately. As a science matures, its theoretical systems tend to change. Instead of merely guessing at the nature of hypothetical "machinery," the scientist can set up a miniature model, mathematical in character, which enables him to make precise predictions about the world. The map I described as an example of a model is in itself a mathematically correct picture of relations in the real world. Through the use of the map, one can make precise, quantitative statements about the distances between objects in the real world, and, with sophisticated relief maps showing the character of terrain, one could make predictions about the length of time it would take to travel and the obstacles that would be encountered. Similarly, the equations that state the Newtonian laws of mechanics enable one to make precise predictions about the length of time it would take objects to fall given distances within the gravitational system of the planet Earth. Models based on the Newtonian equations enable astronauts to steer to the moon. The geometrical models of molecules, physicists' equations dealing with the transfer of heat and energy, economists' predictions about the ebb and flow of supply and demand of commodities in a market—all are examples of mathematical theoretical systems. This book presents

---

1. The concept of *phlogiston* is based on the notion that substances lose something when they burn. A metal was supposed to consist of a *calx* plus phlogiston. When a metal such as sodium burns, it gives off the phlogiston, leaving the calx behind. Since the calx (or, as we would call it now, the oxide) weighs more than the original sodium, it was assumed that phlogiston must have negative weight. A candle, which leaves virtually no ash behind, was assumed to consist mostly of phlogiston with very little calx. The idea of substances with negative weight is not as far-fetched as some accepted concepts in modern physics, for example, antimatter. It just happened that a better, simpler solution was worked out.

few such mathematical theories. They are relatively uncommon in social science, although many economists and some psychologists and sociologists are moving towards their use.

The Nature of Prediction. In some sciences, it is possible to make very precise predictions about the outcomes of an input. The margin of error in most physical and chemical experiments is small. In others, one can do little more than define the *chances* that a particular outcome will result. Such predictions are called statistical. Not every young man fed chicken soup will fall in love, nor will every low front necessarily produce a thunderstorm. In meteorology, as in psychology, a knowledge of inputs improves your batting average. A storm is more likely if the barometer is low than if it is high; it is less likely that your wife will greet you with a smile if you forget your anniversary than if you come in bearing flowers. With both storms and people, a great many factors interact to create an event. When this is true, it is extremely difficult to make predictions that are *certain* to be confirmed.

Predictions are limited by another problem: that of the accuracy of measurement. No measurement is ever absolutely accurate; all have a certain built-in margin of error. Any measuring instrument varies a bit from time to time, depending on the circumstances in which the measurements are taken. This, too, makes it possible that the estimate of inputs could be wrong, or that the measurement of outcomes might be mistaken. Again, you have to state the *chances* that a given input will lead to a particular output. And those chances are, of course, improved where measurement is precise and diminished where it is inaccurate. Of course, we are assuming that all of the measurements are honestly made.

To people who are not scientists, these limitations may be very disturbing. They make the scientist's conclusions seem flabby and uncertain. Worse yet, it is widely believed, even among knowledgeable people, that the social scientist's systems are more complex and his measures more variable than the natural scientist's. And there is some truth to that assertion. Yet the difference is one of quantity rather than quality. Even the natural scientist, with his precise measures and his carefully controlled laboratory conditions, must make statistical predictions most of the time. And many social scientists can operate quite close to the range of predictability of the natural sciences. In his series *The Ascent of Man,* Jacob Bronowski makes the point that science never pretends to absolute and perfect truth. He distinguishes the humility with which scientists face the world from the dogmatic assertions, the total certainty, characteristic of authoritarian belief.

The supposed difference between social and natural science in their degree of exactness is really unimportant. The scientific character of a system lies in the use of observation, the development of theory soundly based on observation, the accumulation of a mass of tested predictions. These are far more important than any arbitrary notions of precision.

Summary

The first part of this chapter has been devoted to an attempt to describe the overall character of any science. As it has been described, a science consists of a series of statements about networks of relations among causes (or inputs) (A) and effects (or outputs) (B). First, it is necessary to classify the characteristics of inputs and outputs, and to measure them. These measurements must then be formulated into statements of a general nature: "If A then B." Networks of these statements are linked by ideas about the character of the "machinery" that is responsible for the reliability with which B follows upon A. The scientist uses such a network of concepts and observations to predict the movement of heavenly bodies as well as the behavior of infinitesimally tiny particles. Presumably, the same approach can be used in studying the behavior of living organisms, including that most fascinating and complex phenomenon, man.

A General Theory for the Social Sciences

Now that we have examined the nature of theory, we can go back to the discussion of social science. I said earlier that each of the social sciences has developed its own set of theoretical ideas or constructs and, indeed, that those ideas are what differentiates any one from the others. Actually, this book deals with the particular theoretical systems of the individual social sciences only to the degree to which they help us work out general notions about man. If you want to see how each of the social sciences—psychology, sociology, anthropology, political science, economics—solves its own problems of constructing useful theory, you will have to read further or take courses in those fields. Of course, I hope that the exposure this book gives you will make you want to explore the individual disciplines.

The next section describes a general theoretical scheme, based remotely on the natural sciences, which I have found useful in thinking about almost every aspect of social science. This is called an "ecological model," because it is derived from the branch of science called ecology.

An Ecological Model

Imagine a pond in a quiet glade in the woods. The water is covered with greenish scum called algae. Darning needles and other flying insects dart over the surface. You can hear a frog croaking as it plops about in the edges of the pond. If you look into the pond, you can see some tiny fish darting around in schools and perhaps a medium-sized fish lurking under a stone.

The pond is a complex system in which the green plants that form the scum draw energy from the sun, use that energy to grow, and release oxygen as a byproduct of their growth. The green plants use up part of this oxygen at night. They also provide oxygen and food for somewhat larger creatures who live in the pond, and these in turn provide food for the fish. The small fish provide food for the frogs and for the bigger fish. Every living thing in the pond is dependent on every other.

The pond is a beautiful example of a stable system. If anything occurs to disturb some aspect of the ecosystem, the pond can usually adjust to the disturbance. So, for example, if there should be a runoff of fertilizer into the pond from a nearby garden, the algae would increase their growth. The population of small animals that eat algae would also increase, as would that of fish. Of course, the degree to which the system can adjust is limited. You could easily kill the pond by adding so much fertilizer that the amount of algae chokes the pond, uses up all of its oxygen, and destroys the ability of the larger organisms to live in it. If you think about the pond as a system, you can see that the growth of the living things in it reacts to changes in such factors as amount of oxygen, temperature, and crowding. Some of the organisms, especially the smaller fish, tend to behave in a way that is distinctly social; they travel in small groups.

We can characterize the environment of the pond as an interaction among three kinds of factors. These are physical (temperature, light from the sun, oxygen concentration), biological (food, the crowding of other organisms, the presence of predators and prey), and social (the interactions among the members of schools of fish). An ecological model defines a system in terms of the interaction among these three kinds of variables.

It is fairly easy to see how such a model can be used to analyze the factors that operate in the interior life of a pond. A similar model can be applied to the world of man. Figure 2.2 describes the components of an ecological model for human behavior. The triangle on the left indicates the social, physical, and biological factors that affect behavior. Ideas about the mechanisms of behavior are enclosed in brackets in the center. On the right-hand side of the diagram are all the observable acts that the social scientist uses as a basis for inferences about mechanisms. Earlier in the chapter, I diagrammed the ideas about love presented by my students. Can you analyze them to see where they fit into an ecological model? Which of the items on the left in Figure 2.1 deal with physical inputs, which are biological, which are social?

It might be worthwhile to develop briefly an example of an ecological analysis of a human problem. Famine has been a continual threat in the crowded lands of East Asia for many years. One of the factors that have made agriculture in that part of the world inadequate for the needs of its population has been the relatively low yields of the wheat, rice, and other grains that the peoples of the area use for food.

In a development that promised to win the battle against starvation, Norman Borlaug, an American botanist working in Mexico, developed breeds of plants that had very stiff stalks and so could support exceptionally heavy heads of grain. These "miracle" grains increase the yield of the land many times. And for a while, they produced enough food to hold forth the promise of an end to starvation.

But there were complications. The new plants do grow remarkably, but they need a great deal of water and fertilizer. It takes money

36

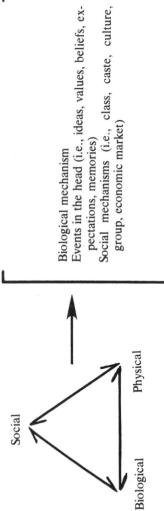

Input (observable)

Social

Physical

Biological

Biological mechanism
Events in the head (i.e., ideas, values, beliefs, expectations, memories)
Social mechanisms (i.e., class, caste, culture,
group, economic market)

Behavior

(*Output*)

Fig. 2:2. A schematic picture of the relation of man and environment

to build irrigation systems and buy fertilizer. Also, it is uneconomical to work very small plots of land in the new way. As a result, millions of poor peasants who work the land in India and elsewhere as tenants and sharecroppers could no longer continue to farm. They could not borrow money to pay for either fertilizer or irrigation. Large landowners found it profitable to take over the cultivation of their own lands. Millions of homeless, disease-ridden people crowded into already overcrowded cities, sleeping on the sidewalks and producing great social unrest.

To complicate things further, the runoff of fertilizer threatens the rivers and ponds of India with the kind of death, called eutrophication, that has turned our own Lake Erie into a smelly cesspool.

The elements of this story fit well into the ecological model we have been using. The new grains create change in the biological environment, as does the growth of algae in the waters of rivers and ponds. The irrigation systems, the fertilizer, the monsoon rains, the burning sun are all aspects of the physical environment. The social environment is characterized by the system of ownership of land that permits millions of peasants to be displaced. It is further characterized by the relation of caste to caste in India, the difference between village and city, the lack of adequate social services.

In the center is man with his ideas, values, and motives. One can easily imagine a group of people with a different set of values and attitudes reacting entirely differently to problems posed by miracle grain and limited water and fertilizer. There are places where the new grains have increased the standard of living of the population with far less social disruption than in India.

Different branches of social science could contribute in their own ways to an understanding of the problems created by the new kinds of grain. A psychologist or psychiatrist might focus on the motives and perceptions of landlords, peasants, and government officials. An anthropologist might provide a broad picture of the culture which could help explain the ability of the society to handle the disruptions caused by the miracle grains. A sociologist might use his analytical tools to define the social systems of city and countryside in great detail. The political scientist might show how administrative organization and concentrations of power affected the way in which both city and country responded. An economist could develop models to describe the distribution of resources; such models would enable us to evaluate precisely the ways the new agricultural techniques have been both blessing and curse. Application of these disciplines might help prevent further disruption.

Some Difficulties in Building the Social Sciences

The discussion so far may have made it seem easy to apply the general principles of scientific method to the development of social science. But there are some major roadblocks. These are not fundamentally different from those faced by natural scientists, but they create difficulties that must be discussed before we go any further.

Values and Social Science

The first problem is that of impartiality and lack of bias in the study of man. The influence of personal values on the work of the scientist cannot be ignored. By and large, most natural scientists have been able to work out their ideas without being affected by problems of values. There are, of course, exceptions. Biologists and physicists in the Soviet Union have had to trim their sails to the prevailing winds of thought which, at times, have ruled out ideas derived from Mendel and Einstein. In the West, the choice of problems has often been dictated by the community's interest in new weapons or in exploration of new environments such as space or the ocean bed. But no social scientist can ignore the possible effect of his own values and ideas. They can influence his observations, making him see the world in a distorted way. They can also affect the interpretation of his findings, the design of his theories, and, most seriously, the conduct of his experiments.

There are critics of the social sciences who say that freedom from bias is impossible. These critics are found both on the political left and on the right. Followers of Karl Marx, who dominate the intellectual life of the Soviet Union and the other "socialist" countries, feel that all of the social sciences in the West are merely justifications for capitalism. And they candidly acknowledge that they use social science in their own countries to support the socialist scheme of things. At the other end of the political spectrum, conservatives have attacked American social sciences because they are used as a basis for criticism of our own society rather than as a support for democratic and capitalist ideology.

It is not easy to deal with these criticisms. How does one achieve freedom from bias? One way is to follow a strict set of rules based on the laws of scientific method. Another is to make sure that the research on which conclusions are based is carried out with careful controls. However, it is probably true that no work in the social sciences is completely free of the influence of the scientist's orientation. Even if the data are derived from properly conducted studies whose controls prevent the preconceptions of the investigator from influencing the outcomes, the interpretation of those data will still be filtered through the ideas, values, and attitudes of the scientist. One of the most important things a neutral observer (if there are any such) can do is to learn how to separate data from implications, to judge the freedom from bias of the investigations which produced the data, and to assess the impact of the scientist's biases on the interpretations.

I try to be aware of my own biases, and I should be candid about them to my readers. Like most American social scientists, I lean towards the liberal rather than the conservative side of issues. You may see some evidence of that leaning in this book. I hope you will be able to recognize the results of that leaning and discount them. Meanwhile, I shall not try to solve the philosophical problem of the possibility of a social science free from bias.

General Laws and Unique Individuals

The second problem faced by social scientists is the need to deal with the uniqueness of each human being. The religious tradition within which we work, the Judeo-Christian heritage most of us share, and the whole intellectual history of the Western world since the end of the Middle Ages all have focused on the individuality of each human being. Religion tells us that each of us is a soul, a child of God. The culture tells us that each of us has a mind and a spirit that are worth cultivating.

Given that tradition, it seems wrong to treat individuals as items in a statistical survey, or as examples of a class or culture. Society tends to reduce our individuality enough. But the very concept of a science demands that the elements studied be comparable to each other. How can you write the "if A then B" laws we discussed earlier in this chapter if no one A is like any other? You need "chemically pure substances." And yet no human being is "chemically pure."

The solution lies in an approach similar to that which makes photography or TV possible. The TV screen shows a large number of dots that can glow brightly or dimly. You can create a picture of an object by making a pattern of dots in which the sections that correspond with the brighter portions of the object glow brightly and those that correspond with the dimmer portions glow dimly. Each of the dots is a standard, interchangeable unit. While the picture that results is not an exact duplicate of the object, it is close enough so that you can recognize Johnny Carson or Barbara Walters without any difficulty. The social scientists' measurements are something like these patterns of dots. While they do not reproduce any one person in all his or her full richness of individuality, they come close enough so that we can describe differences among people from one social group to another and even within the same group. Thus we *can* develop laws of behavior that add up to a science of sociology, psychology, or indeed, any of the social sciences.

Individuality and Laws. Social scientists tend to deal with individuals on the basis of descriptions of populations and general laws. There are some exceptions. As we saw in Chapter 1, the study of individual life histories by psychoanalysts (followers of Freud), clinical psychologists, and anthropologists has led to many general statements that have the character of laws. On the other hand, an attempt to understand human problems by studying individuals is also characteristic of scholars called *humanists.* These include writers, artists, philosophers. Similar approaches are used by many journalists and other commentators on the human condition. I think, therefore, that it is not wise to define the social sciences in terms of commitment to a study of populations, of people in the aggregate, rather than individuals. After all, many humanists come to conclusions about the nature of man and society by taking thought rather than concentrating on individuals.

The real difference between the scientific and humanistic approaches lies in the use by social scientists of controlled observations, formal and systematic theory building, and the testing of hypotheses. That sequence of observation-theory-test can be described as a "rigorous" approach. None of the humanistic disciplines requires rigor, in that sense, although they surely employ rigorous techniques of their own.

In Chapter 1 we discussed the contrast between a playwright and a group of social scientists. It might be interesting to compare the work of a journalist and a social scientist in handling similar problems. A journalist forms impressions from interviews with intelligently but unsystematically selected informants. For example, he may travel through Europe talking to workers, trade union leaders, and government figures in an attempt to understand why it is that so large a proportion of the workers in France and Italy continue to vote for the Communist party. The journalist would "explain" this phenomenon in terms of common sense, intuition, hunch. In contrast, in a study of the politics of Western Europe, Hadley Cantril, an American social psychologist, systematically constructed measures of opinion and attitude, presented these to samples of the population selected on the basis of carefully designed randomized procedures, and made inferences about the reasons for the phenomenon of the Communist vote through the use of fairly rigorous theoretical models.

Each approach has both merits and drawbacks. No matter how insightful the journalist's explanations, one is always tempted to ask him how sure he is that the people he talked with are really representative of the population at large. And there is no question but that the journalist is more prone to distortion from his own biases than the scientist, who at least attempts to introduce safeguards against bias. On the other hand, the social scientist seems to be cold, remote, somewhat less human than the journalist or the humanist. He seems to ignore the rich diversity of human experience.

Both the humanist and the social scientist move back and forth between an analysis of individuals and general statements about people or categories of people. Ideally, the humanistic and scientific disciplines dealing with man should enrich each other. The social scientist can look to the humanist for insights that lead to ways of organizing and classifying his observations and new concepts to tie the classes of observations into meaningful theoretical networks. Interaction between psychoanalysis and literature in the last fifty years has illustrated the way in which humanistic and scientific disciplines may interact. A knowledge of Freud brings new insights to the interpretation of *Hamlet*. Conversely, the heightened sensitivity to the human condition that comes from a reading of Shakespeare might be invaluable to the social scientist trying to understand the interrelations of sons and mothers.

The Fragmentation of Fields

A third problem in the social sciences is created by the inability or unwillingness of scholars working in the individual fields to communicate with one another. There are many ties among these fields, and I have tried, all through this book, to emphasize the continuities rather than the differentiations. Even so, in discussing research or theory, I have been unable to keep myself from using such labels as "psychologist," "anthropologist," and "political scientist."

Scientists did not begin to carry labels describing their fields until the rise of university or college departments in the latter part of the nineteenth century. Many great figures in the early days of the social sciences are associated with the origins of more than one field. But, as the social sciences developed, they tended more and more to consist of sharply delimited areas. The scholars who worked in these areas identified with their own fields. Some of the more parochial among them specialized to such an extent that an individual could be highly sophisticated in one area and quite ignorant of others in which problems similar to his own were examined.

During the period after World War II, there was a move towards interdisciplinary teams in which representatives of several fields were brought together to attack such social problems as crime, intergroup hostility and prejudice, and disarmament. Such groups often spun their wheels endlessly as the members tried to learn how to talk to one another. Interdisciplinary activities are somewhat less common now than they were several decades ago. But many individual social scientists are aware of the problems posed by the boundaries separating such fields as sociology and psychology and make an effort to combine the insights of the different disciplines relevant to their work. As I have said before, I hope that the reader of this book will go on to further inquiry into some of the individual social sciences and, indeed, to some of the attempts to integrate them.

We now turn to a discussion of an issue fundamental in almost all the social sciences: the degree to which characteristics of human beings are determined by biological heritage. Although the impact of biology may seem somewhat remote from the social sciences, it is clear that the social sciences must be concerned with the degree to which people are prisoners of biology or are free to shape their own destinies. And so our next chapter will deal with questions about the basic nature of man.

On Your Own

1. I highly recommend Jacob Bronowski's *Science and Human Values*. It should be especially useful for those interested in the arts or literature since Bronowski tries to show common bonds between art and science. His *Ascent of Man* is also invaluable. If you get a chance to see the TV series or read the book, don't miss it.

2. If the ecological approach interests you, one of the best books on this is Barry Commoner's *The Closing Circle: Nature, Man and Technology*. I would also suggest Rene Dubos's *Man Adapting*.

3. For scientific method I have four suggestions: Dethier, Vincent G., *To Know a Fly* (this might also be useful for the next chapter). Hempel, Carl G., *Philosophy of Natural Science*. Homans, George C., *The Nature of Social Science*. Reynolds, Paul Davidson, *A Primer in Theory Construction* (tough but very good because it works directly with theory in social science).

4. Resurrect a high school (or college) science textbook. Find an example of an input and a related output. What constructs or concepts are proposed to account for the relation? Identify a theory that fits each of the three levels described in the chapter, i.e., classificatory, conceptual models ("machinery in the brackets"), mathematical models.

5. The recent shortage of oil has led to a number of changes that are probably still operating as you read this. Use the ecological model presented in Fig. 2 in this chapter to describe the changes in the social, biological, and physical environment that resulted from the shortage of oil. What changes occurred in people? What were the consequences of all of these changes for behavior?

6. Are there ethical problems in any of the studies described in Chapter 1? What are they? How do you feel about them?

3
Biology and Behavior

It is commonly believed that certain kinds of behavior are "caused" by something called human nature. Among other matters this chapter concerns itself with the notion that there *are* inborn behaviors that occur inevitably and universally among mankind. We will examine the usefulness of the idea that warfare, gambling, machismo, and other undesirable behaviors, on the one hand, and generosity, altruism, spirituality, on the other, are inherent in the biological character of the human species.

To begin, we must define the concept of universal, species-dependent behavior. To do this, it is necessary to detour from the study of man and examine our knowledge of species other than *Homo sapiens.* If one assumes that man is a mammal who shares many of the characteristics of other animals, lessons learned from other species might be applicable to the study of man. That is, if one could demonstrate universal behaviors among cats, owls, or porpoises, one might discover how to search for such universals among people.

Folk wisdom certainly supports the idea of universals among animals. We all "know" that dogs wag their tails when they feel friendly and that cats flick their tails when they are angry. This kind of interpretation of animal behavior has a long history. It was probably very important to the first men, who lived by hunting and food gathering, to learn about animal behavior. If men could rely on animals to follow fixed patterns, the job of hunting them became easier. Even today, hunters and fishermen use such knowledge, waiting for the migration of salmon upstream or the gathering of deer at salt licks. During the next step in human history, when animals were domesticated, the ability to predict the behavior of a creature once one had identified its species was invaluable. In fact, the very fact of domestication implies a high level of information about biologically based consistencies in the behavior of animals.

In historical times, man kept records that demonstrated his growing knowledge of animal behavior. The concept that animals can be expected to show behavior proper to that of their species can be found in the scientific writings of such ancients as the Greek philosopher Aristotle and the Roman poet Pliny. Mingled with observation of real animals was a good deal of myth. Medieval bestiaries include descriptions of the unicorn, which could be captured only by a virgin, or the phoenix, which burnt itself up and then rose triumphantly from its ashes. But alongside these wonderful tales was a sound body of common sense about the real animals living in the forests, the fields, and the barnyards.

Folk wisdom has its limitations. The mixture of myth and reality is hard to sort out without the systematic testing made possible by the scientific method. With the study of animal behavior, scholars began to take the step from folk wisdom to science in the second half of the nineteenth century. Darwin's theory of evolution was originally developed to account for differences in structure among various species of plants and animals. Darwin proposed that such differences occurred because individuals who were successful in coping with the demands of the environment were able to produce more offspring than those who were unsuccessful. As a result of this difference in rates of breeding, adaptation shaped the evolution of biological structures, the character of muscles, nerves, sense organs, skeletons, and glands. This process was called natural selection. Darwin believed that much behavior is an inevitable consequence of the structure of glands, nerves, and other biological systems. He proposed that the behavior of animals evolved through the same process of natural selection. As evolution proceeded, behavior favorable to the species resulted in adaptation and, therefore, superior breeding power. Less-successful behavior meant that the animal would be less likely to reproduce.

One assumption back of this concept of the evolution of behavior is that behaviors, like structure, are passed on from one generation to another. It is usually assumed that the transmission of behavior occurs via "information" stored in genes and chromosomes in the egg cells and sperm. The common word for behavior determined by biological transmission is *instinct,* derived from the Latin word *instinguere,* "to stimulate or urge on." The origin of the word suggests a problem in its use. Among both nineteenth-century biologists and twentieth-century journalists, *instinct* is used to mean both an observable behavior (something on the right side of the ecological model in Figure 2.2) and the inner drive that is presumed to be responsible for the behavior (an item in the center of the model). Thus, instinct is a label applied both to the nest building of birds or the web weaving of spiders and to such inner states as maternal love or desire for power. Since this chapter is concerned with overt behavior, it will deal with that meaning of instinct that refers to behavior. I will introduce some of the ideas of the biologists, comparative psychologists, and scientists called ethologists who have been studying the behaviors that have been called instinctive. The next chapter, which is devoted to the study of motivation, will review the work that evaluates the innateness of motives or drives.

The Concept of Instinct

The uncritical use of this term was very common among both biologists and social scientists of the nineteenth century. Most were ready to accept even highly complex behavioral patterns as arising directly from the biological nature of the organism. There were skeptics, such as British biologist C. Lloyd Morgan, who asked that no instance of complex behavior should be considered inborn if one could discover its origins in either learning or in the effects of external stimulation. Unfortunately, Morgan had little impact during his own time, the last decade of the nineteenth century.

To say that a behavioral pattern is inborn almost demands that one search for the actual biological mechanisms responsible for it. A biologist named Jacques Loeb was able to accomplish this for some simple behaviors. He identified a number of tendencies that he called tropisms; the way a worm turns towards moisture is an example. The mechanism is based on the fact that the two sides of the worm are symmetrical with each other. If one of its sides is stimulated more strongly than the other, the worm tends to turn so that the stimulation is equal on both sides. This movement leads it in the direction of the stimulation. Going back to Darwin, one could postulate that the tendency to move towards desirable and away from noxious sources of stimulation was adaptive and therefore that the behavior was a product of an evolutionary process. This rather simple theoretical scheme has been used to explain the facts that cockroaches avoid light, rats and mice hug the side of tunnels, and worms travel uphill. What looks like a complex instinct is the result of a symmetrical structure and a tendency to move in such a way as to avoid uneven stimulation. Not only is the behavior inborn, but the very character of the organism makes its occurrence inevitable in every member of the species.

Social Darwinism

The application of Darwinian thinking to social phenomena in man followed closely upon the original work in the biological sciences. In Darwin's system, the natural selection that leads to the survival of the fittest operates for both structure and behavior. The social Darwinists, led by Herbert Spencer in England and William Graham Sumner in the United States, believed that the human race was subject to the same laws as lower animals. Strong men triumph over weak ones; so the characteristics of the strong are perpetuated, while the weak die out. By definition, therefore, what *is* is good because it has been adaptive. The rich are superior to the poor, nobles are better than common folk, Europeans should properly dominate dark-skinned "natives" in the colonies. Any soft-minded social action that tries to benefit the weak is eventually harmful to the race. You might find this point of view expressed in the editorial pages of a good many newspapers today. Its attraction for the "haves" is obvious.

Social Darwinism has a bad reputation among most social scientists today. This is partly because the evidence to support its theoretical position has been weak. Even more responsible, I would guess, is its obviously conservative point of view, which is not attractive to most contemporary social scientists. There is a small minority whose position is reminiscent of the nineteenth-century social Darwinists. For example, the American psychologist Arthur R. Jensen has stirred vigorous controversy with his argument that differences between blacks and Caucasians in scores on intelligence tests are biologically based. He has proposed that the depressed social position of blacks is due, not to the heritage of slavery and discrimination, but to their genetically determined inability to function at the intellectual level required by technically advanced civilization. Although Jensen himself denies being illiberal, he does present the conclusion that remedial education for poor members of minority groups is futile. Most social scientists find this argument unconvincing, since it is probably impossible to separate the effects of environmental deprivation from those of genetics, even if the latter does play a role in the present status of blacks and other minority groups.

Behaviorism

Many American social scientists took to instinctivist and social Darwinist positions quite readily. However, there were others who mounted counterarguments. One of the most vigorous came from two Americans, psychologist John B. Watson and sociologist George Herbert Mead. Their position, which they called *behaviorism*, was based on a protest against the nineteenth-century tendency to focus on constructs like "mind" and "image" which could not readily be anchored to objective data. Almost incidentally, however, the behaviorists also took a strongly environmentalist point of view, one that rejected the importance of inborn tendencies in human life and was, therefore, opposed to the tenets of social Darwinism. The contrast with social Darwinism is exemplified by Watson's assertion that he could turn any child into any kind of adult if he had complete control of his training. Watson did accept the idea of some very primitive tendencies arising from the biological nature of the organism, for example, an infant's fright at falling. But he denied the usefulness of the concept of instinct as an explanation for anything more complex. The sociology and anthropology of the day were equally environmentalist in orientation.

stickleback will fight another fish who shows the red belly spot if the encounter takes place near the stickleback's nest. His response at a distance from the nest is more likely to be flight.

2. *Fixed-action patterns.* Uniform sets of movements, characteristic of the species, are called fixed-action patterns. Bird songs are like this: the wood thrush's song differs only in the minutest degree from bird to bird and from time to time. If you want to see a fixed-action pattern, look at a spider weaving its web. Or watch a male and female pigeon dancing and circling as they prepare to mate.

Ethologists sometimes use a kind of slang expression for fixed-action patterns; they refer to them as "wired in." The implication is that a standard arrangement of nerves and muscles develops in each member of a species as a consequence of the normal events in the life history of the individual. Some evidence of this may be found in the fact that the complex flying movements of a locust may be evoked in their entirety when a limited set of neurons in the locust's brain are electrically or chemically stimulated.

3. *Independence of learning.* The third criterion for the species-characteristic nature of a given behavior is its occurrence in a "deprivation experiment." This is a study in which growing animals are deprived of any opportunity to interact with others of their species. For example, it has been found that many species of birds give the standard bird song even if they are raised in isolation and thus have not had the opportunity to mimic adult birds. Even more interestingly, some birds who do not develop the full song typical of their species when raised alone *will* mimic a bird song of their own species but will not mimic the song of another species. A female cat raised by humans without any contact with adult cats usually carries out characteristic nest building shortly before she gives birth. When her kittens are born, she bites the cord, licks the newborn, and presents herself to be nursed. The behavior obviously fits the criterion of independence from learning.

Identifying a kind of behavior as species-characteristic poses questions rather than answers them. If a fixed-action pattern is "wired in," one would like to know what biological structures are responsible and how they operate. If a particular stimulus acts as a releaser, it would be desirable to know what physiological mechanisms react to it and how they trigger the response to the releaser. Geneticists are beginning to learn a great deal about the way in which DNA, a chemical constituent of genes in sperm and egg cells, directs the development of the organism that results when the sperm and egg are joined.

By a kind of metaphor, the potential for development in one direction or another created by variations in the structure of the enormously complex DNA molecule is referred to as "stored information." It is as if the molecule "knows" the way the cells should develop as the organism grows.

The questions which will concern the next generation of biological scientists deal with the process through which patterns of development are shaped by the information stored in the DNA of genes. This is as true for behavior as it is for structure. While our ability to trace developmental sequences is limited, we can, in some instances, show a connection between the functioning of a specific biological system and a particular kind of behavior. For example, it is well known that females of such herbivorous (vegetable-eating) species as deer and cattle eat animal tissues at only one time in their lives; they eat the afterbirth shortly after they have delivered their young. There is evidence that they have an appetite for the protein-rich substance of the afterbirth because of glandular changes that accompany the last stages of pregnancy. Demonstrating the relations among physiological changes at this stage of a new mother's life, appetites, and the eating of the afterbirth is more illuminating than merely labeling this behavior as innate or instinctive or even species characteristic. Such a demonstration is desirable if for no other reason than that an understanding of the mechanism makes it possible to plan intervention if one wants to change the behavior. For example, if one wanted to keep a deer on a vegetarian diet, there are other sources of protein than an afterbirth. The instance is trivial, but the design for understanding of mechanisms as a basis for change is not. Should one, for example, accept aggression as innate or search for its sources in order to modify it? The implication of this position is that no behavior, even species-characteristic behavior, is totally resistant to change.

Relations between Innate Behavior and Learning:
The Ethologist's Viewpoint

To the behavioral scientist, the degree to which species-characteristic behavior may be modified is a matter of the greatest importance. Most people give the term *innate* the connotation of "fixed" or "unmodifiable." Learned behavior is defined as that which emerges from experience; it is usually contrasted with that which arises independently of experience as a result of the operation of genetic mechanisms. This point of view fits the ethologists' position, stated vigorously by Lorenz, that much behavior is universal in any given species and, hence not dependent on the experiences of any one individual.

Lorenz argues that there are two sources for all behavior. One is in the experience of the species as transmitted to the individual by the genes; the other is in the life history of the individual. In both, behavior develops as specific actions turn out to favor survival. For the individual, a learned behavior that helps in the struggle for survival may lead to longer life. In the species, a genetically determined pattern of behavior that gives individuals a better chance to survive through the breeding years increases the number of such individuals and so leads to evolutionary change. The results of experience are stored in the brain for the individual and in the genes for the species.

To Lorenz, the individual's history is never independent of the nature of the species. All behavior requires structures that arise from a process of development. But this development must go through the normal sequences for the species so that the biological systems on which species-characteristic behavior depends may emerge. For example, all normal birds of migratory species fly south in the fall. But a bird that has been deprived of light from birth does not develop a normal retina and so cannot react to the lengthening day that stimulates the glandular changes leading to migration.

If, however, an individual member of a species *has* had a normal history of development, then the resulting biological systems, which are "programmed" in the genes, limit the degree to which that individual's behavior can be modified by the experience of learning. Many examples come to mind. Chimpanzees seem to have subtle brains capable of a high level of abstract thinking. And yet they have never been taught to speak more than a very few words, and those most haltingly. This was true even when young chimpanzees were brought up in a human household. Recently, two young psychologists, Beatrice and Allen Gardner, proposed that chimpanzees do not learn to talk because they lack adequate control over the mouth and tongue. To test this notion, they brought up a young chimpanzee to speak the sign language used by human deaf-mutes. This was, apparently, highly successful. The moral is that chimpanzees as a species have the intellectual capacity to use something like human speech and can therefore learn to "speak" if they are given the appropriate experiences. But they do not have the "wired-in" equipment for verbal speech and so, no matter how intensive the experience, cannot develop *spoken* language.

I have been contrasting learning and the genetic background of organisms as a basis for behavior. Yet even learning is constrained by the organisms' biological character. This can be illustrated by the two most famous experiments on learning, one carried out before World War I by the Russian physiologist Ivan Pavlov and the other designed during the thirties by the American psychologist B. F. Skinner.

Pavlov brought hungry dogs into his laboratory, fed them with meat powder, and measured the amount they salivated when the meat powder was placed in their mouths. He then rang a bell just before each presentation of meat powder. After a number of such experiences, the dogs began to salivate when they heard the bell. In Pavlov's language, the bell had become a *conditioned stimulus* leading to the *conditioned response* of salivating. That is, the salivating had become dependent, or conditional, on the ringing of the bell. While the dog certainly had to *learn* to salivate at the sound of a bell, it was, as certainly, his original tendency to salivate when he tasted meat powder that made the learning possible. Salivating at the taste of food is probably species characteristic.

In Skinner's experiment, a hungry rat was placed in a cage containing a lever and a cup into which a pellet of food or a drop of sweetened water could be placed. At first the animal wandered about manipulating everything in sight. But he was given food only after he depressed the lever, and thereafter, he began to push it more and more frequently. Again, both his tendency to wander about and manipulate objects and his fondness for food pellets and sweet-tasting substances result from his biological heritage. It is that heritage which enables a rat to learn to depress a lever when this act is followed by a reward.

The ethologist Lorenz stresses the fact that the very ability to learn, the skill of an organism in shaping individual behavior to the requirements of the external situation, varies from species to species and is, indeed, a consequence of the history of adaptation that we call evolution. There is fairly good evidence, both from observations in the field and from the laboratory, that different species, in fact even such different subspecies as breed of dogs and cats, differ in their flexibility and adaptability. Most people who know animals will tell you that Siamese cats are different from domestic shorthairs, or beagles from poodles. To an ethologist, these differences are clear evidence both of the operation of evolutionary change and of the biological basis of the ability to learn.

Is Ethology Useful in Studying Man?

It is not easy to make a final evaluation of the ethologists' contributions to the understanding of man. We have to separate two aspects of their work. The first consists of skillful and sensitive observations of behavior in many species—wild, domesticated, and semidomesticated. Man is also included in the list of the ethologists' subjects. The second aspect is the theoretical analysis of behaviors, the use of such concepts as releasers, fixed-action patterns, species-characteristic behavior. We are, of course, especially concerned with the applicability of these concepts to human behavior.

The first kind of contribution is not controversial. Social scientists who accept the relation of man to the rest of the animal world are grateful for the rich data on animal social behavior provided by the ethologists and are willing to learn from them ways of observing human beings. But the usefulness of the theoretical analysis is open to serious question. Certainly the ethologists' stress on adaptation as the key to evolutionary change in behavior helps the social scientist think in ecological terms. That is, it makes him focus on man as an organism adapting to an environment.

The ethologists' emphasis on the innateness of behavior probably makes less of a contribution to the social sciences than the general point of view that stresses evolutionary adaptation. To repeat, the identification of a behavior pattern as having a biological base marks the beginning, not the end, of the process of investigation. Any living creature is the endproduct of a long chain of events. The chain, at least in species that reproduce sexually, begins with the fertilized egg and the DNA in its genes. At every moment in development, the environment in which the organism is living affects its progress. Change the temperature, the acid/base balance, the concentration of salt, and you get an entirely different organism from the one that "normally" emerges. If you do make such changes, the next stage of development is not determined by the genes alone. The genes must operate in a body that has been affected by these changes. So, if you change environment at one stage, the whole history of the organism from that point on is affected.

A good example of this effect of environment on development can be found in the work of Benjamin Pasamanick and his colleagues. They reported that children born in Baltimore in the spring are more likely to be retarded than those born at other times of the year. During the first months after these children were conceived, the mothers suffered the heat of a Maryland summer. The women probably ate less well than usual and were subject to many other stresses that affected the babies they were carrying. These effects may *differ* in different children, depending on their heredity. This study illustrates the point that the important questions about the biology of behavior do not deal abstractly with species-characteristic patterns, but are concerned with the interrelation of genetics and environmental factors in the developmental history of individuals.

The interrelationship of structure and developmental experience was very carefully studied many years ago in a laboratory experiment by the Chinese-American Zing-yang Kuo, who worked on the sources of an apparently instinctive behavioral pattern, the tendency of chickens to peck. In an ingenious experiment, he snipped off a bit of the shell from eggs that contained growing chicks and watched the embryos develop. He discovered that the growing chick is forced by the beating of its heart to open and shut its beak in a rhythmic pattern. This movement forces a kind of pecking. Eventually, the chick pecks its way out of the shell and then goes on to peck at small round objects for the rest of its life. True, the chick's genes are responsible for the development of the anatomical arrangement that, in a normally developing bird, creates this state of affairs. But it is the history of development of each individual chick that leads to the apparently innate pecking response.

Does the use of the word *innate* add anything to this discussion? Lorenz thinks it does. He points out that almost all birds share the same experience within the shell and peck themselves to freedom at birth. But it is only the chicken and its close relatives that maintain pecking as a way of feeding. And the pecking after the chick hatches does seem to be evoked by certain kinds of stimuli that might be called releasers. Thus, the criteria for species-characteristic behavior are clearly met. But pecking can be modified. A chick fed by hand and raised on a wire grid does not develop normal pecking responses. Merely identifying pecking in the chicken as species characteristic (instinctive, if you prefer the older term) does not tell us what aspects of the chicken's biological heritage and normal life experience contribute to this behavior.

This chapter began by stating that a necessary first step in the study of the social sciences is to determine whether there are any universal characteristics of human nature. We have made a long detour into the study of animals in order to develop a framework of ideas for the study of the nature of any species, including man. It is now necessary to ask whether this set of ideas is, indeed, applicable to the study of man. Ethologists and their disciples have, as a rule, not hesitated to make this application. For example, a popularizer of their point of view, the American writer Robert Ardrey, explains a great deal of human social behavior by equating it with the attachment animals show to a particular area, called *territorialism*. Desmond Morris, whose *Naked Ape* and *Human Zoo* have been best sellers, described the fighting of fish and the mating of birds and then analyzed the fighting and mating behavior of man in terms of the same ethological model. Even Lorenz, one of the most sophisticated of the working ethologists, views mankind as condemned to aggressive behavior by the nature of the species. All of these writers use such terms as imprinting, fixed-action pattern, and innate behavior in discussing the human race.

I am personally quite skeptical about the direct application of ethology to human behavior. In order to explain the grounds for my doubts, let me describe a kind of behavioral ladder. Behavior at the bottom of the ladder is simple and relatively inflexible. The higher on the ladder it stands, the more complex and flexible it is. The simplest and least flexible behavior is the reflex: an organism is "wired up" to show specific responses each time a particular stimulus is received. Every living thing, from amoeba to man, has such reflexes. If you want to demonstrate one in yourself, tap your knee and watch it jerk. Or note the way the pupil of your eye contracts when you look at a bright light (you can demonstrate that with a flashlight and a mirror). The phenomenon of imprinting as well as the fixed-action patterns and tropisms described earlier in this chapter represent similarly inflexible behavioral tendencies, but these are probably less dependent on particular nervous and muscular structures than the knee jerk or the pupillary response to light.

The next-higher level of behavioral flexibility is characterized by the modification of a particular reflex or imprinted behavior. I have already described the kinds of modified or learned reactions studied by Pavlov and Skinner. Higher still is the phenomenon of chains of stimulus-response units. Here the response to one stimulus becomes a source of stimulation for the next response in a chain which can include many such units. Think of a trained seal playing "My Country, Tis of Thee." As it blows each note, the sound of that note becomes a cue or signal for the next.

Lastly, there is the formation of concepts. Even such primitive organisms as fish can "learn how to learn," to use the telling phrase suggested by the American psychologist Harry Harlow. Take, for example, an experiment in which a monkey has to learn to open one of two doors. Over one is a red triangle, over the other a black square. If he opens the door under the red triangle, he gets a piece of banana; the other door leads to no reward. He will learn very quickly which door to open. In his next set of trials, the monkey is confronted with a choice of green triangle and red square. The red square is the signal for a correct choice. It should take the animal less time to solve this problem than the previous one. By the third problem, in which the signals are a red circle and a blue square, he will probably make the correct choice immediately. What has happened is that he has acquired the idea, or concept, that the color of the sign matters, not the shape. Harlow calls the development of such ideas the acquisition of a learning set. The development of such learning sets shows a flexibility far removed from the automatonlike character of fixed-action patterns.

Reliable data demonstrating innate reflexes in man are sparse. There is some evidence that, in newborn infants, a sucking reflex, a grasping reflex, and a response to a human face develop independently of experience. A drawing showing a turned up mouth seems to elicit positive responses in very young infants. The early babbling and smiling of infants seem to be independent of external stimulation and occur even in infants who are blind and deaf. But beyond these behaviors in very young human infants, the characteristic behavior of man seems to be quite remote from the fixed-action patterns evoked by releasers described in the work on birds, fish, and more primitive mammals.

Of all the species on earth, man shows the most complex chains of responses, the greatest ability to respond to internal events rather than external cues, the most sophisticated learning sets. In large part, as Lorenz might very well point out, this is due to some unique characteristics of human development. The young child spends a tremendously long time in intense contact with a variety of adults, especially with his parents. During this period, he acquires a language, develops ideas about what his social group thinks he should do, and so learns to think in the characteristic mode of his tribe. Given such a history, how meaningful are such terms as imprinting or fixed-action patterns? Does it mean anything to say that by the age of seven months the infant is "completely imprinted on its mother"? Obviously no human infant shows the kind of automatic following behavior characteristic of a duckling or a chick. The use of the word imprinting is only a metaphor, and a metaphor of slight usefulness at that.

The important point about species-characteristic behavior is that it is possible to predict with a high degree of accuracy what kinds of behaviors to expect just from knowing the species. If you identify birds, fish, or mammals as males of particular species, you also know whether or not two of them will attack each other. The attacking response, a fixed-action pattern, is released by the characteristic signs shown by the males. For birds or fish, this might be the color or the display of feathers. For mammals, it might be such objects as a deer's antlers or a lion's mane. But not so for man. To predict whether two men meeting for the first time will fight or interact peaceably, it is necessary to learn a great deal about the *individual* history of each, about the tradition of his particular social group, about the significance of a variety of learned symbols. Even then the prediction is chancy—especially if the site is a bar on New Year's Eve.

Sexual behavior is another major area in which species-characteristic patterns are common. Yet, there are wide differences through time and space in the characteristic stimuli which evoke sexual activity among humans. Only a species as flexible as man could regard both the voluptuous nudes in Rubens' paintings and the skinny, flat-chested 1920 flapper as sexually desirable. Among many mammals other than man, hair acts as a releaser for mating behavior. And at the moment, large masses of hair in the youthful male seem to be a potent attractant for the opposite sex. A few short years ago, such quantities of hair were marks of advanced age. To call the flowing locks and the beard of the contemporary college student releasers, equivalent to the peacock's tail or the lion's mane, is to use a metaphor which in this instance is meaningless. Hair is a symbol, yes, but one to which the responses are, within wide limits set by biology, almost entirely learned.[1]

Many animals, generally male, respond to signals that identify another animal as a male of the same species, who must be fought off so that the rights to a specific territory may be preserved. Territorial behavior during certain stages in the life history of many species is a highly adaptive way of spacing out individuals so that they fit into the ecological pattern of their habitat. Territorialism creates conditions in which not only food and shelter, but—sometimes more important—psychological comfort, are optimal.

Such popularizers of ethology as Morris and Ardrey apply the term territorialism to the tendency of humans to defend their living space. But the "wired-in," stereotyped tendency of many animals to defend territory is very different from the highly variable character of human spacing. Men do cherish privacy, but they also love company. They differ from one society to another in the degree of crowding they will tolerate. Characteristically, Anglo-Saxon men prefer to stay at arm's length, Latin-Americans within touching distance. A city man survives crowded subways, while his lighthouse-keeping cousin feels crowded if the next inhabited island is within sight. Again, the important difference between man and birds is that if a person knows the species and the stage of breeding activity of a bird, he can predict very precisely the spacing that two individual birds will tolerate. There is no such uniformity among men.

---

1. To make the point even stronger, my comments on hair styles may be out of date as you read this. Are beards still "in" among college men?

The reactions of human beings to strangers have been explained as a species-characteristic rejection of members of outgroups. This is supposed to be equivalent to the tendency of such social animals as ants or baboons to attack individuals from an alien nest or tribe. Of course, human beings do show marked hostility to newcomers, but this is far from universal. Remember the peaceful reception given to Europeans when they landed in the New World. From the natives of Mexico and Peru to the hospitable Sachem Massasoit who welcomed the settlers in Plymouth, the American Indians' first reaction was wonder and friendliness. It was not until the Europeans showed their brutal and exploitative intentions that the Indians became violent. By collecting enough accounts of this kind, one could almost support a universal human tendency to welcome outsiders.

Man, then, is not a "naked ape" any more than he is a fish with lungs or a worm with a backbone. In the complex organization of the human species, there remain traces of all three—ape, fish, and worm. And yet man is a new and unique organism in whom the traces of ape, fish, and worm form a substructure on which the novel character of human behavior has been built. One could almost predict this from looking at the nervous system. Large parts of the human nervous system are indeed equivalent and similar in structure to the nervous systems of more primitive organisms. We have spinal cords like worms. The lower parts of our brains are not very different from those of a fish. Some areas of our brains are similar to the cat's or monkey's brain. But man is unique in having a tremendous structure, that area called the cerebrum, and especially its covering (or cortex), that is enormously more advanced, larger in size, greater in complexity than any part of the brains of any other species. No creature with such a brain could fail to be fundamentally different from all others.

Are there, then, any universal human characteristics? There may be. Most basically human is the fantastic capacity for learning how to learn, for forming complex concepts. This is the basis for the wide-reaching development of human language and for the enormous complexity of human motor responses. The ability to learn a language is universal among humans, except for those whose nervous systems are seriously damaged. Obviously, the particular language that is learned is peculiar to the individual. The ability to perform complex hand-eye coordinations is universal; the particular form of craftsmanship, athletic achievement, or artistic skill is a product of the society in general and the experience of the individual in particular.

The single most prominent characteristic of the human species is its ability to perform those complex internal operations we call thinking. In fact, some writers have argued recently that this ability marked the emergence of the peculiarly human behavioral pattern and that language and tool using arose from thought rather than the reverse. There is much evidence that species other than man are capable of something analogous to human thought. Rats can integrate two separate habits to solve a problem. They can even show behavior that suggests a kind of expectation or anticipation of the future. But the human ability to integrate, to anticipate, to live for the future far surpasses that of any other species. More than all other animals, man lives in time and is dominated by events in his head.

The complexity of man's internal responses is probably also responsible for the enormous subtlety of human social relations. Again, many animals other than man live in social groups. Indeed, research into the social behavior of baboons, chimpanzees, and gorillas increasingly indicates that learning plays an important role in the organization of social groups among nonhuman primates. However, the ability of human beings to transfer ideas from one to another via language results in a uniquely complex social organization. It is man with his language who outstrips any other species in ability to *control* his behavior rather than be pushed about by external stimulation. And it is man who, as a result of these internal controls, leads a life dominated by symbols. Only *Homo sapiens* could fight for an idea like patriotism or religion, could spend energies on the building of monuments to the dead or to the gods. Indeed, only man can be said to have a concept of self, of identity, or of survival. Only man could imagine a religion, could consider the concept of a spirit and of survival after death. In fact, probably only a human being could anticipate death.

In the past, stress on the biological inevitability of one or another kind of behavior has been used as a justification for self-interest. The slave owner claims that hierarchy is based on human nature; the general is attracted to the notion that aggressive behavior is fundamentally human; the patriarchal male describes women as innately incapable of social leadership or creativity. Because of this, most social scientists have tended to distrust ideas about "innate" behavior. But the ethologists' insights should not be totally rejected. Even if the metaphorical use of terms like imprinting or territorialism or releaser for human beings is of limited value (if indeed of any use at all), the notion that man is an adapting organism whose behavior has been shaped by his evolution is a good starting point for the social sciences. The ethologists' concern suggests a search for the limits of variation in human behavior. And if we want to grow as a race, to reduce the forces that lead to war and poverty, to enlarge our creativity, to increase human happiness, it is important that we know these limits.

On Your Own

1. Lorenz, *On Aggression* presents the ethological viewpoint forcefully. Opposing arguments may be found in Montague (ed.) *Man and Aggression*.

2. For an absolutely charming introduction to the ethologists at their best I suggest Lorenz, K., *King Solomon's Ring*.

3. One issue that was barely raised in the chapter was the study of human language. There is a great deal of controversy between such psychologists as B. F. Skinner and Roger Brown, who see language as learned behavior, and a linguist named Noam Chomsky, who feels that there is a deep structure to language which is universal in the human race. Most of the things that people have written about these issues are virtually unreadable except to the expert. Three paperbacks which are reasonably clear are: Carroll, John B., *Language and Thought*. Green, Judith, *Psycholinguistics*. Slobin, Dan I., *Psycholinguistics*.

4. Social behavior in primates is fascinating. We are beginning to get good accounts of their behavior in the wild. However, for our purposes, the most relevant question is their ability to use something like human language. Several psychologists have recently been successful in teaching chimpanzees to "talk" using sign language (the Gardners) or objects with symbolic character (Premack). These attempts are well described in a book aimed at the layman, Emily Hahn's *On the Side of the Apes*.

5. The text suggests that you observe animals engaged in fixed-action patterns. One possibility is that you look for a pair of pigeons carrying out a mating dance. Can you identify the releasers? Describe the sequence of behaviors in both the male and female (the male is the one who puffs up to twice his original size). Observe a second pair. Are the behaviors really identical?

6. Can you find examples of territorial behavior? (Hint: Cats and dogs show this clearly. Do children?) How do you recognize it when you find it?

7. "We will never get rid of war. Man is an instinctive killer." What is your reaction to this statement? Would an ethologist agree? Analyze the statement using the concepts presented in the chapter.

4
Motives

In the last chapter, we examined the thesis that man as a species has some universal characteristics that enable us to predict the behavior of any individual man, woman, or child. That thesis turned out to be true only to a limited extent, and, in fact, to be of little value for the practical task of understanding why people do what they do. The next step, then, has to be an attempt to see what help the social sciences can offer for an understanding of the "why" of behavior. If we look again at the ecological model presented in Chapter 2, we can see that the question of "why" has to be answered in terms of all three elements in Figure 2.2. If you want to know why a person makes one or another choice, performs one or another act, you must be able to describe the state of the environment at the moment of action, the character of the person's needs, and the outcomes of the act. You should then be able to make inferences about inner states which form the basis for a discussion of motives. In order to illustrate this approach, let me tell a story about a specific individual, and then analyze the story in terms of the three-part model in Figure 2.2.

A young woman from a prosperous, upper-class Brahmin family in India came to the United States to be a graduate student at an American university. Like most Indians of her class and caste, she had been brought up to consider the eating of meat disgusting on both moral and traditional religious grounds; she had never actually eaten meat. However, before she came to the United States, she tried to convince herself that she would have to learn to eat meat. She had

67

been told that the traditional balanced vegetarian diet of the upper-class Indian is difficult to achieve in the United States. But, even more, she really wanted to rebel against her traditional family. Eating meat had a hidden significance: it meant becoming more Western, more American.

During the first weeks of her stay in the United States, most of her contacts outside of class and laboratories were with a small group of fellow Indian students who had managed to recreate a corner of India in their apartments. Their furniture was Indian, and the girls continued to wear the sari. They often prepared Indian meals for one another. However, a number of the more emancipated Indian students did eat American food and considered that they were especially daring in breaking away from the old customs by eating meat.

One day a young man invited the heroine of our story to come to dinner with him at a restaurant for her first American meal. She accepted with some trepidation. The young man ordered a sirloin, medium rare. The woman decided that she would have the same. There was a long, strained silence as the food was being prepared. Finally the steaks arrived, swimming in a reddish brown sauce. Our heroine picked up the knife and fork, cut into the slice of almost-raw meat. She sat and stared at it in fascination for a moment and then jumped up, ran into the ladies' room, and was thoroughly sick.[1]

What can we say in nontechnical terms about the motives of our young woman? First, there is no question that she was suffering from a severe conflict. On the one hand, she was probably hungry, since she had not eaten for a number of hours. In addition, she very much wanted to become an American. She was also anxious to impress her young male friend and probably felt that she could do so by imitating

---

1. If this story seems a bit remote, try making up one closer to American experience. For example, think about the problem of a young woman from a farm community who has always been a "good girl." Imagine her coming to a big city, being attracted by a bright, lively group of sophisticates. Think of her conflicts if she were taken by a young man to a party where people use hard drugs (skin-pop heroin, perhaps, or take "speed"). Like the Indian woman in the story in the text, the American girl would be torn by conflict between two kinds of feelings. The first would be a wish to be like her new friends, to experience the intense pleasures of the drug, and to express her emancipation from her puritan family. The second kind of feeling might include both a general wish to maintain the style of life for which she was so rigorously trained and a specific fear of the consequences of taking drugs.

him and eating the steak with cool and easy gestures. Had she eaten the steak, therefore, she would have fulfilled several needs—for food, for heightened self-esteem, and for a sense of emancipation. She may also have had a need to win the friendship and respect of the young man who was her model.

On the other hand, she also had contradictory needs. Her entire past conditioned her against eating the flesh of animals, especially of cows. It was probably a severe emotional shock to face the prospect, not only of eating meat, but of eating it in such an undisguised state. She may very well have felt ambivalent about emancipating herself from the traditions and values of her family, her caste, and her religious group. And so, with the heightened tension of emotional conflict, it is hardly surprising that the outcome was an intense revulsion that led her to reject the meat, both symbolically and, indeed, physically.

A Model for the Study of Motives

Chapter 2 took the position that theory is necessary in order to make sense of the world. We can now put this thesis to a test. In order to develop a theoretical scheme to handle the kind of problem faced by our Indian woman, we might concentrate on her choices and decisions (i.e., to order or not to order the steak; once ordered, to eat or reject it). A theoretical model should enable us to lay out the factors that affect the choice and possibly to predict its outcome.

The first step in making a decision is to think about the consequences of each choice. If you are sitting at your desk and trying to decide whether to do your income tax or go out to a movie, you may visualize yourself hovering over a mass of cancelled checks, receipts, government forms, and a hot miniature calculator. And the other choice, going to the movies, raises the vision of yourself relaxed at the local cinema, munching popcorn, watching the screen.

Three kinds of variables will probably affect your choice of doing your tax return or going to the movies. The first variable is the general value of the kinds of outcomes associated with each choice. For example, doing your tax return on the spot would relieve you of the nagging anxiety caused by an incomplete task. It might also tell you whether you will get a refund. On the other hand, going to the

movies might be relaxing. It could also provide an esthetic experience. The first variable in this instance would concern the general
value you place on getting things done early, on relaxation, or on the
esthetic stimulation.

The second variable is your perception of the probability that either choice will actually lead to a desired outcome. How likely do
you think it is that doing the return early would lead to an immediate
refund, or that going to the movies will lead to a relaxed feeling? The
third variable is the attractiveness of the *particular* outcomes of the
particular choice. How much relaxation do you anticipate from the
actual movie playing at the State or the Bijou, and how much do you
feel the need to relax at the moment? How important to you is the refund you might get by putting in your return?[2]

If one could make a numerical estimate of each of these three
factors, then it might be possible to predict what you would do. The
prediction would be based on a contrast of the overall attractiveness
of the two choices. This would be found by multiplying the generalized value of each outcome or goal (getting a refund, relaxation) by
the perceived likelihood that the goal would be reached (Would
doing the tax early really lead to a refund? Would going to the movies
really be relaxing?), and then multiplying the resulting product by
the attractiveness of the specific goal (How much do you need a refund right now? How much do you feel the need to relax right now?).
The equation for each choice might look like this:

Attractiveness of a choice = $Attr_c$.
Value of the general goal = V_G.
Probability that a choice will lead to a goal = P.
Value of the particular goal = V_{PG}.
$$Attr_c = V_G \times P \times V_{PG}.$$

Why multiply rather then add? Because if any of the terms is
zero, the likelihood of making that particular choice has to be zero.
No matter how large the odds on a horse, you won't bet on it if it has
been scratched from the race (i.e., if its probability of winning is
zero). Similarly, you might want very much to be done with your tax

---

2. One problem that this discussion overlooks is the amount of time between action
and consequence. Going to the movies would be pleasant immediately, while the payoff for doing the tax return would be delayed for a long time. A difference in imme-
diacy of reward could have a great effect on the decision.

return, but if you expect some additional information that might change the figures, you are unlikely to start working on your return.

We will now look at each of these three factors more closely, and discuss some notions about how to measure them.

Generalized Attractiveness of Goals

We can start out by postulating that each person has a number of needs rooted in biological nature and in history. The degree to which these operate independently to determine a person's goals will be discussed a little later; we have already explored that issue to some extent in the previous chapter. At the moment, it is only necessary to note that most people recognize at least some of their needs and that such recognition creates a sense of attraction to, or repulsion from, a variety of possible goals. We are not talking about a momentary attraction to a specific goal—for example, the desire for food or drink. The variable with which we are concerned is the *general* attraction of classes of goals. Can you say something about the importance to you of eating in general, sex in general, sociability? All other things being equal (which, of course, they never are), your answer would provide a partial basis for predicting your behavior.

It is possible to describe a wide variety of goals. Some are quite closely related to the fulfillment of physiological needs; others—such as social achievement, a sense of belongingness, helping others, mastery over self or nature—are remote from biological satisfactions. Paradoxically, there are some kinds of goals that superficially seem unattractive, but that are still effective in moving some people. It is hard to escape the conclusion that some people seem to place a high value on suffering, on solitude, or even on failure.

Measuring the general attractiveness of goals is far from easy. One could simply describe various goals and ask people to rank or rate their desirability. But the weaknesses of such a method are obvious. Even if respondents are candid about their feelings, they may not actually know the force of their attraction or repulsion towards the achievement of such goals as social success, sexual fulfillment, or intellectual creation. A number of techniques have been developed to overcome lack of honesty or candor and also to tap feelings that may not easily be expressed as direct answers to questions. The Thematic Apperception Test (TAT), one of the most widely used, was created by the American psychologist Henry Murray in the mid-1930s. It is now widely used in research and also in helping diagnose the source of trouble in emotionally disturbed people.

The TAT consists of a series of nineteen cards with pictures of different human figures in a number of settings. The expressions on the figures are purposely drawn rather blankly and the settings are sketched somewhat vaguely. A person taking the test is asked to tell a story about the picture. For example, one picture shows a boy looking at a violin in a case. The character of the story told by the person taking the test is used as a basis for tentative conclusions about the generalized nature of his goals. One could guess that someone who places a high value on achievement would be likely to tell a story in which the boy is dreaming about the years of hard work that lie ahead of him and imagining a debut in a concert hall. Someone for whom achievement has relatively little value might be more likely to picture the boy as resenting the time he has to spend practicing when he might be out with his friends playing ball.

One important aspect of behavioral choice has been studied little, if at all. That is the identification of the goals and values related to each of the many choices we have to make. When a person is faced by the necessity for deciding what to do, he has to determine what the possible outcomes of his actions might be and relate these to his ideas and feelings about general goals as well as to the particular outcomes of his choices. Deciding whether to do a tax return or go to the movies is not as clear as it looks. Certain outcomes of working at the tax form are clear—for example, money and freedom from anxiety and a sense of pressure. But doing tax forms (i.e., doing what you are supposed to do) may also be related to a desire to be attractive to authority figures like parents and teachers, or to a need to compete with classmates or brothers and sisters. Not doing the form may be a way of punishing a parent who pushed you into doing things you disliked. In fact, someone who feels guilty without knowing quite why may fulfill a need to fail by not filing a return at all. Later in this chapter you will read more about Freud, whose ideas may be used to explore the kinds of paradoxes I have just suggested.

Expectations

A person's past experiences also provide a basis for a judgment about the likelihood that a given choice will really lead to the achievement of a goal. Expectations may be based on the *objective* probability that an outcome will occur; the likelihood of getting a ten of spades on the next draw is something a good poker player should be able to estimate with great precision. But it is often hard to make such objective estimates, because the outcome of many acts cannot be spelled out as precisely as the draw of cards or the toss of dice. Can you say with any precision just how likely it is that going to the movies tonight will turn out to be rewarding? It depends partly on the vagaries of your mood and partly on the particular movies available as well as on a variety of other intangibles.

Even worse, your subjective expectation of reward may be affected by wishful thinking or by unreal fear. Wishful thinking often leads people to overestimate the likelihood of some pleasant outcome, despite past experience. How many horse players do you know who are overwhelmingly attracted to the long shots in a race? Conversely, people often ignore the likelihood of some unpleasant event because of their desire to choose a course whose risks they prefer to overlook. This is illustrated by the tendency to take another drink for the road, or by the cigarette smoking of a man who has had his first coronary.

In summary, there is a real difference between *objective* probability, which can be measured precisely, and *subjective* expectation. The objective probability of drawing a spade from a deck of cards is one in four. If you desperately need to win, the subjective expectation could be greater than one in four. One could infer your state of mind if you put more money on the likelihood of drawing a spade than was warranted by objective probability. Of course, if you play that way too often, you are likely to lose a great deal of money.

Incentives

Lastly, in trying to predict what kinds of choices people will make, it is necessary to know the *specific* rewards or punishments anticipated from each choice. This has to be done by determining the attraction of a goal at a particular moment. A candy bar has little incentive value after a full meal, much more when a person is hungry. This is related to, but not entirely dependent on, how much, in general, the person likes candy.

Incentive is determined by two kinds of factors. One is internal

—a reflection of the needs of the individual at the moment. How hungry do you feel, how flush do you feel, how lonely are you? The second is external, based on your evaluative reactions to the display of potential rewards or punishments. In some ways the world may be seen as a great cafeteria, the incentive value of each dish on the line a function of one's hunger and of the attractiveness of the food.

An Indian Student's Dilemma

We will now go back to an analysis of the problem faced by the Indian woman with whose story this chapter began. She was clearly faced by a conflict between two tendencies: the tendency to eat the steak before her and the tendency to reject it.

The tendency to eat the steak was reinforced by two generalized motive or value systems. The first stems from the experience that eating allays hunger. The second is related to the symbolic value of eating new foods as a way of demonstrating assimilation into a new culture.

The first generalized motive system, however, was associated with a low expectation that eating *steak* would actually allay her hunger, since the student had never eaten meat before. Further, the particular object before her, the rare steak, appeared extremely unattractive to her. Therefore any tendency for her to choose to eat the meat was based on the second of these motive systems, the desire to acculturate. She undoubtedly had a very high expectation that eating the meat *would* result in her feeling Americanized and giving that impression to others. In addition, she may have thought that eating the meat would make her seem suave and sophisticated. If all of this were true, eating the steak would have high incentive value.

However, the tendency not to eat was also quite strong. The generalized value placed on not killing and not eating animals had been reinforced by her entire life history. Her vegetarianism was based on a complex system of values in which the eating of meat was symbolic of barbarism, of everything strange and foreign and inferior. In fact she may have had mixed feelings about traveling overseas, an act forbidden to an extremely orthodox Brahmin. Furthermore, her expectation of violating her value system if she ate meat was at the highest possible level, very likely 100 percent. One might say therefore that the incentive value of not eating the meat was extremely high.

Biological Factors in Motivation

In discussing incentives, I commented that the attractiveness of a particular goal (say, eating snails) is a function of the level of internal needs at the moment (How much biological hunger do you suffer?) and your learned reactions to the goal (Is eating snails something to which you are accustomed?). But the notion of biological hunger, or need for food, needs closer examination, especially in view of the general skepticism expressed in Chapter 3 about the likelihood that any human behavior is "stamped in," in a biological sense. It is now necessary to discuss the possibility of biologically determined *motives,* as distinguished from behaviors. The idea that there are biological drives—notably hunger, thirst, sex, and possibly aggression— has often been proposed. The following section examines the validity of this concept for one of these drives, hunger.

An Analysis of "Hunger"

The desire for food is a good starting point for an evaluation of the concept of innate or biological drives. A great deal of evidence has accumulated to show that both the onset of eating and its termination are controlled by centers in a portion of the brain called the hypothalamus. When a certain small area in the hypothalamus is destroyed in rats, the animals eat themselves into a state of almost fatal obesity. Another center in the hypothalamus which controls the beginning of eating can also be identified and destroyed. The rats that have been subjected to this manipulation never begin to eat; they starve themselves to death in the presence of plentiful food. Both centers are probably stimulated by substances in the blood that respond to physiological needs for food. They are probably stimulated by the centers in the brain that react to the outside world and thus enable an individual to respond to cues that set off learned or habitual reactions to food.

Normal people also maintain a balance between responses to external cues and to internal, physiological stimuli to eating. I have already defined the incentive value of food at any given moment as a mix of the physiological state of the organism at that moment and the attractiveness of the food. When you have just eaten, even the most interesting dishes do not attract you. On the other hand, even if you are quite hungry, you are not likely to eat food you have not experienced in the past. During World War II, American soldiers who had not been given survival training starved in the jungle despite the fact that they were surrounded by potential sources of food which they either did not recognize or to which they could not respond because of negative reactions acquired in early childhood.

Sometimes the balance of response to internal and external cues is disturbed. When that happens people can get either very thin or very fat. It sometimes happens that adolescent girls lose the desire for food almost entirely. They continue to be very active. Their weight may drop alarmingly, as much as fifty or sixty pounds in a few weeks. This condition, which is known as *anorexia nervosa,* has been attributed by psychiatrists to rejection of the emotional demands of growing up. The end result is not dissimilar to the self-starvation resulting from an operation on the hypothalamus of a rat.

The opposite problem, i.e., obesity, is much more common. The research of an American psychologist named Stanley Schachter has led to some interesting insights into differences between people who are overweight and those who are not. A normal person usually eats when he receives internal biological cues that he is in need of nourishment. These cues include such changes as increased contractions of the stomach or lowered levels of sugar in the blood. The latter seems to affect the "eating center" of the brain. In addition, most normal people have learned to react to the passage of time as a cue to eating; they tend to get hungry at times when they usually eat. As a result of these mechanisms, the normal person seems to be able to control the amount of food he takes in and so maintain his or her weight at a remarkably constant level. There seem to be built-in biological and psychological safeguards that stop the normal person from eating more than is needed for adequate nourishment.

The obese person responds in a very different way. According to Schachter, obese people are strongly affected by externals, the odors and sights that signal the presence of attractive foods. They also eat in response to internal cues that have nothing to do with food. For example, Schachter has discovered that when obese college students are subjected to stress, they eat much more than normal students under similar stress. On the other hand, obese students are more likely to skip meals on the weekends when they are not actually in the presence of food. Obese Jewish students have reported that they do not feel a need for food during a day of ritual fasting, Yom Kippur, if they spend that day in the synagogue and are not exposed to the sight or smell of food. "Normal" students, on the other hand, said that they felt ravenously hungry even while they were at their prayers.

In another experiment, Schachter polled the flight crews of French airliners traveling from Europe to the United States. These people leave Europe in the forenoon and have lunch early in their flight. They arrive in the United States many hours after their last meal, but, because of change in time zone, the time in New York is early afternoon. Normal, i.e., nonobese, air crew personnel do not find it possible to wait until the usual hour for dinner. Their insides are growling, and so they usually eat when they arrive, even though this is not a usual time for a meal in New York. On the other hand, the overweight airline personnel find it easy to wait for dinner *since* there are no external cues to make them want to eat.

In a most ingenious experiment, Schachter invited college students to participate in a study in a closed laboratory cubicle. The students arrived about an hour and a half before suppertime. The clock in the room was speeded up so that the subjects thought that suppertime was upon them while they were engaged in the experiment. Normal subjects did not eat from a bowl of crackers that was made available to them because they did not feel hungry or because they did not want to spoil their appetites for dinner. Obese subjects, on the other hand, were unable to resist the attractions of food. These attractions were made more legitimate by the clock; this external cue had more control over the obese subjects than over the normal.

Are There Any Biological Drives?

In general, the evidence argues that there is no such thing as a purely biological drive in humans, at least among adults. It is also probably true that there are no drives completely independent of man's biological nature. Even so clearly life maintaining an activity as eating is shaped by the individual's experiences. Schachter's subjects, like the fictional Indian woman with whom we began, eat or refrain from eating on the basis of a complex mix of biological states and learned reactions.

It has been traditional among social scientists to divide motives into "primary," or biological, and "secondary," or social, categories. They tend to define the life-maintaining motives as primary and identify these as the sources of eating, drinking, breathing, eliminating, propagating the race. They call the drives to achieve, to win power, to be friendly, to gain social status, or to acquire worldly goods "secondary" or learned.

It seems to me that this classification into primary and secondary drives does not work well. As we have seen in the previous discussion, the behavior that is supposed to be based on primary drives is, in large part, learned. The biological components in eating, drinking, eliminating, sex *seem* of the utmost importance, but the notion that these drives are independent of learning does not bear close investigation.

But the opposite argument also applies to the concept of learned drives. None of the "secondary" drives is totally independent of man's biological nature. Achievement or power needs, drives towards social affiliation, esthetic drives can all be related to the character of glands and nerve cells. All trace back to a childhood in which the dependence of human infants, the need for warmth and food, the first stirrings of sexual interest were tied to socially approved behavior. In the last analysis, all behavior is related, closely or remotely, to the need for survival.

It would seem appropriate, then, to regard all drives as having both a biological and a learned, or social, component. The job of the social scientist, working with the biologist, becomes one of finding out how the biological nature of man expresses itself in his complex social motives.

Is a Rational Model for Motivation Adequate?

The discussion of motives up to this point has been based almost entirely on the notion that people reason and that they can talk about the reasonable basis of their choices. I have asked you to assume that individuals making choices are able to determine the level of attractiveness of different kinds of goals, their expectations of achieving these goals in one or another choice, and the incentive value of the outcome of these choices. Having gone through a computation in which each of these factors is multiplied by the others, people would then be expected to select the choice that has the highest product.

Unfortunately, it is doubtful that most human beings ever act this way. Even if they do weigh the attractiveness of choices, they may often be unaware of the reasons for the relative desirability of one or another goal system. And, as pointed out, there is often a considerable discrepancy between subjective expectations and objective probability of the occurrence of outcomes. Social scientists who wish to study the motives of individuals must, therefore, take into account a wide variety of "unconscious" forces.

An Introduction to the Theories of Freud

For a discussion of the nonrational in motivation, we must turn to the founding father of psychoanalysis, Sigmund Freud. In a book of this kind, it is impossible to give a comprehensive account of Freud's ideas. However, it seems desirable to describe some of his basic concepts, if only in an elementary manner, because they have been so influential in the thinking of most social scientists and because they are interesting in themselves.

Development

According to Freud, the individual human being begins as a defenseless creature. The primary source of pleasure is the mouth. The infant receives pleasure by sucking at the breast. He has the illusion of dominating the world by crying. The infant is actually helpless, but he or she is able to exert some impact on others by crying, cooing, or gurgling. This stage was labeled the *oral* stage by Freud. It lasts until the child begins to walk and move around in the household.

In the second stage, the child, whose life up to that point has been an innocent paradise, must begin to submit to social restraints. In Freud's view of this development, the major social restraint is toilet training. Whereas the infant in the crib was able to eliminate at will, he or she must now learn to curb both bladder and bowel. While it is true that curbing the desire to eliminate is unpleasant, the child soon acquires a sense of mastery over himself and over the universe by learning to control his elimination. Thus a new pleasure center emerges in the child's life, and a new source of pleasure control, the anus. Freud, therefore, calls this second stage the *anal* period.

In the third stage, the child begins to discover the pleasures of manipulating his or her genitalia. At about the same time, the child begins to develop intense emotional relations of a differentiated kind with the parent of the opposite sex. According to Freud, little boys at this age have fantasies of marrying their mothers, little girls their fathers. The traumatic discovery that the parent of the opposite sex is already taken leads to strong feelings of anger and resentment. However, in normal development, identification with the parent of the same sex becomes an extremely powerful source of emotional rewards. Thus little boys learn to delight in feeling masculine and little girls in feeling feminine. Part of this delight arises from their acting like the parent of the same sex and, indeed, pretending that they are this parent. Thus, to Freud, the third stage of development, the *phallic,* is characterized by a fixation on the sex organs as a source of pleasure, by a conflict in which the parent of the opposite sex is desired, and by a solution of that conflict through identification with the parent of the same sex. You may remember the brief note on a Freudian analysis of *Mourning Becomes Electra* in Chapter 1. The conflict in this stage is named *Oedipal* after Oedipus, the hero in Greek mythology who killed his father and married his mother.

These stormy events are followed by a period in which sexuality is repressed, the *latent* period. The child's playmates are primarily children of the same sex. He or she is busily occupied with acquiring the skills necessary to function in society, usually through some kind of formal schooling. The child learns how to live with others in organized social groups.

The latent period ends at puberty with the child's transition to biological maturity and the beginning of the stage identified by Freud as the *genital* phase. At that point, he or she begins to substitute a person of his own generation for the forbidden partner, the parent. In normal development, as maturity is gained, the substitution leads to love, marriage, and the formation of a new family.

As is well known, Freud attributes many of the troubles of psychologically disturbed people to failure to resolve adequately the tensions generated in each of these various periods. People who are psychologically sick either slide back to an early stage in development or never move beyond it. Thus Freud views the alcoholic as an infant perpetually sucking at his bottle, trapped in the dreams of oral pleasures and total dependence. The obsessive compulsive is seen as lost in a hopeless struggle to control himself and to manipulate the outside world in an orderly way. He repeats over and over again the traumas of his anal period. The homosexual has been unable to resolve the conflict between a desire to be like the parent of the same sex and the desire to possess the parent of the opposite sex.

The Geography of the Spirit

Freud developed three major theoretical concepts defining different aspects of "mind." The first of these is the *id*. This is supposed to be a system of biologically based drives that are in large part unconscious. To Freud, each individual has enormous drives both towards sexual activity and towards destruction. Both the sexual drives, which Freud calls *libido,* and the destructive drives generate the force behind almost all activity, although in most human beings the effect of these forces is channeled by learning. Unlike the young child, the socialized adult cannot express his sexual or destructive drives in a straightforward and uncomplicated way. In Freud's system, these unconscious drives represent something like a powerful stream of water that must find its outlet somewhere. If dammed in one direction, it flows in another.

The second construct is the *ego.* The ego is the system of learned, organized activities. It is the individual as executive, shaping his or her life, acting in a purposive manner to fulfill conscious goals. Actually, Freud himself was not terribly interested in this aspect of human function; it remained for some of his followers, especially his daughter Anna, to stress the importance of the ego in understanding human functioning. You may be familiar with the popular use of the term "ego" to indicate a sense of self-importance. While few psychologists or psychiatrists use the word that way, there is a germ of meaning in the popular use. The ego includes the individual's sense of his own individuality, the expression of his feeling of worth, and the techniques he has acquired to create a functioning concept of himself.

Lastly, Freud describes the *superego* which represents the internalization of the parents' systems of values. To some extent, a small boy actually "becomes" his father rather than merely trying to be like his father. He includes within himself, often unconsciously, the system of goals and, even more, the system of prohibitions he has seen in his parents as he has grown up. Except that the superego has many unconscious components, it may be equated with conscience in its function as a source of prohibitions. Since it is a source of values, it may also be equated with a person's ideals.

Defense Mechanisms

Another important component of Freud's design for an understanding of human motives is his concept of *defense mechanisms*. Freud began with the observation that both the id and the superego often give rise to intense anxiety. People are upset by unacceptable attractions to potential sources of sexual satisfaction. In order to survive, to prevent emotional collapse, people have to develop ways of resolving their anxiety. Some of Freud's most acute observations were made when he identified techniques for maintaining emotional balance; it was these which he called the defense mechanisms.

The names Freud gave to the defense mechanisms have become part of everyday vocabulary. *Sublimation* refers to socially productive activity that drains off the energy of the libido and prevents destructive anxiety. For example, someone who takes cold showers and runs around the track to distract himself from forbidden sexual urges is sublimating. So, presumably, is the person who rejects the usual pattern of family life in order to devote himself or herself to scientific, artistic, or religious pursuits. The man who beats his wife because he cannot let himself even think hostile thoughts about his boss is *displacing*. The expression of aggression towards a defenseless person gets rid of anger and permits the person to maintain balance. *Reaction formation* occurs when someone does something which is opposite to what he really wants. A person whose defective toilet training leaves him with an urge to be messy can defend himself against this by becoming compulsively neat.

The defense mechanisms are familiar modes of adjustment to all of us. When they become too powerful, the result can be serious maladjustment. This is the Freudian explanation of the origins of much neurotic behavior. A detailed discussion of psychopathology is beyond the scope of a primer. If this brief glimpse interests you, the books on abnormal psychology cited in the bibliography in this chapter would make rewarding reading.

How Useful Is Freudian Thinking to Social Science?

Freudian terminology and Freudian ideas have become part of

the general vocabulary of most educated people. When social scientists assume that people cannot always talk intelligently about all of the factors that determine their choices or the intensity of their reactions, they are using a simplified version of the Freudian approach. The basic idea that the character of an adult is shaped by the interactions of the very young child with the members of his family seems obvious to us now. It caused waves of horrified reaction when it was first proposed in part at least because the notion that infants could have sexual interests was so incompatible with the Victorian idea of the angelically pure child.

But Freudian ideas have their limitations. His description of the life history of an individual is very much that of an upper-middle-class Viennese in the late nineteenth century. It is bound to the character of one culture[3] at one particular time. And so, although the idea that the adult is shaped by the history of the child is widely acknowledged by social scientists, the universality of the Oedipal conflict or of the latent state is somewhat more controversial.

Freudian Ideas and the "Values ×
Expectations × Incentive" Theory of Motivation

The relation of Freudian thinking to the model for drives presented earlier in this chapter is fairly clear. The generalized systems of goals or values that are the first term in the model are related to Freud's concepts of both the id and the superego. The procedure for measuring the strength of generalized motives by analyzing stories evoked by pictures (i.e., the TAT) has already been described. This procedure is especially valuable because it can tap unconscious as well as conscious values. The rationale for this is based on Freud's concept of *projection* as a defense against the anxiety roused by some motives. Projection occurs when people attribute to others feelings or ideas that they sense in themselves but cannot express because they violate potent taboos. A man who desperately desires sexual fulfillment but who is barred by religious or social restraints may react by perceiving a convenient scapegoat as vigorously sexual. Presumably, ideas that cannot be expressed directly can be brought out indirectly if they can be attributed to people in a TAT picture.

Expectations, the second component of our model, are probably

3. The concept of culture will be explored in detail in Chapter 5. The limitations of Freudian thinking will appear in clearer perspective after you have read that chapter.

similar to components of the ego in a Freudian system. They represent the results of learning, and they are an important basis for action. The fact that Freud was relatively little interested in the ideas and values we described as expectations may very well represent one of the most serious weaknesses of his system.

Similarly, except to the extent to which incentives have symbolic characteristics derived from events in early childhood, Freud was also relatively little interested in the specific incentive value of individual goals. However, Freudian concepts help expand our idea of incentive, since they point to the possibility of symbolic incentives. The steak in the story with which we began clearly had enormous symbolic significance to our heroine. Its rejection represented ties to her family, just as eating it represented ties to a brave new way of life. We could easily have used the Freudian vocabulary of id and superego to describe the conflicts raging within her soul.

This discussion has dealt with the contributions and the weaknesses of Freudian thinking from the point of view of the social sciences. To summarize, Freud makes us focus on the early history of the individual, but his indifference to the adult's relation with his social environment limits the usefulness of his system. This is especially true because of Freud's roots in a particular time and place. However, this limitation is not required by the theory of psychoanalysis: it is true only of Freud's own work. Such followers of Freud as Eric Erickson and Erich Fromm have developed psychoanalytic systems which incorporate socio-cultural factors.

Freud also forces us to remember that we can't always trust what people say about themselves; we have to use indirect approaches such as free association, analysis of dreams, and projective tests if we really want to go deeply into motives. His lack of attention to the thinking as well as the feeling man limits the value even of this contribution. Still, no one interested in studying human behavior can ignore the contributions of Freud to our concepts and techniques for working with motives.

An Application of the Value-Expectation-Incentive Theory to Analysis of a Social Motive

The discussion in this chapter so far has been largely abstract. A good way of applying the conceptual scheme for motives to a human problem might be to turn to a motive that is primarily social. The motive I have chosen is the drive to achieve, a subject that has been the focus of an enormous amount of investigation by social scientists and whose understanding is vital to the exploration of many social issues.

The measurement of the need for achievement began with an adaptation by Henry Murray's disciple, David McClelland, of the Thematic Apperception Test, which was described earlier in this chapter. McClelland chose a limited number of TAT pictures and presented subjects with some concrete questions about the stories they imagined when they saw the pictures. He asked them to say something about the character of the people in the stories, the reasons they were doing what they were doing, and the outcome of these actions. He then proposed that the strength of the subjects' desire to achieve could be determined from the nature of the themes in their stories. If a person describes the individuals in the picture as planning, thinking about the future, overcoming obstacles, then he or she is clearly fixated on achievement. If the individual telling the story describes people as experiencing, feeling, reacting to the world but not acting, then his or her need for achievement is considered low.

McClelland's first studies were devoted to a search for ways of demonstrating that the analysis of fantasy really does provide a measure of need for achievement. He found that people who were in a situation that called for striving, for example, students awaiting an examination, wrote stories that included more references to striving, planning, and working towards the achievement of goals than people in a relaxed, unstimulating environment. These studies supported the notion that the analysis of fantasy is valid, that it really measures the need for achievement.

McClelland next began using the projective test to measure the first component of our motivational scheme, the *general* attractiveness of achievement as a goal. In many studies, he found that people whose need for achievement was high, as measured by the projective test, behaved differently from people whose need for achievement was low. For example, in a game like darts or ring toss, high-need achievers tended to take moderate risks in situations where they could estimate the likelihood of success or failure. Individuals with a low need for achievement tended either to take very slight risks or to jump to the other extreme and play the longest of shots. In talking to subjects in these experiments, it became apparent that people who take moderate risks are really focusing on winning, especially if they feel that they themselves can be responsible for the win. Those who have little need for achievement are often motivated by a strong need to avoid failure. They seek out situations in which they have virtually no risk of failure or situations in which the likelihood of success is so slight that they do not feel any shame over failing.

Another approach to the study of achievement was developed by a psychologist named Julian Rotter at the University of Connecticut. He discovered that it is possible to characterize people on a scale of attitudes that he labeled *internal/external control*. People who have a feeling of *internal control* believe that they themselves are responsible for their fate in most instances. 'They see the world as one in which they can achieve their goals by exercising skill. In contrast, people who are *externally oriented* are fatalists. They believe that they cannot have any control over their own fate, that the arbitrary workings of outside authorities determine whether or not they succeed or fail, whether they prosper or are impoverished.

Both success and failure affect people differently, depending on the level of need for achievement and of internal or external orientation. To someone who has a strong need for achievement, success *increases* willingness to undertake more and more difficult tasks. Failure has an immediate tendency to make high-need achievers work harder, but in the long run makes them drop down to somewhat less challenging tasks.

In contrast, people whose primary motive is a need to avoid failure are not impressed by success because they do not really believe in their own capacity to continue to succeed. If they win by taking very slight risks, this merely reinforces them in their tendency to avoid choices that would really threaten their feelings about themselves. If they fail after taking extreme risks, this merely confirms their expectation of failure.

What this means is that success and failure have much greater effect on people with a high need for achievement and on internally oriented people than on those whose need for achievement is low or who are "externals." Another way of putting this is that high-need achievers are more sensitive to the rewards and punishments that flow from their efforts than are people low in need for achievement. In some ways, belief about control (i.e., internal/external orientation) and need for achievement seem to go together, even though the measures by which they are determined are very different. I hope I haven't given the impression that one should regard the high-need achievement, internally oriented people as the "good guys" and the low-need achievement, externally oriented people as the "bad guys." But there is no question that the former have both the motivational structure and the beliefs that seem to go with success in the conventional sense in our society.

The Motives of Adolescents in the Ghetto

We can apply the ideas we have just defined to an analysis of a serious and difficult social situation, the dilemma of black adolescents in the ghetto. Schooling there is usually inadequate and to take advantage of what schooling is available they must exercise enormous personal force. On the other hand, they are surrounded by the attractions of life on the street, especially the withdrawal from competition represented by the use of drugs. Choices are rarely simple, but one might summarize the dilemma of ghetto teenagers by saying that one of their choices is to work harder at school, try to enter a skilled occupation or a profession, try to achieve the rewards of middle-class American society. Taking a different road, they can drop out of school, earn subsistence wages at unskilled work or survive on public assistance, and make a goalless life palatable through the use of drugs. A third choice is to refuse to join the ranks of drug-ridden dropouts or to strive for advancement in society, but instead to work with radical political groups to change the society.

You may get some feeling for the application of the concepts presented so far in this chapter by using them to evaluate the decisions taken by young people in the ghetto. It has been determined in a number of surveys that young ghetto men and women tend to be externally oriented. That is, they tend, very realistically, to be fatalistic about the possibility that their own efforts can really have an impact on their lives. They probably vary widely in need for achievement and need to avoid failure.

It is difficult to make and sustain the choice to work hard as an individual and try to "make it" in our society. Even if the value of making it is in general extremely attractive, and the specific incentives are extremely desirable, the expectation that this choice would really lead to success is probably very low for ghetto youth. And, the incentives are often far removed. That is, the young black adolescent who decides to stay in school must reconcile himself to working for incentives that are years off, very hard to achieve, and emotionally remote. The immediate incentives—high grades in school, scholarships, admission to a desirable educational institution or training program—may be attractive, but, again, the expectation of the likelihood of reaching them is small. On the other hand, even if the value generally placed on the purposelessness of the dropout's life may be low, the incentives of the street are present and attractive, and the expectation of achieving them in the dropout's life are very high. Thus it is hardly surprising that relatively few ghetto youngsters choose the path of hard work and individual advancement.

Even though the product of motive × expectation × incentive rarely gives young people in the ghetto a powerful tendency to choose hard work and education, the alternative is not necessarily apathy and withdrawal. As I indicated, there is a third choice for some adolescents with high need for achievement but low expectation that the standard path will be rewarding. That alternate is affiliation with such groups as the Black Panthers of the late 1960s. Consider that choice. The goals of a heightened level of personal pride and of belonging to a valued group are probably high in most ghetto youngsters. The success of street gangs attests to this. The expectation that political activity will achieve the long-range goal of the "revolution" may indeed be low, but the incentives of approval from peers, of a sense of purpose to life, and of a variety of immediate rewards are certainly attractive, and the expectation of achieving such returns from membership in a radical group is probably very high. For many black adolescents with high achievement needs, the product of motive, expectancy, and incentive for this choice is undoubtedly decisive.

Efforts at Intervention

Even though the last decade has brought little fundamental change in the ghetto environment, a considerable social effort has been devoted to bringing as many young people as possible into the mainstream of American society. Objectively, black boys and girls now enjoy considerably expanded opportunities for education and entrance into the skilled trades and professions. The returns from this effort may or may not be disappointing. If one is a pessimist, the glass is half empty; to an optimist, it is half full.

Two psychologists at the University of Michigan, a husband-and-wife team named Patricia and Gerald Gurin, have been central figures in the effort to evaluate the success of attempts to educate young people in the ghetto. They found it easy to identify the reasons for the frustrations in this effort. Even people with a low expectation of success are sometimes encouraged by success to work hard in situations other than the specific one in which success occurs. Therefore, one should expect that any training effort that gives boys and girls the experience of succeeding ought to have a considerable impact. On this basis, much of the psychological and sociological training devoted to ghetto youth has been designed to give them some feeling of success and to increase their expectation that striving will actually lead to the social and vocational goals they are encouraged to adopt.

Unfortunately, the typical point of view in the ghetto is one of external orientation or fatalism. This is very different from the *pathological* fatalism that one sometimes finds among middle-class people who suffer from a lack of internal strength. It is instead a realistic fatalism which stems from the actual experience of powerlessness in the face of government, trade unions, landlords, police, and the educational establishment. Several experiments have shown that a sense of fatalism usually disrupts the impact of objective successes on expectations. These results suggest that, unless the external orientation of ghetto youngsters is reversed, attempts to promote education and training will have relatively little impact.

What Can Be Done?

To effect real improvement in the lot of the inhabitants, one should change both the ghetto environment and the people who live in it. To see where these changes might be beneficial, let us consider each of the three components of motives: general values, expectations, and incentives.

Research on social change suggests that it is very hard to affect basic systems of values. These have their roots deep in the culture, and, for individuals, are based on years of experiences. It may be that values can be changed by heroic efforts. But short of revolutionary upheavals in societies or years of individual psychotherapy, we have to accept the idea that, if change in motives is to take place, it must be based on changes in expectations and incentives rather than in values.

In some ways, the easiest factor to work with is incentives. To improve incentives for achievement among the young in the ghetto, it would be desirable to introduce enough short-term rewards so that staying in school and working would be more attractive than the pleasures of the street. The young people would have to have experiences in which they actually *did* exercise some control, win rewards about which they really care, achieve some sense of freedom of choice. Experiences such as these might lead to an increase in internal orientation and achievement motive.

It would be foolish to pretend that small improvements in school experiences can have much effect if the unemployment rate among young men and women in the ghetto hovers about fifty percent. The community must solve the long-range problem of integrating the part of the population now left out of the affluent society before young people can believe that a lifetime of meaningful and rewarding work lies ahead of them. Nevertheless, the problems posed by the discussion of achievement motive and internal/external orientation are real ones. Even if we do get rid of racist barriers entirely, even if we do provide opportunities, we still have to encourage people to go through the newly opened doors. A whole generation will be stunted unless ways are found of erasing the crippling results of growing up in a deprived minority.

The next section of the book attempts to present some concepts which may be used to characterize social systems as a whole. We need these concepts in order to study the way children grow up to acquire the values and expectations of their social groups.

On Your Own

1. Hall on Freud is fine but don't be afraid to tackle the master himself. Freud wrote well and there are some good translations. You will undoubtedly find a number of books by him either in the library or in paperback bookstores. Start with the *Introductory Lectures,* the *Psychopathology of Everyday Life,* or *Dream Analysis.*

2. If McClelland intrigues you, you may be interested in a procedure called "motivation workshops" in which people learn about the nature of motives and also work

through a series of exercises or games in which they learn to improve the level of their achievement or affiliation motives. Two sources of materials are: Educational Ventures, Inc., Middletown, Conn., which publishes a series of handbooks for "reaching real goals" developed by Alfred S. Alschuler and Diane Tabor of Harvard. McClelland, David C. and Steele, Robert S., *Motivation Workshops*.

3. A very traditional view of motivation from a biological point of view is John L. Fuller's *Motivation: A Biological Perspective*.

4. Think of an instance in your own recent past when you were aware of being torn over the choice between two options. Using the approach described on page 69, try to estimate in some terms the level of your general values for the outcomes of each choice (perhaps on a scale from zero to eleven). Then check your expectation of gaining these values (chances in 100) if you chose one or the other outcome, and rate the incentive in each outcome (again on a scale from zero to eleven). Does what you finally chose make sense in terms of this analysis?

5. Can you identify your own level of need for achievement? Is it high, low, medium? Does your behavior fit McClelland's description of people in the high, low, or medium category of need for achievement? For example, do you like to take moderate risks, or are you someone who avoids risks entirely or gambles regularly on long odds? Do you plan or let things happen to you? Do you feel rewarded when you have the opportunity to overcome obstacles? N.B. This question does *not* imply that it is necessarily good to have high need for achievement.

6. Go back to the literary work you analyzed for the first study question in Chapter 1 and identify the defense mechanisms you find in some leading character's behavior. Is he compulsive (or is she)? Does he (she) engage in projection, sublimation, displacement? How do you make this identification of defense mechanisms? What are the consequences of the defense mechanisms for the story? You may have to read pages 85–97 of Hall's *Primer of Freudian Psychology* to answer this question since the chapter gives very few details on the defense mechanisms.

7. Analyze your own eating patterns using Schacter's scheme. Do you respond to internal or external cues? Are you moved to eat only by really attractive food or do you eat primarily because you feel hungry? Does your weight bear out Schacter's prediction of the differences in eating patterns between overweight and normal people?

8. A continuation of the work on black adolescents has recently been reported by Gurin and Epps. It provides a remarkably insightful analysis of the intellectual and emotional problems of black college students. See *Black Consciousness, Identity, and Achievement* by Patricia Gurin and Edgar Epps.

Section III
Society

5
Culture and Behavior

The previous chapter began with a story about a student from India transplanted to the United States. The purpose of this story was to provide some raw material for an analysis of motives. Actually, there was no need to make the story revolve around a student from a foreign country; a similar story could easily have been constructed using the experiences of an American student moving to a university for the first time. I chose to write about an Indian in the hope that an exotic protagonist would attract your interest more than someone from an everyday background. Also, the picture of a familiar world seen through the eyes of a foreigner makes things that are usually taken for granted stand out. In a sense, it was almost necessary to invent a foreign visitor to make you take a fresh look at the character of motives, just as Montesquieu in *Persian Letters* invented a visitor from Persia to put into relief the contradictions of pre-revolutionary French society.

But telling a story about a student from India makes the assumption that the reader has a little knowledge of what an Indian girl might be like. It is not entirely safe to generalize about people, but it is likely that if you knew that someone is female, young, from the subcontinent of India, and of high caste, these pieces of information would go a long way in helping you make some reasonably good predictions of the person's reactions to a variety of circumstances. The more you knew about India in general and the person's community within it in particular, the better your predictions would be.

Of course, if you had to predict a person's actions, you would obviously be in the best position to do so if you knew that particular individual well. You could assume that a person's actions in any given situation would be similar to his or her previous actions in similar situations. However, if you observed a *number* of people in the same social group, you might become aware of similarities in their behavior. You could then use your knowledge of these similarities. Knowing that a person *is* a member of a given group, you could then predict that he will probably (*not* certainly) act as his fellows usually do.

Let us trace the way a newcomer might learn about the customs of a group. Imagine that you live in New York or Chicago and are visiting the family of one of your friends who has moved to the city from a small town in Kansas. You notice on the very first day of your trip that your host does not lock his doors at night. To someone living in a big city in the 1970s, this *is* startling. But the failure to lock doors is not the only bit of startling behavior. You also discover that your friend's family leave their automobile in front of their house with the key in the ignition and the doors unlocked. Tools are left in an open tool shed behind the house. There are no bars on the windows or other ways of guarding the household from intruders. Your friend's fifteen-year-old sister is allowed to walk through town by herself to do an errand late at night. Few parents would let a fifteen-year-old girl walk out alone in the middle of New York or Chicago after dark.

From all of this evidence you might conclude that your host had a set of ideas about the world somewhat different from your own. As someone living in the middle of a big city, you fear invasion of privacy and value being closely protected. You anticipate that anything you leave lying around is likely to be stolen. Your friend and his family, in contrast, seem to be open, secure, and trusting. But up to this point, you have no way of knowing that this characteristic is not peculiar to your friend and his immediate family.

As you stay in the town, however, you notice that the behavior of your friend's family is not unique to that family. No one seems to lock doors or bother with bars on windows or with burglar alarms. Everyone seems to leave garage doors open, displaying a tempting array of automobile and gardening tools. Nightfall does not seem to be an occasion for withdrawing into the safety of one's own home or sticking to brightly lit avenues. And so you conclude that there is a real difference between the customs of the small town and those of the city. Further, the difference lies not only in customs, but in ideas. We have not directly reported on this difference, but the kinds of ideas that characterize small town or big city can be inferred from the differences in behavior we have discussed. And we have included some description of differences in the environments of the two social settings. All of these differences could be summed up by an anthropologist as differences in *culture*.

The Concept of Culture

Among social scientists, anthropologists have been most active in studying the kinds of differences among communities that impress a visitor from the city to a small town. The key concept anthropologists have brought to this inquiry is the notion of "culture." Unhappily, there are about as many different definitions of culture as there are anthropologists. The definitions use various elements of the ecological model shown in Figure 2.2. That is, culture has been defined in terms of variation in the environment (the left side of the diagram), of classes of behavior (the right side of the diagram), and of ideas (in brackets). Figure 5.1 presents the relation between the various definitions of culture and the ecological model.

Anthropologists interested in the careful description of different societies are called ethnologists. They define culture in terms of such material characteristics as housing, means of transportation, implements, and ornaments. They also focus on rules of social interaction, thus delineating the social environment. Of course, the distinction between the ethnologist's approach and one that focuses on behavior is an arbitrary one, since behavior (the right side of the ecological model) helps define the social environment which is one of the most important aspects of the input side of the diagram. Most classical anthropology in both Britain and the United States was devoted to field studies in which the often exotic details of life among the dying remnants of primitive peoples were captured for posterity. You can get the flavor of this kind of approach to culture by going to the ethnological sections of natural history museums. In the best of these, you will find skillfully designed dioramas showing the lifestyles of Indian

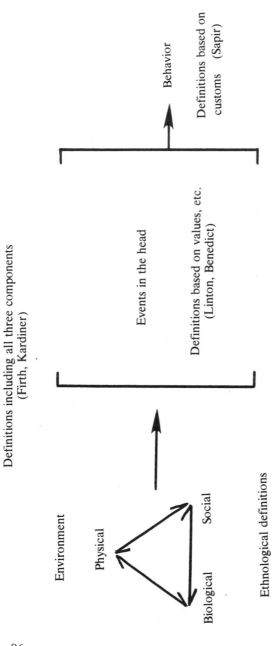

Fig. 5:1. Definitions of Culture Related to the Ecological Model

Definitions including all three components
(Firth, Kardiner)

Events in the head

Definitions based on values, etc.
(Linton, Benedict)

Behavior

Definitions based on
customs (Sapir)

Environment

Physical

Social

Biological

Ethnological definitions

or African villages. At their worst, you will see miles of dusty cages filled with feathered headdresses and simple agricultural implements. This approach to culture clearly uses classificatory or type one theoretical systems (see Chapter 2).

If we wanted to apply the ethnological method to the story with which this chapter began, we could define the culture of small town and big city by means of descriptions of artifacts and of the physical and social environment. We would describe differences between one-family houses open to the world and high rise buildings with carefully locked apartments, between tree-lined streets with vistas of fields and hills and crowded avenues and dirty subways.

A second approach to culture focuses on the output or behavioral side of the ecological model. This point of view is expressed in a definition proposed by one of the fathers of American anthropology, Edward Sapir: "Culture, as it is ordinarily constructed by the anthropologist, is a more or less mechanical sum of the more striking or picturesque generalized patterns of behavior which he has either abstracted for himself out of the sum total of his observations or has had abstracted for him by his informants in verbal communication." Sapir emphasizes the fact that observations of behavior have to be organized into patterns or categories, either by the social scientist or by the people on whom he relies for insight into the society being observed. Again, this yields type one or classificatory theory. If this kind of approach to culture were used to analyze the city dweller's visit to the small town, it would produce a focus on behaviors such as the locking or not locking of doors and windows, the freedom of movement after dark, the modes of address among family members and between family members and strangers.

An entirely different point of view defines culture in terms of ideas (the list in brackets in the diagram of the ecological model). Such anthropologists as Ralph Linton or Ruth Benedict characterized culture as consistent patterns of thought, dominant attitudes, and values. This psychological approach to culture uses observations of behavior and environment as a basis for inferences about "events in the head." Benedict, for example, contrasted the calm, controlled "Apollonian" system of values of Zuni and other Pueblo Indians in the American Southwest with the dynamic, activist "Dionysiac" values of their neighbors, the Navajos. In the story of the visit, we could define the values of the small town's culture as open, trusting, friendly, the city as suspicious, unfriendly, closed.

An interesting and rather sophisticated approach to definition of culture which employs all three components of the ecological model is that of the English anthropologist Raymond Firth. His picture of culture includes characterization of the group's social structure, social controls, rules dealing with the way individuals interact, material goods, and, lastly, codified knowledge of the group, its social standards and its systems of values and goals. From this point of view, a comprehensive picture of a community's culture must be built from descriptions of the physical, social, and biological environment, of consistencies of behavior, and of those events in the head that can be inferred from behavior.

Individuality and Culture

For any one individual, the culture in which he or she has grown up provides a general model for behavior. However, each person's behavior is the product of his or her own unique experiences. It seems a truism to say that culture must be rediscovered by every member of each generation.

One implication of this truism is that the generalizations of social scientists about the typical behavior of people in any society are a poor basis for dealing with individuals. The descriptions of cultures deal with the statistical *mode*. The word *mode* deserves a moment's attention. If a fruit stand had fifty bushels of apples, fourteen bushels of pears, and three each of peaches, avocados, and mangoes, it would certainly be obvious that the typical fruit on the stand was the apple. If the stand were somewhere in the northeastern United States, it would also be a fair guess that most of the fruit on the stand was grown locally. That description of the fruit stand would, however, be incomplete. It would fail to note that the energetic proprietor had invested in at least two varieties of produce from faraway places, the avocados and mangoes. In order to give a complete picture of the stand, it would be necessary to describe, not only the typical fruit, but also the extent of diversity. Similarly, a description of only the modal or typical behavior of a society leaves much to be desired. The friendly, trusting small town we described undoubtedly includes some individuals who are habitually suspicious of their fellows. And the picture we drew *was* oversimplified; would these friendly people accept a young man with beads and long hair?

Nevertheless, modal behavior, and the ideas associated with it, set the background against which diversity must be interpreted. A suspicious mother who was reluctant to let her teenage daughter go out unaccompanied after dark would be somewhat deviant in a small town, quite typical in the center of a big city. Such a mother would be a poor source for someone trying to define the culture of a small town. Only as a comprehensive picture of the behavioral patterns of a group emerges, though, can the social scientist make the judgment that one person is, and another is not, characteristic.

Summary

Most people living in the same society share a set of ideas about appropriate behavior in that society. These ideas, the behavior with which they are associated, and the environment that provides the setting for the behavior are all necessary for a complete definition of the culture of a society. While different anthropologists tend to emphasize one or another of the three components of culture, it seems desirable that all be included. The next stage in this discussion requires a look at the ways the elements of a culture are transmitted and shape the life histories of individuals.

Socialization and Enculturation

Anthropologists use two terms to describe the process by which an infant acquires the characteristic beliefs, values, and behaviors of the society. The word *socialization* refers to the process in its most general sense. It is usually used to describe the experiences of growing up shared by most members of a group. *Enculturation* refers to the specific process by which the character of the culture is transmitted to each member of the group.

Social scientists from disciplines other than anthropology have dealt with one or another aspect of individual growth and development. Freud's ideas about emotional development have already been introduced. The great Swiss philosopher-psychologist Jean Piaget has proposed concepts that have had a great impact on our understanding of the development of thought. He has also dealt with the growth of moral judgment, play, and creativity. Both Freud and Piaget believed that their ideas about development were applicable to all human beings. Within the general pattern shared by all humans, however, there are characteristics unique to each social group. The discussion that follows focuses on ways of describing these unique aspects of individual cultures.

An elegant formulation of the impact of culture on personality was created by Abraham Kardiner. His theory integrates Freud's ideas about personality with concepts of culture derived from the work of such anthropologists as Ralph Linton and Franz Boas. Kardiner was a psychoanalyst turned anthropological theorist, and his system is characterized by a synthesis of many points of view. Like Raymond Firth, Kardiner used all three components of the ecological model in defining the relation of culture and behavior. He called the various aspects of the environment *primary institutions.* These he related to the character of the individual by positing a *basic personality structure* or *modal personality* shared by all members of a society. One important consequence of basic personality is the system of ideas and beliefs common to a social group, which Kardiner calls *secondary institutions.*

Primary institutions affect the individual through a series of *key integrational systems.* These describe the factors that affect an individual's reaction to crucial events of his or her development. They include the transition from newborn status to infancy and from infancy to childhood, the indoctrination of the young into adult status, the modes of organization of production which influence an individual's work, recreation, and family life, and, finally, withdrawal during old age.

Basic personality is described in Freudian terms. The character of id, ego, and superego and, especially, the nature of defense mechanisms are considered by Kardiner to be shared, in part, by all members of a society. Common characteristics of personality are based on the key integrational systems characteristic of the primary institutions of a society.

Secondary institutions include the systems of belief that derive from a society's religion, science, art, and philosophy. Kardiner goes on to study the way these secondary institutions derive their character from the basic personality typical of a society and thus from the nature of the primary institutions. The whole system feeds back upon itself. Government, for example, provides a series of primary institutions that affect individuals. However, Kardiner considers the nature of ideals about government to be elements of the secondary institutions.

During his long tenure at Columbia University, Kardiner stimulated many social scientists who attended his seminar on culture and personality. Under his direction, several carried out extensive field investigations in which the techniques of anthropological study were combined with a focus on individuals. One of these studies, by Cora Du Bois, provides a good illustration of the usefulness of Kardiner's analytical system. She worked with a group called the Alorese, a primitive people living in what was then the Dutch East Indies, now a part of Indonesia. She lived with the group for two years, learning its language, observing its customs, and gathering lengthy life histories from many of its members. In addition to the observations and life histories, she used a variety of psychological tests.

I will abstract only one small finding from the two volumes of Du Bois's report, but that gives the essence of Kardiner's approach, as she applied it. The women among the Alorese raise most of the food by cultivating small garden patches in the jungle. The work is very hard and time consuming since the jungle is an enemy against which continual effort is required. Women in many cultures are the main providers of food, but they solve the problem of child care by bringing their children with them to the fields, often in a device like the Amerindian papoose carrier. In Alor, mothers desert their children shortly after childbirth. The infants are left in the often indifferent care of siblings as young as five or six years of age. The fathers are busy with a complex "financial" game involving bride prices and dowries, which require long conferences between debtor and creditor. They expect to be fed by their wives but do not participate in caring for the young. The consequence of this pattern is a basic personality characterized by anxiety, suspicion, mistrust, lack of confidence, and repressed hatred. The primary institution responsible for this is the system of care for infants, a critical key integrational system. The basic personality leads to a set of secondary institutions in which relations between spouses are viewed as necessarily hostile. Religious beliefs do not include any concept of a supportive or loving deity.

In a discussion in Kardiner's seminar, several of us asked how

Alor would be affected by the introduction of the papoose carrier, in which mothers could bring their children with them to work. This device might alter the key integrational system but, as we shall see later in the chapter, there is much question whether people with the basic personality characteristic of Alor would be willing to use it.

Another illustration of Kardiner's system, in which basic personality links primary to secondary institutions, may be found in the widespread similarities among societies in which the family is organized along father-centered, or patriarchal, lines. The patriarchal family is characteristic of most of the societies that descend from the great migrations of the Iron Age out of central Asia. These migrations apparently brought patriarchal families to Western Europe, the Mediterranean basin, India, and China along with the domestication of large animals, the wheel, and the use of iron tools.

In almost all the societies descended from the Iron Age invaders, the history of individual development is similar to that described by Freud. That is, a child typically grows up in a setting in which a dominant father is the final source of authority within the family. A boy has to grow through a painful process of suppressing his desire to dispossess that dominant father and possess his mother; each girl must cope with her wish to kill her mother and marry her father. Presumably, a successful resolution of this conflict results in an internalization of the values of the parent of the same sex and an attempt on the part of the child to model himself or herself after this parent.

We have already discussed this sequence in Chapter 3. The consequences for the personality of the individual are, according to Kardiner, those described by Freud. The patriarchal family also shapes the character of the secondary institutions. Religion, one of the major secondary institutions, revolves around a father-god who is the source of all authority. Presumably, in a society in which there is no strong central male figure in a family, the traditional religions of the Iron Age cultures, with their father-gods like Zeus and Jahweh, would have relatively little attraction. Or, at least, it would be necessary to change the basic structure of the family in order to make the religion anything more than an alien transplant. Similarly, governmental structure in these societies usually centers on a dominant male figure, the "father of his country." His name may be king, emperor, president, or chairman, but under any of these names he is a substitute for the godlike father who figured so strongly in each individual's early history.

In contrast, groups in which the young are not shaped by a dominant father as chief authority—for example, the Trobrianders described in Chapter 1—do not easily adapt to patriarchal forms of government, nor do they convert readily to such religions as Christianity or Islam. In such groups, religion typically revolves around a set of beliefs about ghosts or spirits who are temporarily present after death. These ghosts should be placated since they may interfere capriciously in human affairs, even though they are not really powerful. The governmental structure, such as it is, usually consists of a loose alliance of families.

Kardiner's system has many of the strengths and weaknesses of the period of the thirties during which it was developed. It provides a valuable synthesis of Marxist, Freudian, and anthropological thinking. Kardiner dealt with the entire span of human life; in that respect, he advanced beyond Freud's fixation on the experiences of early childhood as the basis for the development of personality. Kardiner was aware of the importance of economic and sociological factors in behavior. In fact, many of his analyses of the impact of primary institutions on personality provide a good model for the integration of economic and individual-oriented aspects of social science.

But there *are* weaknesses. Kardiner was limited by his Freudian scheme for describing personality. Like many students of culture and personality, he assumed that studying a few members of a group provides an adequate basis for defining typical behavior. We search in vain, for example, for evidence that *most* Alorese were really as crippled emotionally as the ones interviewed by Du Bois.

Lastly, correlation does not necessarily imply causality. That is, merely demonstrating the occurrence of a particular pattern of child rearing and finding a personality characteristic that seems to be derived from it, does not *prove* the causal connection. For example, it seems reasonable to relate the neat, formal, almost compulsive character of Japanese behavior to the extremely rigorous toilet training carried out by Japanese families. Ruth Benedict, in her well-known book on Japanese society written shortly after World War II, *The Chrysanthemum and the Sword,* made such a connection. However, many Japanese-American children are subject to the rigorous early toilet training characteristic of Japan but share most of the personal traits of Americans—including the sloppiness. If we are to make real progress in studying the impact of society on personality, it will be necessary to examine trends in whole societies and to work with the complex ecological interrelations of environment and person through entire life histories. The next section describes an ambitious attempt at a systematic study of one aspect of the relation of culture and behavior.

Culture and the Achievement Motive

The achievement motive, as measured by David McClelland, was introduced in Chapter 4. You may remember that McClelland measured need for achievement in individuals by recording and analyzing their interpretations of ambiguous pictures. Achievement needs were indicated by interpretations stressing planning, overcoming obstacles, and striving towards goals. These studies form only part of McClelland's twenty-five-year effort to analyze the factors that affect the level of achievement motives and to identify the consequences of the motives. His work illustrates the interrelation of social and physical environment, ideas, and behavior.

We have already described the first stages in McClelland's work. The next step in his researches applied the concept of need for achievement to societies rather than individuals. McClelland was intrigued with the possibility of describing the overall level of need for achievement in a society by analyzing such artistic and literary materials as poems, plays, and stories. If one could measure the typical level of achievement need in a society, it might then be possible to examine both the factors that lead to differences in this need from one society to another and the consequences of such differences.

McClelland's techniques were varied. In one study, for example, he analyzed stories in fourth-grade readers from more than twenty-five countries. He chose fourth-grade readers because he felt that these were sufficiently complex to represent the ideology of the country and yet simple enough that it would be relatively easy to discover uniformities in the motives expressed by the stories. He was able to rank these countries in accordance with the level of achievement needs shown in fourth-grade readers published in or around 1925. He then ranked the countries according to industrial production in 1925 and found no tendency for those countries high in need for achievement to show high industrial production or vice versa. Next, McClelland measured the rate of industrial growth in these countries over the next several decades. He discovered that the level of need for achievement in 1925 was an excellent predictor of the relative amount of industrial growth over the subsequent fifteen years. Apparently the motivational climate of a country does not relate to its present prosperity but can be used to predict its economic development in the near future.

McClelland went on to test the relation of need for achievement and economic development in a number of other ways. He had found in previous studies that one could measure achievement needs of individuals by analyzing their doodles. Apparently, individuals high in need for achievement show closed, complex forms in their doodles while individuals low in need for achievement show continuous, simple forms. The same kind of analysis was applied to the decorations on Greek vases. It turned out that Greek cities enjoyed explosive economic growth about one generation after their vase decorations began to look like doodles from people with high levels of need for achievement.

McClelland then turned his attention to an analysis of literature. He was able to make inferences about the level of need for achievement in ancient Greece, in Spain, and in England by analyzing the themes found in poetry and plays. In both England and Spain, he found that the rises and falls in industrial activity, measured in various ways, tended to track the level of need achievement in literature but to follow it by about a generation. The same kind of association was evident in ancient Greece. The striving heroism of the heroes of Aeschylus antedated the period of rapid expansion in Athens by a generation. The plays of Sophocles, and especially those of Euripides, written when Athens was at its height as a commercial power, were introspective and stressed internal conflicts rather than the heroic. In fact, when these plays were being produced, Athens was already sliding toward a period of decline as an imperial power.

McClelland tried to explain the relationship between need for achievement and the growth of a community. His thesis was that individuals with a high level of need for achievement would be good businessmen or entrepreneurs. The evidence for this thesis was obtained from studies of risk taking; individuals high in need for achievement tended to take moderate risks. This was especially true under circumstances where they could control the outcome of choice by the exercise of skill. In contrast, individuals with a low need for achievement tended either to take no risks at all or to gamble by "going for broke." McClelland reasoned that if this were so, any community that has many people with a high need for achievement would value a business orientation and would encourage risk taking. Such a society would have great potential for expansion. A society with few people high in need for achievement would be stable but static. The emphasis would be on conservation rather than growth.

But this does not tell us how need for achievement develops in individuals or, indeed, why there seems to be a regular rise and fall of both need for achievement and economic and political expansion. The former question was answered by studies of the relation between patterns of child rearing and achievement need. By measuring achievement need and then asking questions about his subjects' early lives, McClelland demonstrated that children who were reared in an atmosphere in which independence was encouraged tended to develop high need for achievement. These children were urged to make up their own minds and take responsibilities for their decisions, and they were rewarded for the consequences of this independence. In contrast, societies that minimized children's abilities to make their own decisions and to take responsibility for them tended to produce individuals who were either reckless gamblers or cautious conservatives.

The reason for the cyclical nature of achievement need then becomes apparent. In a society that is poor but adventurous, parents make their children independent, thus encouraging high need for achievement. The boys grow up to become prosperous men of affairs and turn the rearing of their children over to servants or slaves. A servant's rewards are dependent on his ability to ingratiate himself into the good will of his charges. Servants and slaves usually tend to spoil children by smothering them with care rather than giving them responsibility. As a result, children raised by servants rather than by their own parents tend to be low in need for achievement, a generation of introspective intellectuals or idle spendthrifts. McClelland suggests that the institution of slavery is probably responsible for the decay of the societies in which it takes hold.

However, even the existence of a relatively high level of need for achievement in some individuals in a society is not enough to make it possible for the society to grow. In order for entrepreneurship to establish itself, the society must have a climate in which people with a high need for achievement can find an appropriate outlet for their energies. Thus the impact of high need for achievement is negligible within communities where class position is all-important and in which status cannot be earned but can only be obtained by birth. Further, McClelland points out that entrepreneurship and the taking of moderate risks imply a state of affairs in which people can reasonably expect that taking risks could pay off. That means, therefore, that people must anticipate social stability and must have faith in one another's trustworthiness. Otherwise they would find it hard to carry out long-range entrepreneurial plans. We will explore the implications of McClelland's notions for an analysis of social change at a later point in this book.

The Effect of Differences in Culture

How might a knowledge of differences in culture enhance one's ability to predict and control the behavior of others? We began this chapter with a story about a city person's visit to a small town. His puzzlement over the behavior of his hosts was probably due to his failure to expect the way of life to be very different from the one to which he was accustomed. If he had been sensitive to differences of culture, he might better have understood his experiences. More importantly, he might have been spared the embarrassment of failing to fit easily into a new way of life.

An anthropologist named E. T. Hall has written a charming and insightful treatment of the problems raised by contact among people from different cultures, a book entitled *The Silent Language*. He became aware of the problem when he worked for the U.S. State Department for many years on the task of training Americans to participate in the foreign aid program that arose from the post-World War II Marshall Plan. From his experiences with the training of Americans for work in the Middle East and other areas, and from his own scholarly work, Hall derived a concept of culture defined in terms of communication, "the way man reads meaning into what other men do."

Hall worked out the dynamics of communication by defining a series of "primary message systems" which vary from one culture to another. These systems delineate the variety of verbal and nonverbal cues that are used to exchange ideas. The message systems include information about the use of time and space, attitudes towards subsistence, sexuality, play, defense against danger, and the proper way of exploiting material things. Most important is the way learning takes place. Hall differentiates three kinds of learning: formal, informal, and technical.

The primary message systems are interrelated. For example, territoriality, the use of space, is related to defense, since many living spaces are arranged so as to fulfill the perceived needs for defense. The layout of a medieval castle illustrates such an arrangement.

Since learning is so important, Hall's discussion of its characteristics is worth looking at. To Hall, formal learning is carried out by precept. Parents, teachers, and other authority figures give the growing child a carefully worked out system of rules. These rules do not necessarily have to have a rational basis; they define the proper ways of doing things. Examples include grammatical systems (why *not* say "he goed"?), taboos, religious systems. Formal learning is also used to transmit concepts about proper emotional responses. Children are instructed (not always in so many words, but still quite consciously) to look sad at funerals, gay at weddings. Boys are instructed in proper ways of acting manly; girls learn proper ways of meeting men, eyes downcast or direct.

Informal learning does not require language. It arises from the child's imitation, or modeling, of the parent or other figure. A girl might be *told* how to deal with boys, i.e., given a formal set of rules. Or she might pick up the proper ways of dealing with boys by watching her mother, her older sister, her favorite aunt. Similarly, boys develop a sense of proper masculine behavior from their fathers or older brothers or uncles; many of the patterns that are most characteristic of masculine or feminine behavior are never put into words.

Technical learning is based on the logical working out of rules or systems. The schoolboy who applies the principles of scientific method and logic as he is learning physics, the apprentice artist who uses ideas about esthetics to develop his skills are engaged in technical learning. There is some formal learning here; in both instances, teachers present the principles, which are often taken on faith. But the working out of rules and their consequences is a matter of logic and experience rather than automatic conformity to the precepts of an authority.

The three kinds of learning lead to three kinds of awareness, ways of perceiving the world. Formal awareness consists of taboos, traditions, explicit notions as to what *is* obviously right. Informal awareness is subtle and tenuous. It is based on patterns that vanish if one focuses on them, patterns derived from tone of voice, gesture, inflection, or choice of idiom. Technical awareness consists of an understanding of scientific or artistic rules.

Hall notes that formal systems are very rigid and hard to change, since they are founded on the strength of "sacred" documents or traditional authority. The legitimacy of the texts or authorities must be rejected before formal systems can be altered. Hall gives the example of an agricultural agent trying to convince Indians near Taos, New Mexico, that they should plow in the spring when the soil can be broken up easily. This attempt at persuasion was unsuccessful because, unbeknown to the scientifically oriented agricultural agent, this group of Indians believed that the earth is pregnant in the spring and must be protected. They saw plowing as a violation of the pregnant earth. Therefore, spring plowing ran counter to a whole religious system; it could not be examined on the basis of a rational evaluation of its merits. To the agent, the problem was one of technical learning. To the Indians, it engaged many aspects of their formal system.

Informal systems also are very difficult to change because it is hard to affect what is not clearly verbalized. Thus, for example, it is extremely difficult to change the interrelations between the sexes because, in addition to the formal systems that define the proper roles of men and women in each society, there is an enormous body of informal, hardly conscious feelings and forms of interaction that have been acquired by "osmosis" and that permeate almost every aspect of a person's style of life. How do you get people to change deep-seated patterns of which they may not even be aware?

Technical systems, on the other hand, can be changed very easily, since no emotion is involved in them. If a body of knowledge has been acquired through reasoning, then presumably, demonstrably superior reasoning can supplant the previous system. It is worth commenting at this point, however, that one of the most difficult obstacles for someone trying to change a society by means of communications derived from technical knowledge is the support given to traditional behavior by both formal and informal systems. As we noted, the agricultural expert perceived spring plowing as a purely technical issue; his Indian audience did not. Nutritional improvement is rendered difficult by vigorous taboos (based on formal systems) and deeply ingrained taste preferences (based on informal systems). For example, it is almost impossible to use the large number of cows in India as a source of food because of the taboo against eating the flesh of a sacred animal. Similarly, throughout the world it has been almost impossible to get communities suffering from protein deficiency to eat foods enriched with fish meal because their inhabitants find the taste of fish unpleasant. We shall come back to this issue again in discussing change in culture later in the chapter.

Time, Space, and Bargaining as Forms of Communication

Some of Hall's most interesting insights come from his analysis of the use of time and space in different cultures and from his discussion of bargaining. Hall points out that, to an American, time moves rather rapidly. If you have an appointment with an American and are only a few minutes late, you still need to apologize. A stronger apology is needed for a delay of a quarter hour, and to keep someone waiting an hour is an insult. In contrast, among Arabs, an hour's delay represents the psychological equivalent of a five or ten minute delay among Americans. A day's delay requires a fairly strong apology and it would be insulting to keep a person waiting for a week. If Americans and Arabs have to do business, the brief delays that seem negligible to the Arab leave the American fuming. On the other hand, the American's insistence on the urgency of scheduling time annoys the Arab. To the patient Arab, the American's need to fill time and his requirement that people focus on one thing at a time are bewildering.

The use of space is also a vehicle for communication. Hall has defined a new science, *proxemics,* as the study of the way people's position in space communicates ideas and feelings. The "Pan-American Waltz" is an example. Latins tend to stand close to each other as they talk. In fact, it is common even for men among Latins to touch each other. Americans, on the other hand, keep their distance. It is rather uncommon for American men, except under somewhat special circumstances, to make physical contact. Therefore, when an American and Latin are talking to each other, the American tends to edge back, giving the Latin the impression that he is cold and rejecting. The Latin, on the other hand, tends to edge forward, giving the American the impression that he is trying to be too intimate. Next time you are in a public place like a shopping center, observe the distances between people. Do men or women stand closer to each other? Are there any differences among different ethnic groups?

Differences in rituals of bargaining also illustrate Hall's thesis that a variety of behaviors may be used as subtle forms of communication. To an American, a bargaining situation is one in which each of a pair of antagonists has a concept of the absolute limit to which he or she is willing to go. After the presentation of offers and counteroffers, the bargainers end by splitting the difference. An American seller tends to set his own demand much higher than the point at which he expects to end because he knows that the final result of the bargaining session is likely to be well below the first price asked.

In many Middle Eastern countries, especially in that characteristic place of commerce, the bazaar, the routine of bargaining is much more subtle. A kind of unspoken understanding defines a fairly narrow range of variation within which the final price will emerge. Each bargainer's offer has symbolic significance. If the prospective buyer sets the proposed price too high, he gives a signal indicating that he is naive and is therefore a fit subject for trickery. If he offers too little, he is being insulting. Men and women who are used to dealing with the bazaar avoid these errors; they can easily communicate the seriousness of their intentions by the kinds of bids they make. An American caught in the bazaar is as unable to handle the implications of bids and counterbids as an Arab would be to cope with the interactions in an auction sale at Parke-Bernet's or Christie's.

The implication of Hall's work is obvious. If one is to navigate in a culture different from one's own, one should attend to the formal and technical systems described in the documents about the culture. But one must also try to enter into the informal and extremely subtle patterns of communication involved in posture, gesture, use of space and time, the myriad symbolisms of even the most apparently trivial kinds of interaction.

The Possibility of Change

Except for an occasional hint, most of the discussion in this chapter has revolved around a description of cultures as they exist. And yet cultures change. Any society that remains completely inflexible in the face of changing environment is doomed to extinction. The history of man has been one of almost continual evolution of societies. Two questions are intertwined in any discussion of change in culture. The first deals with spontaneous change. It asks about the sources of change as a society reacts to internal and external forces affecting its stability. The second deals with deliberate attempts to bring about change and seeks the reasons for the success or failure of such attempts. An understanding of change is critical today as the human race faces the problem of adapting to the new situations created by the explosive growth of population, the fantastic increase in technology, and the new potential for universal destruction created by nuclear armaments. We will return to the question of a society's flexibility in the last section of the book.

There are two ways in which society may change. The first is through *internal evolution*. A society may develop new ways of doing things as it adapts to changing environmental circumstances or, indeed, as a consequence of the evolution of existing forms. The second is *diffusion*. A society may adopt new forms of social or technical organization from its neighbors or from its commerce with distant strangers. It may also be forced to adopt new forms by conquerors.

The most dramatic changes result from the intrusion of one group into another. Examples of this kind of diffusion include the explosive spread of new religious systems—the growth of Christianity, Islam, and Buddhism—as well as the almost universal spread of the American culture of Ford and Coca-Cola. Diffusion occurred early in the history of the race. It is fascinating to read the work of archeologists who have traced the spread of new metals, grains, and domesticated animals from their origins. On the other hand, one should not ignore the fact that evolutionary processes within societies can also give rise to change. The artistic explosions of fifth-century Athens, seventeenth-century Holland, or late-nineteenth-century France, or the sudden expansion of Elizabethan England cannot be accounted for solely by external influences. Similarly, the marked changes in American society that followed the introduction of the automobile, and the accommodation of European society to the development of printing represent internal evolution.

A Case Study in Cultural Change

What are the reasons for change? As a first step in developing general principles about the determinants of change, I should like to discuss a specific instance described by the famous American anthropologist Margaret Mead. In 1928 Mead visited a group of people called the Manus, who live on a small island off the coast of New Guinea. She described them as a Stone Age people, leading lives of almost complete isolation. They lived in houses on stilts in a warm lagoon, an arrangement that was convenient in some ways but very limiting in others. They lived off agriculture and fishing. And they were almost totally illiterate.

Mead found the Manus an extremely active people. They were alert, lively, curious. The children were free to range about. As a consequence of living in the lagoon, they learned to swim and paddle canoes at about the same time that children in other societies begin to walk. During the years between five and fifteen, they passed freely through the community from family to family, were dealt with very affectionately, and were subject to relatively little discipline. However, on arrival at sexual maturity their lives changed dramatically. Marriage for these people was based on a system of high bride prices paid in a currency of shark's teeth. Young boys always went into debt in order to be able to marry. As a consequence, they were subject to lifelong slavery to pay off the debt. Both men and women resented the pressures created by this system. The contrast between the free life of the children and the highly confined life of the adults was very painful. The result was a high level of hostility between husband and wife. In marked contrast to the children, the adults were sullen, hostile, and perpetually quarreling.

The Australian government, which held the area in trust, demanded the payment of taxes in money. As a result, during the brief period between childhood and marriage, many of the young men left the community to engage in contract labor in order to raise the money for taxes. However, they were little affected by this experience and, after their brief period of contract labor, usually reentered the Manus society and participated in the typical pattern of reluctant and hostile marriage.

When Mead left in 1928, she felt that she would never make contact with Manus again. She felt sad at breaking her ties with these people, whom she described, for all their internal hostilities, as attractive and emotionally receptive to her. But she knew that their isolation and lack of literacy meant that she could not communicate with them from her own world.

Mead returned to Manus after World War II to find an incredible change. Where she had previously seen a primitive, grass-skirted, Stone Age community, she now found a neat village, not on the lagoon but instead on the land. There was a series of huts in an open square, with a small, steepled church the most prominent structure. The people were dressed in what was an unmistakable copy of Western costume. What had happened?

The series of events began with World War II. A fairly large number of the young men who had left the community for indentured service were trapped behind the Australian lines. The Manus village itself was behind the Japanese lines. Thus, instead of returning to the village after one or two years, the men remained away for five or six. During this time, because they were bright, curious, and talented, they became valued members of the Australian and American combat teams. Manus men were in great demand for such jobs as driving trucks and assisting in the maintenance of automobiles and other vehicles. Many of them learned to read and write. But the most dramatic influence was that of the American way of life. Manus boys not only saw American men and women in free and affectionate exchange, but they also saw Hollywood movies. The picture of American life, idealized as it was, gave them the notion that life could be different.

When they returned, they were reluctant to enter into the traditional patterns of the old culture. For a while, things were quite confused. One of the most usual reactions of a Melanesian community to this kind of stress in the past few years has been a so-called cargo cult. The South Seas communities had observed Western cargo ships come to the ports and unload vast quantities of goods. Their reaction was an intense belief that, if they threw away all of the paraphernalia of their old cultures, a cargo ship would come and miraculously give them enormous amounts of goods from the Western world. As a part of the cargo cult, there was usually a vision of the overthrow of domination by Europeans and the assumption of power by the local aborigines.

The Manus people were briefly subject to a cargo cult and did, indeed, throw away many of the old shark's-tooth necklaces and other symbolic objects from their old way of life. However, the cargo cult did not last long. Manus was fortunate in having a leader, a man named Paliou, who had been caught behind the Japanese lines during the war and had had the experience of organizing many of the New Guinea natives into work crews for the Japanese. Only one of his parents was from the Manus people, but he had a great deal of affection and admiration for his Manus relatives.

It was he who mobilized a kind of revolt among the young. They announced that they were simply going to abolish all the rules of the previous culture. They moved their houses from the lagoon to the shore. They engaged in intensive agriculture. They abolished bride prices and passed laws forbidding quarrels between husband and wife. They started a school and insisted that all children attend it and learn to read and write. What is more important, they engaged in negotiations with the Australian government to permit the establishment of local governmental councils on a democratic basis.

Why was it that the people of Manus were capable of this dramatic change? Mead believes that the reason was that, in their early treatment of children, they had created free and strong personalities who were curious, investigative, and practical. The same contact with American and Australian culture in other New Guinea groups has led to slow and often unsuccessful attempts at adaptation to Western ways once the original pattern of their society had been shattered. The marked success of the Manus in contrast to many of their neighbors was probably due to the fact that the Manus people emphasized independence and skill in their early development.

The contrast between Stone Age Manus and contemporary Manus, a contrast that had developed in less than one generation, was symbolized by the fact that Mead on leaving in 1954 looked forward to sending the book she would write about them to her friends in that community. And, during another visit in 1968, Mead learned that the Manus community had continued to prosper. After an initial period of reluctance, the Australians cooperated in the establishment of local, semiindependent government groups. And the Manus people are taking the lead in the first steps of New Guinea's people towards self-determination and eventual membership in the United Nations.

We began this section by asking what it was that makes change in a society possible. To use Hall's terminology, we really were talking about change in other than technical systems, since the adoption of such technical changes as the use of bicycles needs little explanation. On the basis of her work with the Manus, Mead concluded that cultural change takes place along lines made possible by the already existing culture of the community. Her argument is similar to McClelland's. Both make the point that change must be compatible with the basic ways of thinking and interacting in a society. If the new ways mesh with the old, then they can easily be introduced. Otherwise, change is unlikely. This point will be explored more thoroughly in the sections of this book on community decision and on alternate forms of societal organization.

"Simple" and "Complex" Cultures

Many of the illustrations in our discussion of culture and behavior, although not all, have been based on relatively simple societies. At this point in the book, it is necessary to shift attention from general discussions of culture and behavior to an examination of the complexities of "advanced" societies. Advanced societies are characterized not only by complex technology and systems of knowledge but also by variations in culture among such subgroups as classes, castes, and regional and ethnic groups. Therefore, it is important that we examine the tools for studying internal variation in advanced societies and also look at the implications of such diversity for behavior. The next chapter will be devoted to a discussion of the social organization of complex societies.

On Your Own

1. Both books by E. T. Hall are available in paperback. Both are wonderful. They are *The Silent Language* and *The Hidden Dimension.*

2. The chapter discusses Margaret Mead's *New Lives for Old.* It is available in paperback. You can also get the flavor of the grand old lady of American anthropology from almost anything else she has written. Available in paper are: *Sex and Temperament in Three Primitive Societies; Coming of Age in Samoa; Cooperation and Competition Among Primitive Peoples; Male and Female; Growing Up in New Guinea.* Most paperback bookstores carry them.

3. Honigman's *Personality in Culture* is very textbookish, but it is well written, easy going, and, mostly, quite interesting.

4. If you really want to stretch your mind, Anthony Wallace's 1970 revision of his *Culture and Personality* is very good but tough. The earlier edition (1961) is probably not available, but if it were it would be easier. Cora Du Bois's original report on Alor, *The People of Alor,* is available in paperback.

5. An American businessman goes to India and lives and works there for many years. As he passes his sixtieth birthday he decides to change his way of life. He takes off all his clothes, puts on a loin cloth, takes a begging bowl, and spends his days sitting in the central square in Calcutta. An Indian businessman goes to the United States and lives and works there for many years. As he passes his sixtieth birthday he decides to change his way of life. He takes off all his clothes, puts on a loin cloth, takes a begging bowl, and spends *his* days in Times Square in New York. Which of the two is abnormal? Why?

6. For one day, pretend that you are a visitor from mainland China. Use the various definitions of culture in the chapter to guide you in asking about the significance of everything you see. Does this help you realize how much meaning there is in even the most apparently simple acts?

7. Even though the use of handguns in crime has increased and we have had a number of horrifying assassinations in the past decades, the United States has not been willing to institute even so mild a measure of gun control as universal registration of weapons. Use the concepts of culture and behavior in the chapter to identify those characteristics of American culture that may be responsible for this unwillingness. Do not attack or defend gun registration on its merits; the issue is not whether it is good or bad but why most U.S. legislators won't even consider it.

6
The Anatomy of Society

An observer without technical training in the social sciences, asked to answer the question, How many different kinds of people do you know?, might be a bit puzzled as to how to begin answering. He would probably resolve his puzzlement by establishing some sort of rule. For example, he might list people by their occupations—doctors, lawyers, auto mechanics, bakers, and so on. Or he might group people by their religion, national origin, age, or sex.

If you were to stop him at this point and ask him to try to find new rules for classifying people, he might find this a bit difficult, but, after some thought, might say, "There are the people who get their names in the papers and live in the good part of town and those who sleep out on Skid Row." If the observer came from an old, settled community, like a town in New England or in the old South, he might go on along these lines in a fairly detailed way, telling about the old families who have lived in his part of the country since the beginning of settlement and who receive a great deal of respect; the newer people who have money and important professional and management jobs, but whose families have not had their money for a long time; the solid, respectable people who aren't well off but who belong to a good church; and so on down to the kinds of people who live on the wrong side of the tracks.

What we have been doing in this exercise is to try to get ideas about the structure of society by looking at differences in the way people regard each other. Social scientists refer to the examination of the levels, layers, functioning groups in a community as the study of social stratification. If you were as addicted as I was to the television program "Upstairs, Downstairs," you had a thorough exposure to the realities of one kind of social stratification.

Actually, the notion of "strata" in a society is a metaphor. If you go down to a river that has cut a deep gorge into the earth, you can see the layers of stone that were formed during different geological ages. These are called strata. The idea that society is in some way built of a series of levels like the layers of geological strata sometimes helps us make sense of many aspects of social environment. But we should never forget that it *is* a metaphor and that the social strata or classes do not have "real" existence, but are actually constructs in the sense that we defined them in Chapter 2. In addition, the strata in the rocks are sharply defined, their boundaries clearly visible. Social strata may be as clearly differentiated. But there are societies in which the borderlines separating social layers are vaguely defined and indistinct.

Some of the ways in which social scientists define the character of the layers of society can be derived from an analysis of the answers you may have given to the question posed at the beginning of the discussion, i.e., How may different kinds of people do you know? In the following section, I will try to sketch a number of the better-known systems used by social scientists for studying the structure of society. It may seem to you, as the discussion continues, that the different ways of defining class or social strata are contradictory at times and that at others they overlap. Try to bear with this until we finish outlining the various ways of defining class. I shall try to make sense of the variety of systems at the end.

Class as Social Function

At parties you may have played "The Game" in which people are asked to answer the question, Who are you? While there are great individual differences in the way the players answer this question, one of the most usual is for people to tell about their occupations or their ways of making a living. Since work or preparation for work occupies more time than any other single activity and is the focus for a tremendous expenditure of energy, it is hardly surprising that most people answer the question, Who are you?, by describing their occupations.

Unless occupations can be grouped according to some under-lying pattern, they are not terribly useful as a basis for defining the structure of society. There is an almost infinite variety of occupational titles. One classification used by the U.S. Government lists over 3,500 separate occupations. But occupations can be put into categories, and these can then be used as a basis for defining social classes. Of several approaches to this task, the best known is derived from the work of Karl Marx, the German scholar who helped found the socialist and communist movements in the middle of the nine-teenth century.

Basically, Marx proposed that contemporary societies consist of two major classes. One class is composed of people who make a liv-ing from the ownership of land, factories, or businesses. The other is composed of those who have nothing but their labor to sell. Marx was aware that one could classify more finely within these two categories. He knew that there are large proprietors and small proprietors and that there are working people of different levels of skill and wealth. However, it seemed to him that the fundamental issue was a group's relationship to what he called the means of production. The most im-portant differentiation in Marx's system is between those who make a living by exploiting the work of others through their ownership of land or factories and those whose living comes from doing productive work.

At this point I should define two additional terms—*role* and *status*. In real life, role means exactly the same as it does in the theater. An actor's role is the part he plays. In the theater, his actions are largely determined by the script. He has to memorize every ac-tion, every word that projects the particular function of the character he is playing. In the real world, the script is rarely set down as pre-cisely as that of a play. But each of us learns a set of expectations of the things we have to do to play out the requirements of our position in life. Much, although not all, of our behavior is determined by these expectations.

The word status refers to the position in society to which roles are attached. It implies a kind of ladder, often called hierarchy, in which some positions (or statuses) are generally considered "above" others. There are two kinds of status. One, called *ascribed* status, is derived from birth into a particular group. The son of a duke is auto-matically a member of the nobility; the eldest son will acquire the status of duke when his father dies. The other kind of status is *achieved*. This is won by the efforts of the individual. Seven years of apprenticeship make one a plumber. There are problems, of course. Any soldier who graduates from officer candidate school acquires the status of a member of the officer class in the United States, although he may not enjoy quite the status of a West Pointer. In England, an older and more stratified society, a man who does not come from the right kind of family is not quite considered an "officer and a gentleman" even though his technical education may entitle him to a commission.

Back to Marx. As I said above, to Marx, role, in the sense of social function, was the only important source of social stratification. And in modern capitalist societies, social roles are basically organized into two groups or categories, the exploiters and the exploited. However, a genuine social class arises when a group of people who share the same relation to the means of production develop a sense of common interest and go on to create some form of political or economic organization, a political party or a trade union. This provides a focus for their attempts to protect their interests. As a class acquires a sense of togetherness (Marx calls it class consciousness), it can develop ideology, religious or ethical beliefs, even forms of art. Its members tend to regard each other highly and to have hostile or rejecting feelings towards outsiders. But the *primary* phenomenon is the relation of an individual through his social function to the organization of productive activity, i.e., his status as worker or owner. Everything else characterizing a class is secondary to this relationship and arises from it.

Marx felt that new forms of society evolve out of the struggle of social classes to realize their interests. The liberal democracies, for example, resulted from the rise to power of industrialists and merchants. He assumed that the working class would emerge victorious in the next stage of social evolution and that from the victory would come a classless society. This would presumably end the history of social evolution based on the conflict of classes.

The years since Marx's first analyses have hardly borne out his prophecy. It is well known that the division of the so-called socialist states into social classes is almost as profound as the class division in the capitalist societies of Marx's own day. The Yugoslav experience, as described by Milovan Djilas in *The New Class,* illustrates this phenomenon. The organization of a socialist society requires the development of a class of bureaucratic managers and political leaders. As they become clearly distinguishable from the mass of the population, they acquire many of the characteristics of a ruling class. Any visitor to the supposedly classless societies of Eastern Europe is struck by the differences between the style of life of industrial workers, housed in wooden shacks or barrackslike apartment houses, and that of the scientists, artists, government leaders, and managers, living in comfortable villas and driving large, black automobiles.

A number of American sociologists have drawn on Marx, but they have modified his point of view considerably. Among them, Kingsley Davis, Wilbert E. Moore, and, most prominent of all, Talcott Parsons share a position that may be called "functionalist." That is, they describe society in terms of the way social mechanisms operate and sustain themselves. They all tend to view differences in social functions as arising from the needs of society. These differences result in jobs that vary in the amount of training they require and the amount of responsibility they confer. According to these sociologists, society must decide which of its functions are most important and then, somehow, must reward most heavily the people who carry out those functions. They recognize that this scheme breaks down when important but unpleasant functions are carried out by slaves or immigrants, people who have no other choices. But they regard these exceptions as relatively unimportant. Like Marx, they derive social strata from role, or social function. Unlike him, however, they deny that any advanced society could ever really be classless.

There have been a few attempts to create something genuinely approximating a classless society. Most notable of these are the Israeli kibbutz and contemporary China in the period since the Cultural Revolution. In both of these societies, the emphasis on equality is such that a vigorous effort is made to reduce the shame attached to unskilled, manual labor and to reduce the rewards usually given to brain labor. Of course, many other societies, including both the socialist countries and our own, reject the concept of class in their official ideology. However, the realities do not always fit the ideology. We will return to the discussion of the success or failure of the Israeli and Chinese experiments in the last chapter.

Status

I suggested earlier that one possible source for the metaphor about social strata is the layers of rock in the gorge of a river or in some other setting that shows geological strata. An obvious point about this metaphor is that one stratum of rock is *higher* than the other. If the metaphor is to be pursued, one would have to assume that one *social* stratum is in some way "higher" than another. The noted German sociologist Max Weber added the concept of *status groups* to Marx's ideas about the economic origin of social class. These are groups that have a sense of community, as do Marx's classes, but that consist of people distinguished by a common level of *prestige* within the larger society. Through such techniques as interviews and projective tests, one can delineate a community's perception of its class structure and then develop a model of a society based on variation in prestige, or, as Weber calls it, "honor."

It is not always easy to place people in a hierarchy of prestige. In small communities, where everyone knows everyone else, a picture of the hierarchy can be worked out fairly simply. Even there, however, people's perception of social classes distant from their own tends to be hazy. To the very poor, distinctions between old and new money mean little. To those on the top of the heap, the differences between upper-middle and lower-middle class may also be hazy. In big cities, where most people do not know each other and therefore are not aware of family or personal reputation as a basis for status, people tend to respond to subtle indicators of membership in groups of greater or lesser prestige. These may include the accent with which people speak, the particular idioms they use, their clothing, table manners, and drinking patterns. Often, evidence of the awareness of social distinctions is itself an indicator of status.

Interaction as a Basis for Social Strata

If social strata are functioning groups, then one way of defining them is to ask who associates with whom. W. Lloyd Warner, whose work was described briefly in Chapter 1, is the best known of the social scientists who use this approach. His work is reported in a series of books dealing with his investigations during the 1930s of a small town north of Boston that he called "Yankee City." It is no longer a secret that the town was actually Newburyport, Massachusetts. Warner, drawing on his background as an anthropologist, began by interviewing large numbers of people to find out who visited with whom, who belonged to which clubs, and who made up a variety of informal social groups. He traced a network of associations within the town which enabled him to describe six strata. Each stratum consisted of a group of people who interacted a great deal among themselves and relatively little with people in other strata.

The highest group, called "upper-upper" in Warner's terminology, consisted of the descendants of Yankee ship owners who had made their money in the first part of the nineteenth century and who lived in fine old homes on the main street of the town. You may remember that we identified O'Neill's Mannons as part of this class. Just below this group were the "lower-uppers," people who formed the bulk of the prosperous professionals and managers of the largest local industry, a shoe factory. Although many of these people were as wealthy as the first group, they were not included in "upper-upper" society because of their relatively recent arrival in the town or recent rise to affluence.

The next level consisted of the "upper-middles." These were the college-educated professionals and owners of moderate-sized businesses. They lived on side streets, had relatively few pretensions to being "society," but were still included by the elite of the town in certain large groups, including the Chamber of Commerce and the United Fund. Beneath the "upper-middles" were the "lower-middles," the owners of small businesses and the white-collar workers in the town's industry and commerce. Most of these people had less education than the individuals in the strata above them. They were not invited to attend even the large formal events in the social life of the town. But they were active in their own churches and in various service clubs of a less prestigious kind than those with which the upper strata were affiliated.

Next came the "upper-lower" class, solid, stable working-class people, churchgoers who lived in sound but old housing. Their social associations were centered primarily in their churches. The very bottom of society consisted of the "lower-lowers," people who were quite isolated from social contacts with the rest of the town. Their associations were informal, across the back fence on the part of the women and in the bars among the men. Their educational level was low, they worked sporadically, and they were often on the wrong side of the law.

While the primary sources for the delineation of strata came from descriptions of social association, each group shared other characteristics. People in a given class tended to live in the same kind of neighborhood, to have roughly the same level of education and similar occupations. As a shortcut to estimating a person's class position, Warner developed an index based on some of these secondary characteristics. Such indices have been widely used. Although the components may vary, the indices usually include measures of occupation, education, and area of residence. But these characteristics are used to assign people to classes whose identity was originally derived from social association. To Warner, a person belongs to a class if he "has gained acceptance as an equal by those who belong in that class." Support for the use of the shortcut measures is based on the correlation Warner and others have found between measures derived from such indices and those directly linked to social association.

The shortcut indices based on education and occupation result in definitions of social class that superficially seem not very different from those proposed by functionalists or Marxists. However, for Warner the *central* fact is social association and the other phenomena flow from that.

Ideas as a Basis for the Definition of Class

From our discussion of culture in the previous chapter, you might expect that one important way of defining social class would be on the basis of ideas, values, and attitudes. In the 1940s a psychologist at Princeton named Richard Centers discovered that people who had similar occupations and similar educational levels sometimes behaved differently because they identified with different classes. In a nationwide survey, he asked people to identify themselves as members of the upper class, middle class, working class, or lower class. He found that among people with similar characteristics on objective scales of income, occupation, and education, some identified themselves as "middle-class," others as "working class." The latter generally had more radical political positions than the former. To Centers, therefore, the central factor in defining social strata is a shared set of ideas. While other theorists, for example, Marx, do not deny the importance of ideas, they believe that ideas derive from those other aspects of a person's lifestyle that define social class; to them, ideas do not form the primary basis for a person's location in a class system.

How Can a Person's Social Class Be Identified?

The previous discussion suggests that there are at least four different ways of locating a person in a class system. One of these uses his economic role. Another searches for groups that consider him an equal. A third asks about his patterns of interaction at work and at home. A last procedure uses ideas and the groups with which the ideas are shared. The existence of these four approaches must seem thoroughly confusing. Of course, if all these factors were perfectly correlated, life would be very simple. We would then find that anyone who is an owner, in the Marxist sense, would also have a set of social associations, a level of prestige, and a set of ideas consonant with his or her economic position. Unfortunately the correlations are not quite perfect. Was Franklin Delano Roosevelt a good example of an "upper-upper" class person? Or Eleanor? In origins, yes, but in beliefs and social associations obviously not. Were Centers' shopkeepers who held radical political ideas middle class or working class? What can one make of Park Avenue radical chic? Is the notion of social class, then, a useless one?

Several people have suggested that it is not very useful. In a perceptive discussion, American psychologist Roger Brown has suggested that each of the criteria that we have used to describe social strata is in fact a continuum. For example, think of classifying people according to their height or weight. You could set up artificial criteria for classes of height, such as tall, medium, and short. Or, for weight: heavy, medium, and light. However, it makes far more sense to say that people form a continuum from the lowest weight or height in a group to the highest. In order to describe somebody's physique, it might be better to give his actual height and weight than to place him in an artificial grouping. Brown thinks of status, occupational classification, variety of ideas, and patterns of social interaction as providing similar continua along which people can be placed. He proposes that most of the discussions of social class have been based on artificial distinctions created by social scientists rather than on actual groupings in the real world. Although this is an attractive point of view, it seems premature to discard the idea of social strata or classes entirely. Placing people in such groups can be extremely useful. In the remainder of this chapter, I shall show how classifying people according to large, crude groupings such as "lower-middle" class or "upper-upper" class has provided insights in the study of such diverse phenomena as mental health, child rearing, and political behavior.

The problem is that these classifications provide nice statistical associations for comparing the characteristics of groups but are of less value for the study of individuals. However, even for individuals, the broad groupings utilized by social class theorists provide a good working basis for the first step in understanding and predicting behavior. Yet how can we choose among all these different ways of placing people, of defining class structure?

A Solution Based on the Ecological Model

One way to solve the problem is to go back to the ecological model. A description of social classes that ignores the changing characteristics of the total environment in which behavior takes place is a poor basis for predicting the activity of real people in the real world. The ecological model suggests that one or another dimension becomes important in determining class position depending on the nature of the environment at the time.

Think about a Midwestern city like Kansas City, Missouri. As it happens, the social class structure of this city was investigated rather carefully by R. P. Coleman and B. L. Neugarten, a team of social scientists who used Warner's approach. They were able to identify at least nine social levels in which associations within groups were much more frequent than associations across groups. And they found that a simple score based on education, occupation, and area of residence gave groupings very similar to those produced by association. However, there are probably many circumstances in which the general pattern of association would be a poor predictor of people's behavior and in which the cruder index based on education and occupation would be even poorer.

Imagine, for example, that there were a major strike in the city. Probably most of the people who have anything to do with the industry that is struck would take sides on the basis of economic interests. Under these circumstances, a Marxist could probably predict people's behavior fairly successfully from an analysis of their economic stakes in the outcome of the strike. There would, of course, be exceptions; but the Marxist or functionalist definition of class would work quite well.

Assume now that the strike were settled and a controversy were to arise over busing to accomplish school integration. The town that had previously been divided along one set of lines would again be angrily divided, but along a completely different set of lines. People who were drawn together by the economic issues of the strike might now be separated by race or ideology. At this point, a Marxist analysis would be of relatively little value. In fact, a European social scientist would probably be totally bewildered by the fact that blue-collar workers (e.g., factory or service workers) might line up with upper-class conservatives on one side of the issue, while intellectuals, some people in the professional and commercial groups, and, of course, most of the blacks in the community would line up on the other side.

How can we generalize from this instance? The rule seems to be that the dimension along which people fall into social strata is determined by the characteristics of the ecological systems that affect their behavior at a given time in a given place. Therefore, it is not fruitful to identify any particular person as being a member of a class in general or abstract terms. The question to ask is, What kinds of groupings are important in determining this person's responses to the pressures of the environment at the moment at which you are trying to identify his membership in a class? This approach enables one to understand what would make a person behave like a member of the middle class at one time, like a member of the working class at another, and would make his affiliation to a racial or religious group the most important factor in his behavior in yet another set of circumstances.

This approach also provides a model for studying the conflicts that so often arise when people are torn among the demands created by their affiliations to more than one social group. A poignant example of this kind of situation is the conflict faced by black professionals or businessmen. By virtue of their education and occupation, these men and women are clearly middle class. And they have generally been accepted into the prestige groupings and professional associations appropriate to their status.

As members of a subordinate group in a racist society, however, black professionals are often torn internally. There are many times when they identify as blacks with people who are poorer and less skilled and, therefore, presumably in a different social stratum. At other times, they affiliate with their fellow professionals. While some circumstances might easily determine whether the black professional reacts as a black or as a member of an occupational group, there may be situations in which neither reaction is prepotent. The result can be acute internal conflict, not easily resolved.

The discussion of the problem of the black professional introduces the concept of caste. A caste is a social group whose members have an irrevocable identification. Unlike class position, which can sometimes be determined by individual effort or failure (i.e., achieved status), caste membership is based on birth; that is, status is ascribed. Of course, the distinction between class and caste is not as sharp as it seems. In the English society described in "Upstairs, Downstairs," position in the nobility, which is a caste, is clearly determined by birth. Yet, the young woman who married James Bellamy does seem to move into the upper caste by virtue of her individual gentility as well as by her marriage. Still, no miracle of education or economic improvement could ever make one of the servants a social equal to the granddaughter of an earl.

Societies differ in the rigidity with which they maintain their strata. At one extreme of rigidity lie India and Medieval Europe. In such societies, the ideas about caste are widely held and virtually everyone can be placed almost immediately through a variety of signs. At the other pole, we have societies that reject the very idea of social strata or any other kind of inequality. We have already mentioned the Israeli kibbutz and contemporary China as examples of such societies. In some ways, the United States lies between these two poles. Our ideology demands that we be a caste-free society, but virtually everyone recognizes that the reality in our country is one of deep social divisions. The only thing that tempers the rigors of these divisions is the possibility, more or less completely realized at different times, that people can cross the boundaries of class.

Virtually all societies, even those most committed to equality, recognize the kind of stratification that is based on social function. The major difference among societies, both in ideology and in reality, is in the degree to which differences in social function are genuinely derived from achieved rather than ascribed status. The least class-ridden societies are those in which there is *genuine* opportunity for anyone to achieve any status of which he or she is capable, no matter who his or her parents, no matter what his or her origin in racial, religious, or social groups. I include *her* quite purposely for obvious reasons; a society in which only men can rise is obviously not really open.

Some Applications of Ideas about Social Strata

Social scientists have done a great deal of research in which they have tried to relate a number of different kinds of behavior to position in the social system. I should like to tell you very briefly about three of those areas. In all of these researches, the definition of social strata is some simple version of one of the classifications we have just discussed; but it usually works, in the sense that class does turn out to predict behavior. The first area is the relation of social class to the way people bring up children. The second relates social stratification to mental health and mental illness. The third area concerns social class and political behavior.

Social Class and Child Rearing

In the previous chapter, we discussed the variation in the paths by which children in different cultures are led to become fully enculturated members of their societies. Families from various social strata within a single complex society also differ in their patterns of child rearing.

An example of such differences may be found in the contrasting methods used by middle-class and working-class parents to rear their children in our society. Traditionally, middle-class people have raised their children in a highly disciplined manner, whereas work-ing-class people, especially members of minority groups like blacks, have tended to be somewhat permissive. Mark Twain provides a vivid picture of the difference by contrasting the households in which Tom Sawyer and Huck Finn were raised. Huck Finn's struggles with the severity of middle-class nurture in the Widow Douglas's establish-ment provide the raw material for a masterpiece that is quite realistic despite its comic exaggeration.

One characteristic of middle-class society is its dependence on technical experts for advice on everything, from gardening and the purchase of an automobile to ways of bringing up children. A major source of technical expertise has been the material issued for the general public by the federal government. The Children's Bureau, a division of the Department of Health, Education, and Welfare, has, for many years, been publishing pamphlets providing guidance to parents. Those dating from the years before 1930 urge mothers to schedule feedings strictly, to avoid picking up babies who are crying, to begin toilet training at six months. Surveys conducted immediately after World War II confirmed the rigor of middle-class methods of bringing up children and the relative permissiveness of the working class.

A Contemporary Picture of Middle-Class Child Rearing. The mid-thirties saw the beginning of a remarkable change. Under the in-fluence of Freudian thinking, middle-class mothers began to be con-cerned about the psychological well-being of their children. After World War II, the influence of the widely used book on child care by Benjamin Spock reinforced the tendency to avoid frustrating children by means of rigid schedules. The use of corporal punishment became taboo. The later pamphlets from the Federal Security Agency reflect these changes. They focus on the importance of the emotional rela-tion between parent and child and, generally, reinforce a tendency to increased permissiveness.

Surveys of middle-class mothers during the fifties and sixties in-dicate that they tend, at the verbal level at least, to stress the goals of happiness, flexibility, and internal control. They worry about the mo-tives behind their children's acts rather than responding directly to the actual behavior. And they feel very self-conscious about the use of discipline. Nevertheless, their children must be socialized.

Middle-class parents begin early to reason with their children, to use explanations rather than corporal punishment when children break rules. But there is a hidden agenda in the verbal explanations and the endless cajoling. The potency of middle-class control over children lies in the threat of withdrawal of affection. Punishment is not a swift and rapidly passing reaction to wrongdoing; it carries with it the possibility of intense and long-lasting disapproval, loss of love.

Rewards also often operate over a long time scale. They may require long periods of waiting (If you are good, there will be a new bicycle for Christmas). They hinge on a careful assessment of behavior at home and in school. Middle-class children are given a great deal of responsibility for their actions. They often have to earn their rewards by planned and systematic behavior. In view of such training, it is understandable that many middle-class children develop high levels of need for achievement. In many ways, the manner in which middle-class children are brought up is a good preparation for middle-class styles of life. The middle-class child is going to have to work hard in school and postpone gratification in order to achieve the training that will permit him to enter middle-class occupations. Once he has done this, he will be expected to show initiative and to work on his own in order to solve problems.

Working-Class Patterns of Child Rearing. The studies that have compared middle-class and working-class ways of bringing up children have focused on "upper-lower" class families, in Warner's terms. That is, the father generally has a skilled or semiskilled blue-collar occupation, belongs to a trade union and a church, and maintains a relatively intact family structure. In families of this kind, the mother typically stresses conformity, neatness, good manners, control of the externals of behavior. She usually controls her child by physical means or by inviting the father to administer punishment rather than by employing explanations or threatening to withdraw affection.

The working-class pattern of child rearing is also a preparation for working-class styles of life. Since working-class occupations rarely require long-range planning or provide opportunities to exercise initiative, high levels of need for achievement are not required for success. What is needed is the self-discipline to stick with routine, repetitive tasks. The stress on control in the rearing of children is probably ideal preparation for such occupations.

Both casual observation and formal investigation support the picture of contrasting patterns of child rearing in middle-class and working-class homes. The children of middle-class homes, especially little girls, are permitted to dress sloppily, characteristically appearing for school in unironed blue jeans. Little girls from working-class homes are more often dressed in neatly starched dresses.

It has often been true that middle-class standards tend to diffuse through the entire population. The role models provided by the mass media are certainly derived from middle-class practice. Thus, one can expect that the wives of factory workers living in the new subdivisions in the suburbs may be assimilating towards middle-class norms, with their emphasis on personal expression rather than neatness and cleanliness. The distinction I have just described may be more appropriate to the sixties, when the studies were carried out, than to the state of affairs today.

These findings hold for the statistical comparison of groups. Many families in both middle and working classes are undoubtedly exceptions to these norms. However, families that represent exceptions probably also view themselves, and are perceived by others, as exceptional. The middle-class mother who pays overly strenuous attention to neatness and manners or who uses physical punishment to control her children probably thinks of herself as bucking the tide of permissiveness. Similarly, the working-class mother who permits her child to be sloppy or to engage in boisterous behavior probably is aware that she is deviating from the norms of her neighborhood and her friends.

It should be emphasized that the distinction just drawn is between middle-class and upper-lower-class families. There is a large population of lower-lower-class people characterized by social disorganization, one-parent households, a lifestyle shaped by the culture of urban or rural slum. In this stratum, parents' control of their children is marked by lack of continuity, by sporadic violence and equally sporadic shows of affection. In this world, marked by what the American anthropologist Oscar Lewis calls the culture of poverty, one finds neither the tight controls of the upper levels of working-class society nor the pressures towards achievement characteristic of the middle and upper classes.

A further distinction must be made between two kinds of

middle-class families. The middle class of which we were speaking above is in large part that of the white-collar employees of large corporations and the professionals, people associated with the sciences, the arts, education, and communication. A study in Detroit carried out several decades ago noted that there really were two kinds of middle-class people. One kind, the "new middle class," consisted of individuals whose values were organizational. The other kind, the "old middle class," had the traditional values of nineteenth-century America. Typically, the old middle class consisted of small proprietors, independent professionals; the new middle class consisted of employees of the large corporations that make Detroit their headquarters. Parents in the old middle class tended to behave more like the working class of today, treating their children with greater rigor and exacting a greater measure of conformity to the externals of proper behavior.

Social Class and Mental Illness

One of the most dramatic findings in the literature on social stratification has been that people at different levels in American society have different kinds of mental illnesses. If you look at the nature and distribution of mental illness, the big dividing line lies between the lower-lower-class and the rest of society.

An extensive study of mental illness and social class was carried out in the early 1950s in New Haven, Connecticut, by two investigators—a sociologist, August Hollingshead, and a psychiatrist, Frederick Redlich. They started out to test several hypotheses. The first was that the prevalence (that is, the number of existing cases) of mental illness is related significantly to an individual's position in the class structure. The second was that the types of diagnosed psychiatric disorder are connected to class structure. The third was that the kind of treatment administered to patients is associated with position in class structure. The fourth was that factors in the development of psychiatric disease differ among social classes. These hypotheses assumed an ability to place people in social classes. They also assumed a classification of mental illnesses and the availability of techniques to study their development in individuals.

Hollingshead and Redlich, like most investigators in this field, distinguished two major categories of mental illness, neurosis and psychosis. People who are neurotic respond to the pressures of their environment by an exaggerated kind of defense along the lines described in our discussion of defense mechanisms in Chapter 3. Thus, they may become extremely anxious, compulsive, or develop psychosomatic symptoms. On the whole, though, they maintain control over themselves and are able to continue functioning in their own worlds, although many are so miserable as to seek psychiatric treatment. In contrast, the psychotic is someone who loses touch with reality. He may have delusions or visions or hear voices. He often does not know where he is. He may also suffer from extremely exaggerated feelings, fly to the heights of elation or sink to the depths of depression. In general, psychosis represents a severe breakdown of an individual's controls, whereas neurosis represents controls so exaggeratedly strong that they cripple the individual.

Hollingshead and Redlich began by communicating with all treatment facilities and private practitioners likely to have cared for patients from New Haven. Their team was able to locate virtually all those who were in treatment during a six-month period in 1950. Interviewers then sought out these patients and their families and gathered information necessary to place them in one of five social classes. The basis for class distinction was the kind of shortcut index derived from the work of Warner to which we referred earlier in the chapter. In this instance, the index used education, occupation, and a characterization of the person's area of residence. Class I consisted of upper-class people; the data did not permit Warner's distinction between upper-upper and lower-upper categories. Classes II and III were respectively upper and lower middle class. Class IV was upper-lower class, the kind of working-class people whose child-rearing behavior was described in the last section. Class V consisted of lower-lower-class people.

Two findings emerged from the classification of patients in treatment. The first was that psychosis was increasingly prevalent as one went down the social scale. The rate of psychosis, adjusted for age and sex, was almost three times as high in class III as in classes I and II, almost ten times as high in class IV as in the uppermost group, and notably higher yet in class V. The second finding was that the prevalence of neurosis, adjusted for age and sex, was highest in classes I and II, decreased in classes III and IV, and then showed a slight increase in class V. However, the large number of psychotics in class V created a tremendous disparity in the proportion of psychotics to neurotics in that group as compared with the others. There were almost nine times as many psychotics as neurotics in class V; the differences in frequency of the two kinds of ailment were much smaller in the other groups.

It should be noted that these data concern treated prevalence, i.e., the rates are derived from a count of the number of patients under treatment during a given period. The number of patients in treatment may be affected by the length of time the person remains in therapy as well as by the social factors that determine the availability of treatment. Therefore, epidemiologists are wary of making inferences about the causes of disease from prevalence data, particularly data on cases in treatment. The investigators did get some information about the rate at which new cases of mental illness were identified. Although there was no clear trend across the entire social class spectrum, there was a break between class V and the rest of the community. Class V showed a higher incidence of psychosis and lower incidence of neurosis than classes I-IV. These findings have been confirmed in other places and through the use of other techniques.

What can one conclude from the work of Hollingshead and Redlich? Some of their interviews support the notion that the natural history of mental illness is very different for people at the bottom than for those higher up in our society. This difference may account in part for the excess of psychosis among lower-class and of neurosis among upper-class patients. In order to be identified as a neurotic, a person has to be able to talk fluently about his emotional problems with professionals in the field of mental health—psychiatrists, psychologists, or social workers. This is obviously easier for someone who is well educated and shares the values and beliefs of the professionals than for someone of different background. Working-class people typically reject the notion of psychological causation of their complaints and the associated talking-out therapies. They may acknowledge difficulties with "nerves," but they see these problems as biological in origin and demand medical treatment. All of these factors tend to reduce the likelihood both that working-class individuals with emotional problems would be diagnosed as neurotic and that they would remain in treatment for lengthy periods of time.

The history of the psychotic is also affected by social class. The same emotional problems may lead to very different results among people from different social strata. The working-class person who suffers disorders in cognition or who becomes withdrawn gets into difficulties with family and job that are rarely identified as psychologically based. Eventually, he or she behaves in a bizarre manner that disrupts social ties. The police are often involved in the sequence of events in which a working-class person acts out, is labeled psychotic, and is placed behind bars in a public mental hospital. The characteristic course of events in 1950, when the New Haven studies were done, was long-term confinement with relatively little treatment. Today the working-class psychotic is treated with drugs or electric shock and released into the community with little insight into his or her problems. The revolving door in the mental hospital is ready to receive the patient back again as soon as these problems result in further social disruption.

Middle-class people who break down are rarely subject to this brutal regimen. For one thing, the increasing sense of pressure and inability to cope often lead to attempts to get help from family physicians. Psychiatrists and psychologists are available to those for whom kindly words and tranquilizers are inadequate. Middle-class people and their advisors are aware of the availability of free clinics and so utilize them more than working-class patients.

The burden of this discussion is that much of the difference between class V and the rest of the population in prevalence of neurosis and psychosis, which was found in the New Haven study and elsewhere, is due to differences in the way society treats these two groups. Equivalent disturbances in behavior are labeled differently among patients from class V and from groups higher in the social scheme. And the length of treatment also differs. Class V psychotics remain in treatment much longer than those from the upper groups. Middle-class neurotics also are treated for many years, especially if they see psychoanalysts. Both the difference in labeling and the difference in length of treatment affect prevalence, since both influence the number of individuals identified as suffering from a particular disease in any given period of time.

Thus the first, second, and third of Hollingshead and Redlich's hypotheses were confirmed by their study. To examine the fourth, which deals with the origins of mental illness as a function of social class, one must turn to a different kind of data. In a perceptive study of the early history of psychiatric patients, another team working with the New Haven group, the psychiatrist Jerome K. Myers and the sociologist Bertram H. Roberts, contrasted the pattern of family dynamics in class III and class V patients suffering from psychosis and neurosis. They reported that the typical class III person who broke down had been subjected to unbearable pressures to achieve from his family. However, his family had not given him the support needed to prepare him to fulfill the demands of middle-class value systems. These middle-class patients were anxious because they could not satisfy their mothers' demands and because they did not get adequate support from their fathers. They felt enormous pressures to move upward in society, beyond their parents' level of accomplishment, but had not acquired the strength to enable them to fulfill these needs.

In contrast, the class V people who broke down usually came from families in which they felt little love, affection, protection, or stability. The lack of loving care and affection resulted in a sense of neglect and, in consequence, a low feeling of self-worth. When people think relatively little of themselves, they are poorly equipped to handle the tensions of a complex world. Lower-lower-class people, by and large, do have to cope with economic hardship, with the vagaries of an uncertain labor market, and with the random brutalities of slum living. An inability to cope may very well lead to withdrawal, to outbursts of violence, to the kind of disorientation that we label as psychosis.

We can see, therefore, that there is a meaningful connection between our picture of the way people bring up their children and the consequences for the mental health of these children when they are grown. The implications for preventive psychiatry are fairly considerable. They argue that lower-lower-class children need more nurturing than they are getting and that middle-class children, perhaps, should be subjected to less pressure.

Social Class and Political Behavior

One of the most widely believed dogmas based on Marxist thinking about social class is that economic interests lead to class consciousness, which in turn leads to political activity. Much of the political life of Europe revolves around parties organized along class lines. .Virtually all of the socialist and communist movements of the world, following the principles presented by Marx and his co-workers, accept the thesis that workers will become aware of their common needs and will therefore join together to achieve power in order to fulfill these needs. Of course, the various followers of the Marxist dogma differ about the way this search for power should be conducted. But there is very little difference of opinion about the relation between economic interests and their expression in the po-litical process.

Marx predicted that the working class would become increas-ingly impoverished. This prediction has not been fully confirmed. A growing army of lower-lower-class people, outside the class structure in many ways, has been accumulating in the slums of American cities. In Western Europe, however, blue-collar workers have become in-creasingly prosperous. In the United States the group we have called class IV, the unionized, skilled and semiskilled workers, has also been able to win an ever growing share of the good things of life. There have been suggestions that the working class, in consequence, should lessen its sense of class consciousness and its affiliation to the traditional workers' parties. This has not been found to be true in a number of studies of political process in Europe. For example, an in-tensive study of prosperous automobile workers in England, carried out by a team of sociologists headed by J. H. Goldthorpe, found that, even though the modern industrial worker in England lives more comfortably than his nineteenth-century ancestor, he still thinks of himself as a member of the working class and has the tradi-tional allegiance to socialist parties.

Goldthorpe and his colleagues also found that blue-collar and white-collar workers show very different patterns of interest and association. They report, for example, that blue-collar workers tend to do their visiting within the family, whereas white-collar workers tend to have a much wider pattern of social contacts. Blue-collar workers say they are interested in having their children advance through education, but actually they do relatively little to encourage their children to study and, in fact, seem quite unconscious of young children's needs for an environment conducive to schoolwork. In contrast, the parents in white-collar families are extremely supportive of their children's scholarly activities. Blue-collar workers show relatively little interest in leaving the characteristic occupations of the manual laborer, whereas white-collar workers are interested in upward mobility. Lastly, Goldthorpe found a fierce loyalty to the Labour party, which calls itself socialist, among manual workers. There was more political flexibility among white-collar workers.

In sum, then, we find that the Marxist prediction that "workers" will have a high sense of class consciousness and will engage in appropriate political activity was confirmed for blue-collar workers in England but not for white-collar workers.

The effect of social class membership on political behavior in the United States is more complex than in Europe. A number of studies carried out in the thirties and forties did show that members of the working class tended to vote for the Democratic party, which they regarded as being "for the common people." And, as we noted in discussing Centers, they were joined by many professionals and merchants who regarded themselves as affiliated with the working class. Thus, from the time of the New Deal on, the Democratic party held the loyalty of a majority of the country.

In general, where economic interests are concerned, the pattern continues to hold. That is, as long as the issues of the political process are clearly related to unemployment, or to prices, there is a tendency for people from working-class families to vote for the Democratic party and its populist position.

However, since the 1950s, many political battles in the United States have had relatively little to do with economic issues. This has been especially true when the fear of domestic or foreign communism or the tension among races or ethnic groups became an important consideration in determining people's votes. Under these circumstances, it is common to find that many working-class people, especially blue-collar, Roman Catholic workers, desert the Democratic party in order to vote for someone who exerts a strongly anticommunist or antibusing appeal. This pattern of voting is certainly puzzling to anyone whose ideas of class are based on Marxist notions.

The fact that working-class people, on the whole, are less sympathetic to nonconformists and less concerned with civil rights than middle-class people has been confirmed by several national surveys. This is not inconsistent with the pattern of child rearing we described earlier. If the rearing of working-class people emphasizes the need for control, orderliness, and conformity to external demands, then they would certainly tend to reject deviant social and artistic positions as well as behavior that is outside the accepted boundaries.

Note again that we are confirming the usefulness of the ecological model. The stratification that revolves around economic positions is useful as long as the political struggle is based on economic issues. But when these conflicts deal with considerations other than the economic, analysis of social strata on Marxist lines is no longer useful, and it becomes necessary to look for other sources of social division. Under these circumstances, therefore, such factors as ideology or social association become more important.

This chapter has dealt with the broad question of the anatomy of a complex society. The next step in our inquiry requires that we focus down on the detailed content of interaction among individuals. We have to shift from a study of the anatomy of society to a study of its functioning.

On Your Own

1. A good basic summary of the data and theories of social class is M. M. Tumin's *Social Stratification*. If you are interested in the details of Warner's approach, his group has published a paperback that outlines their method. This is *Social Class in America* by Warner, Meeker, and Eels. A nice treatment of social class in the growing suburbs is William M. Dobriner's *Class in Suburbia*. Both of the New Haven studies described in the text are available in paperback through Wiley's Science Editions.

2. Some of the most vivid descriptions of lower-lower-class life are found in the work of Oscar Lewis. He deals with the group of people who move back and forth between Puerto Rico and the slums of cities in the northeastern United States, primarily New York City. A good introduction is his *La Vida: A Puerto Rican Family in the Culture of Poverty—San Juan and New York*.

3. Warner's description of social class in Yankee City has a fictional analogue in J. P. Marquand's *Point of No Return*. This story, which revolves around the impact of social class barriers on the lives of people in Newburyport, gives a detailed picture of the mores of the town. Marquand spent his early years there and knew it well.

4. Can you identify your own position in American class structure using each of the schemes presented in the chapter to describe social class? Find an incident in your own life in which each of the three major ways of defining class (social function, social status, ideas) would have predicted your behavior.

5. How homogeneous is your social life? Make a list of your own friends and your parents' friends. Identify their class position. How many people from strata other than their own do your parents count as friends? Visit with any regularity? How about you? What are the implications of your answer to this question?

Section IV
The Dynamics of
Social Action

7

Social Interaction

Now that we have discussed the organization of society in a general way, we can turn to an examination of face-to-face interactions among people. These are the basic units of any social system, the day-in-and-day-out encounters that form the working elements of society. We have already anticipated this discussion of social interaction. For example, we explored the interaction among the members of the Mannon family in Chapter 1. In Chapter 4 we watched the impact on a young Indian woman of her date's sophisticated taste in Western food. And in Chapter 5 we saw how the interactions between a visitor and his hosts in a small town enabled the outsider to learn about the culture of a community new to him. Now it is time to build up a systematic approach to social interaction.

We begin with the ecological model. This tells us that each person's behavior is affected by the social, biological, and physical environment, by the person's background of ideas, values, and attitudes, and by feedback from his or her own actions. In dealing with social interaction, we focus down on social environment, on the impact of significant others (to use a phrase from the technical language of sociology) on behavior. A number of questions can be posed. What determines how people perceive each other? Why do people like or dislike others? How do people reward or punish each other as they come into contact, and what is the effect of the rewards and punishments? Lastly, what kinds of systematic language can we use to describe informal and formal groups?

To provide some raw material for discussing these questions, I shall use a fictional account of the experiences of a young woman who has recently completed her first year of work after graduating from college. She has been attending a human relations training program run by her corporation. Her instructor has asked her to describe her experiences at work since she joined the company. Here is her paper:

My name is Susan Green. My job with this company was my first since I graduated from_____College near New York City. Since the college I went to was big and impersonal, it was hard to get to know people there. I enjoyed my courses in mathematics and computer science, but I knew that unless I went out for extracurricular activities I wouldn't have many friends. Besides, I was told that it wouldn't hurt in getting a job if I had experience other than classroom and computer center work. So I spent a lot of time on the college newspaper. I did make lots of friends there. We not only enjoyed working on the paper, but we also went out together.

When I first joined the_____Company, I felt a little bit lost. This was the first time I was out of school, and it felt strange to be on my own. It was really wonderful to find somebody in my department who had graduated from the same college I went to. It turned out that this girl, Ginny Stover, was a senior programmer and a really important person in the department. She was also an editor of a little weekly paper put out by the employee association. But that wasn't really why I liked her. The thing that attracted me was that she was such a nice person. For one thing, she knew my older sister very well because they had been in the same class in high school. So she sort of took it on herself to make me feel at home, to tell me where things were, and to give me some tips about which of the higher-ups to avoid and what kinds of projects were worth trying to get into. One of the nicest things that happened was that she turned out to be interested in playing the guitar, and so we had a great deal to talk about since I also like to play the guitar.

After I had gotten used to my job, I decided I would try to join the staff of the employee association's newspaper. I asked my friend Ginny whether I would be able to work on the paper even though I was a newcomer. She said she thought that there wouldn't be any trouble getting me in. So the next time there was a staff meeting, I went down to the newspaper headquarters. It was a little room in the basement of the building and was crowded with desks and typewriters. There was a great bustle of people wandering around doing all kinds of things that looked very important. I had a little bit of an idea of what it was like to be on a newspaper, although the college paper had been a much simpler operation than the staff newsletter.

I sat in on a meeting of the staff of the paper that first time. The editor-in-chief, a girl named Sandy, was the chairperson of the meeting. It was a little funny to hear her called chairperson, but everybody there was pretty much into Women's Lib. They discussed things like who would be taking on what kinds of stories and how they would be able to get enough money from the employee association so they wouldn't have a deficit. It was clear after a while that Sandy ran things with a pretty tight hand. She didn't pay very much attention to what other people said. In fact, most of the time she just gave orders.

After the meeting, my friend Ginny introduced me to Sandy and said that I would be interested in working on the paper. Sandy said they needed people to cover department beats. I said that I would be interested in doing that. Sandy said, without even looking at me, "We need somebody to cover the sales department because the girl who was supposed to do it got mono." I said that I wouldn't object to covering the sales department, but I didn't know if I would be very good at it since I had never been interested in anything but math and computers. Sandy said that she would send me some material on how to go to the section heads of the sales department and that she expected me to come back with a story every time they had something important to get into the paper. I thanked her very much and said I was looking forward to working on the paper. Sandy said that things were very busy, but that I should always come and talk to her whenever I had any problems. But I didn't get the impression that she really wanted to be disturbed.

For the next two or three weeks, I spent a lot of my spare time working quite hard on the paper. I tracked down the supervisors of every one of the sales sections and tried to get them to tell me about what was going on in their department. Some of them were very nice people, and others brushed me off and looked terribly busy. The most interesting time, though, was when I went to the newspaper office with my friend Ginny on Tuesday nights. That was the night when the paper was made up. Everybody was working frantically to get all of the stories in shape and to get a layout of the paper ready to be taken down to the printer. Sometimes it would be three or four in the morning before everything was ready, and one of the girls who had a car would drive the copy to the printer's in town.

It was very exciting to feel that I was part of all this activity. I looked at the world a little differently because I was a member of the newspaper staff. A lot of my opinions about the company were changed because of things I heard the girls on the paper say. One of the most important things, of course, was that most of the girls on the paper were strong for Women's Lib, something I had never thought about very much for myself. I found myself listening to them and then thinking about things that happened to me. For example, once I talked up in a department meeting when one of the supervisors made a sexist statement. I never would have had the courage to do that before, but, watching some of the other girls on the paper, I got the idea that it would be good to assert myself.

Even though the first three or four weeks were very exciting, after a while I started getting a little bit tired of the work that I had to do on the paper. I really wasn't very interested in sales, and the stories I wrote always got chewed up, probably because they weren't very good. Several times I got nasty comments from people in the sales department about whom I had written a story because they said I hadn't gotten the details right. One of the other things that happened was that I started getting more and more disillusioned with the Women's Lib ideas of the people on the paper. It seemed to me that they were so busy worrying about being badly treated because they were women that they missed out on a lot of things. It was especially hard to take because, at about the same time, I was beginning to get very involved in a big project that was headed by Alexandra, one of the senior people in systems, to set up a new data-processing procedure. The girls on the paper didn't think much of this. They thought that it was a bad thing for women to focus on data processing because that was a second-rate kind of occupation, a kind of clerical job that had traditionally been held by women. A couple of times, I had to tell people on the newspaper that I couldn't handle a story or come to a meeting because I had to work overtime or because we had just been given some time on the computer to try something out. They gave me a hard time. In fact, after a while I almost hated to show up.

The thing that really disillusioned me with the newspaper was a big campaign they put on over the business of sex discrimination. Traditionally, most of the employees have been women, but the senior supervisors and systems experts have been men, with one or two exceptions. The people on the paper, probably because of their Women's Lib attitudes, were very unhappy about this state of affairs and wanted to start a lawsuit to force the company to promote more women. We had a knockdown, dragout fight in a staff meeting over the stand that the newspaper should take. Sandy and most of the other people who counted on the paper thought that we should come out strongly for the lawsuit. A couple of the rest of us thought that women would have to upgrade their skills to win promotion and that a lawsuit was a waste of time. I remember walking out of that meeting and thinking that I would probably have to drop out of the newspaper even though I had enjoyed being part of the group.

Leaving the newspaper was easy because I was getting more and more involved in the systems work and had started to feel a lot closer to some of my friends who were going to go on for master's degrees at night and who were spending a lot of time in the computer center. I spent more time with Alexandra working on our project. At about that time, I told Ginny that I was very sorry but I would have to give up working on the paper.

An Analysis of Susan's Story

Susan's paper went on to analyze her experiences in terms of the concepts to which she had been exposed in her training program in human relations. At this point, however, I would like to discuss Susan's experiences from the point of view of a social scientist and apply to them some theoretical ideas derived from the study of group processes.

Person Perception

It is clear from Susan's story that she was immediately attracted to the alumna of her college, Ginny. She admired, if she didn't particularly like, Sandy, the editor-in-chief of the staff newspaper. You get a hint that she also was attracted to Alexandra, on whose project she started working towards the end of the period described in the paper. It would be interesting to use Susan's experiences to define some of the things that determine whether one person will be attracted to another. Figure 7.1 presents some of the concepts that help answer that question. It was drawn from a widely used textbook in social psychology written by P. F. Secord and C. W. Backman, a sociologist and a social psychologist.

There are three columns in Figure 7.1. The first column tells you something about the external events that influence attraction or liking. The second column tells you something about the events inside the head of the perceiver, and the third column tells you a little bit about the sorts of behavior from which liking or attraction can be

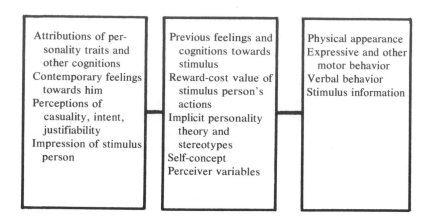

Fig. 7:1. Factors in forming impressions of personality

Source: Second, P. F., and Backman, C. W., *Social Psychology,* New York: McGraw-Hill, 1960.

inferred. The three columns of this table fit neatly into the three components of the ecological model presented in Chapter 2.

Susan's story doesn't say very much about physical appearance, but research on the sources of attraction suggests that most people are attracted to those who fit their own ideas of beauty, repelled by those whom they regard as ugly. These are very personal ideas. Each social group defines its general concepts of beauty or ugliness, but each individual acquires a unique set of ideas about what is beautiful and what is not from his or her own experiences.

Research on the factors that determine attraction also indicates that, in the early stages of their acquaintance, people tend to be attracted to others who share a common background. A social psychologist, Theodore Newcomb, who worked with students in an experimental dormitory at the University of Michigan, reported that new arrivals were drawn to each other if they came from the same part of the country, planned to study the same subjects, or lived in rooms next to each other. From Susan's story, we can see that Susan would easily be attracted to Ginny. They had gone to the same college and shared many mutual acquaintances. To Susan, Ginny was an island of familiarity in the bewildering sea of novel experiences and people she encountered in her first job.

As time goes on, however, a feeling of liking tends to come from the sharing of ideas rather than from such superficial attractions as coming from the same part of the world. As people work or play together, they experience each other's moods, learn about each other's opinions, watch each other make decisions. These shared experiences may be rewarding or punishing or, at times, emotionally neutral. As the interaction progresses, each person forms an internal picture of the other based on inferences from observed actions. Thus, Susan inferred from Sandy's behavior at the first meeting that the editor-in-chief of the newspaper was a rigid, unyielding person, and she was probably repelled. The later interactions reinforced this first impression.

One item in the first column of Figure 7.1 is "Expressive and other motor behavior." This reflects the fact that we rely on much more than what people say as a basis for forming impressions. As we noted in Chapter 5, nonverbal behavior has been studied intensively by anthropologists, sociologists, and social psychologists. Gesture, eye contact, distance maintained between people, even the position of hands and arms communicate feelings and affect impressions. For example, one could imagine that Sandy (the editor-in-chief) probably did not look directly into Susan's eyes very often as they were talking, but rather kept her own eyes straying towards her work or towards other people in the crowded room. Sandy may very well have folded her hands over her head, a position that experts in this field assure us is often interpreted as an attempt to create a sense of superiority and distance. On the other hand, one would expect that Susan's friend Ginny probably did look directly into her eyes when the two of them were talking.

As we shift from the first column of Figure 7.1 to the second, we move from inputs to the ideas, beliefs, and motives that affect the way one person reacts to another. There are four items in this column, each reflecting either the influence of events in the perceiver's past or the immediate effect of currently held beliefs.

First is "Previous feelings and cognitions toward the stimulus." Each of us has a repertory of habitual reactions that are called into play by the stimuli described in the previous discussion. Perhaps we have always liked people with New England accents or always disliked people with red hair. More seriously, we have all had experiences of developing positive or negative impressions of people. The factors that determined these impressions in the past left us with learned reactions to others.

Next is "Reward-cost value of stimulus person's actions." This is a way of saying the obvious: if people treat you well, you are likely to develop positive feelings towards them. If people treat you badly, the consequence is likely to be negative impressions. Susan's first contact with the editor must have had a damping effect on her feelings about that young woman. No one enjoys being manipulated, and Susan did have the feeling that her own interests were being disregarded.

The kinds of ideas we hold about the nature of personality, whether formulated or not, also affect our perception of others. Secord and Backman use the phrase "Implicit personality theory and stereotypes." Some of the categories used to classify people are held almost universally in any given social group; others are based on individual experiences. We also develop some concepts about the sort of behavior we can use to classify people into these categories. Psychologists have identified two main ways of dealing with personality. One way, a *trait* approach, assumes that people have characteristics that they maintain no matter what the environment in which they are behaving. If you followed this approach, you would characterize people as dominant or submissive, friendly or unfriendly, anxious or stable. That is, if you subscribe to an "implicit personality theory" that leads you to classify people according to their traits, then one of the things you do when you meet a person is to try to fit that person into your set of traitlike categories. Psychologists who use this approach are the American Raymond Cattell and the Briton Hans Eysenck.

Another approach to personality, which has been used more recently by such psychologists as Albert Bandura and Walter Mischel, working at Stanford University, is a *social learning* approach. Rather than characterizing individuals as dominant or submissive, the approach asks about the kind of situation in which people have learned to be dominant or have learned to hold back. It makes the assumption that any one person may be dominant in some situations and submissive in others. Someone who holds to this social learning point of view is less likely to label people with trait names but is more likely to try to look at the causes of their behavior in the situation in which it takes place.

We aren't given much information about Susan's ideas on the nature of personality. She does hint at a trait approach. You get the impression that she immediately labeled Sandy as a cold and domineering person. She does not indicate that she saw Sandy's behavior as determined by the demands of her editor's role. If Susan had been a believer in social learning theory, she might have tried to find a different Sandy in the informality of the lunch table or the staff picnic.

The last item in the middle column of Figure 7.1 is self-concept. You don't get very much information about what Susan is like from the way she writes, but there is some implication that she has relatively little anxiety about herself, knows her own mind, and tends to be active rather than passive. I suspect that one of the things that determines whether she likes people or not is the sense of security she brings to her first interactions with them. For example, the fact that she reacted negatively to Sandy may have been due to the friction that inevitably is generated when two strong people meet. Perhaps someone who felt less secure about herself would have been ready to hero-worship the editor-in-chief rather than to react negatively.

Secord and Backman's third column describes the outcome of the process of impression formation. The first item merely states that attributions of personality traits and other personal characteristics result from the operation of the variables described in the first two columns. The second item, "Contemporary feelings toward him," takes cognizance of the fact that impressions, as has been implied in much of our discussion, lead to feelings. The last deals with a complex matter to which the next section is devoted: the attribution of causality, intent, and justifiability to another's actions. Looking at Susan's story, we can apply these variables by saying that Susan attributed the traits of friendliness and helpfulness to Ginny, that this led to positive feelings, and that Susan interpreted Ginny's behavior as being caused by a desire to be helpful. In contrast, Sandy was perceived as autocratic and hostile; this led to negative feelings. Although Susan does not spell out her attributions, one gets the impression that Susan assumed that Sandy meant to *use* her but was indifferent to her as a person.

Attribution

The previous discussion demonstrated that people respond to stimuli and operate on these inputs, transforming them into impressions on the basis of their ideas and past experiences. Several theorists have tried to organize the data derived from studies of people's perceptions of others. The precursor of most modern theorists in this area was Fritz Heider, a German psychologist who fled the Nazis and came to the United States. He suggested that people have a need to think of others in a consistent and sensible way. So, for example, we tend to respond positively to people who are liked by our friends, negatively to those whom our friends dislike. If we learn that someone is a member of a group of whose goals we disapprove, we are less likely to perceive the good things about that person and more likely to perceive the bad. Could you be completely impartial about someone who is introduced as a member of the American Nazi party or of the Mafia? Heider saw this need for consistency as a source of what he called "cognitive balance."

Beyond a tendency to maintain cognitive balance, there is the process of trying to make sense of another's behavior, summarized in the phrase about attribution in Figure 7.1. In discussing the interpretation of nonverbal behavior, I noted that the gesture of hands folded over head may lead one to think that the person making the gesture is trying to convey a sense of superiority. One way of phrasing this statement is to say that the observer attributes meaning to the gesture. This is not always a straightforward process. There is a tale of two businessmen meeting on a railroad platform in Czarist Russia. One asks the other, "Where are you going?" The other answers, "To Minsk to buy butter." The first replies, "Why are you lying to me? I know that when you go to Minsk to buy butter you always say you are going to Pinsk to buy eggs. I overheard you buying your ticket—you actually *are* going to Minsk today. So why are you lying to me?"

Heider proposed a basic distinction between two sources of attribution. One is based on an observer's inference that a particular behavior is due to the internal disposition of the other person. The other is based on the inference that the behavior is due to external pressures. In the story about the two merchants, the accusation of lying is clear evidence of the first process.

A contemporary American psychologist who has worked with attribution, Harold Kelley, begins with Heider's formulation. He goes on to work out the character of attribution in two circumstances. In the first, the perceiver has the opportunity to observe another person's behavior a number of times. He or she then carries out a kind of scientific analysis similar to the formulation of a functional relationship we described in Chapter 2. That is, the observer looks for consistencies of behavior over a variety of external circumstances. If these are found, an attribution based on internal disposition is made. ("Why are you lying to me?" assumes a number of instances of lying.) If there is no such consistency, behavior is attributed to the force of circumstances.

When an observer has only one chance to watch someone's behavior, according to Kelley, attribution is based on a process he calls "discounting." The observer searches about for explanations and discounts or rejects the less plausible ones.

A study carried out by two social psychologists, John W. Thibaut and Henry W. Riecken, illustrates the process of discounting very nicely. In this study, American college seniors were asked to try to persuade another student, who was actually a confederate of the experimenter, to give blood in a Red Cross drive. For some of the subjects, the other student appeared to be a freshmen, low in status in the university. For others, the person to be persuaded was a graduate student, high in status. All the confederates agreed to give blood. The subjects were then asked to explain the behavior of the person they had just persuaded. They tended to interpret the behavior of the "graduate student" as due to his generosity, an attribution to an internal factor. They indicated that they could not see any external cause for the graduate student's yielding to persuasion. For the "freshman," the difference in status, an external cause, was identified quite consistently as the reason for yielding. In each instance, the subjects discounted the less plausible explanation.

Now that we have discussed the determinants of the impressions people form of each other, we can move on to look at the interplay of action and reaction as people engage in social interaction.

Interaction

There is a wonderful old story from the Jewish ghetto about two old men who meet for the first time in years. They gaze at each other. Each says, *"Nu"* ("Well"). There is a long silence. Finally, as they part, one says to the other, "It's a pleasure to be able to open your heart." Clearly, a great many things happened between these two men that would not be captured by a court reporter's transcript of their conversation.

In Shakespeare's *As You Like It,* Jacques says, "All the world's a stage, and all the men and women merely players." This is a somewhat hackneyed truth, but a truth nevertheless. We are playing roles every moment of our waking days and, perhaps, even during our dreams. This is true even when we are by ourselves, but it is more marked when we interact with others.

Erving Goffman, a noted American social scientist, has devoted a lifetime to careful descriptions of the rules people follow as they engage in interaction. He too sees the world in theatrical terms. Each of us performs a series of rituals, patterns of behavior that vary little and that have symbolic character. The significant people with whom we interact understand the meaning of the rituals and mesh their rituals with ours. Goffman has travelled widely, studying people as they adapt to the role of patient or attendent in a mental hospital, prisoner or guard in a jail, innkeeper or tourist in a resort. He has sketched the rules that determine the permissible contacts we make with those we meet in the street or in public conveyances. His theatrical vocabulary is extended to take account of the fact that some people in a given setting are participants in an interaction; some are audience; some, like elevator operators or waitresses, only part of the scenery. Recently, Goffman has used the modern technology of videotape to record interactions and develop an extremely precise system for describing the minute details of encounters among people in natural settings. His approach tells us relatively little about individual differences, but it provides an enormously subtle and rewarding vocabulary for the study of social interaction.

Contingencies of Interaction. Much behavior is ritualistic and varies little from time to time. (Think of the way people routinely say, "Have a good day," to the bank teller or supermarket checkout clerk.) However, a great deal of social interplay is affected by mutual exchange of reward or punishment. I would like to work through an

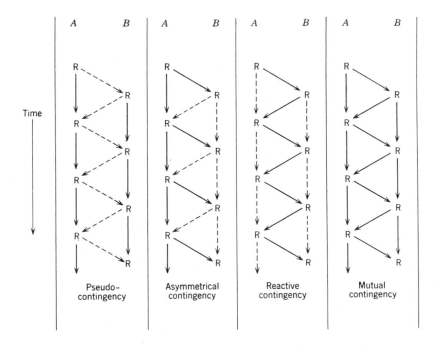

Fig. 7:2. Classes of social interaction in terms of contingency

Source: Jones, E. E., and Gerard, H. B., Foundations of social psychology, New York: Wiley, 1967.

interesting scheme that describes a number of patterns of mutual exchange, even though it requires a new set of terms. This scheme, described in Figure 7.2, was developed by social psychologists Edward Jones and Harold Gerard. It deals with contingencies of interaction. One can define a contingency as an "iffy" state of affairs. If my smiling at you depends on your smiling first, then my smile is *contingent* on yours.

In order to trace through this complex scheme, I will comment on each of the columns and provide some illustrations of their application to situations you may recognize. The diagram as a whole is about two people whom we might call A and B. For example, in the story we told at the beginning of this chapter, think of Susan as A and the various people she interacted with as B. Each *R* stands for some piece of behavior; the psychologist's jargon is "response." As each individual comes into an interaction, two kinds of factors affect him or her. The first is a set of plans, a set of motives which, as we have described them in Chapter 4, consist of values placed on one or another outcome of the interaction and expectations of the likelihood of these outcomes. The second is the impact on each person of the *other's* behavior.

A solid line linking one of a given individual's R's to another's implies that a person's behavior is responsive to his or her own plans. A solid line from one person's R to the other's R in the next row implies responsiveness to one's own plans or to the behavior of the other person.

The first column is labeled "Pseudocontingency." In pseudocontingency, each person responds in terms of his own plans and pays very little attention to what the other person is saying. I'm sure you have had the frustrating experience of talking to someone who apparently had not heard a word you have been saying. If you charge on without regard to what your opposite number has done or said, the interaction represents an example of pseudocontingency. Another example of pseudocontingency is the parallel play of two eighteen-month-old children in a sandbox.

The next column, labeled "Asymmetrical contingency," involves an interaction between two people, A, who responds only to his or her own plans, and B, who does react to A. I think we could consider that Susan's interaction with the editor-in-chief fits this pattern. You may remember that the editor-in-chief didn't even seem to hear that Susan was expressing an interest in the work of her own section but blindly went ahead telling Susan to report on the sales department. In contrast, Susan did respond to the editor's statements;

she had to say yes or no to the request to take on the assignment she was offered.

The third column, headed "Reactive contingency," is one in which each person plays a kind of Ping-Pong with the other. That is, each person ignores his or her own plans and responds only to what the other person is doing. I think this sort of interaction is fairly rare. Very few people are completely willing to subordinate themselves to the desires of another. However, I suppose that when two people meet for the first time and are very uncertain about what they want of each other or, indeed, what they can possibly expect of each other, it may be that almost everything that happens in the meeting depends upon what each says to the other.

The fourth column, headed "Mutual contingency," represents the highest level of sharing between people. In this, each party in an interaction reacts both to his or her own plans and to the behavior of the other. I think that the way in which Susan interacted with her friend Ginny when they first knew each other might be an example of mutual contingency. They both yielded somewhat in their behavior, but each continued to carry out her own plans. That is, to Susan, Ginny was a source of information about the new work environment and an introduction to a wider circle of friends and activities. As a result, Susan had to shape herself somewhat to Ginny's "Women's Lib" ideas. To Ginny, Susan was a fellow college alumna who needed some help. And Ginny had to go along with Susan's expressions of independence in order to be able to provide this help adequately.

I think we can see from this discussion that there are two sources of interaction between people. One of them, called *outcome control,* involves the simple manipulation by one person of another by means of promised rewards and punishments. Susan's behavior was shaped by the editor-in-chief, temporarily at least, because the editor-in-chief held out the promise of a position on the newspaper, an outcome that Susan desired. The second source of interaction is called *cue control.* It is a reaction to the stimuli presented by another person rather than to the promise of reward or punishment. An example of this pattern may be found in Susan's reaction to Ginny. The warmth and friendliness were a part of what attracted Susan, but probably the most important source of attraction was the fact that Ginny was a familiar face in an otherwise strange scene. It was the familiarity that first made it possible for Susan to approach Ginny and try to become her friend.

The scheme we have just explored helps us deal with the events in immediate, face-to-face contact among individuals. But the impact individuals have on each other goes far beyond the momentary effects we have been describing. People are influenced by the groups to which they look for support or from which they obtain a sense of social identity. Our analysis now turns to a discussion of long-lasting influences on individuals from social groups.

Reference Groups

Social scientist Herbert Hyman coined the term *reference group* more than thirty years ago to describe a group of people from whom an individual derives ideas, values, and expectations. A reference group can consist of people who meet face to face. But it may also consist of individuals whose contact is not immediate and personal. For example, to many members of the medical profession, the American Medical Association forms a kind of reference group, a source of general ideology as well as a guide to specific behavior. This is true even if the individual physician has never been to a meeting of the American Medical Association. It is a reference group because he has become a member, reads the publications of the association, and hears through his contacts with other physicians about the ideas championed by the association.

Most people are members of more than one reference group. The pattern of a person's memberships in reference groups may be a fairly complicated affair. Figure 7.3 is a diagram of some of the reference groups that are important in Susan's life. Some of the groups are quite central; I have indicated these with solid lines. Others, given dotted lines, are important, but as background rather than immediate influences.

One of the critical questions to ask about an individual's relation to a reference group is the sort of role he or she plays in it. We have already discussed the concepts of role and status in the previous chapter. You may remember that a status is a position in some social group, a role is the set of behaviors called for by that position. Roles can be defined in terms of the expectations people have of each other.

One point that should be remembered is that roles do not come

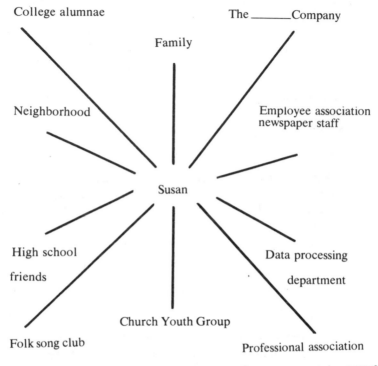

Fig. 7:3. Reference Groups in Susan's Life

singly. An outstanding American sociologist, Robert A. Merton, has developed a concept of *role-set,* the complex of roles associated with a given status. For example, Susan's status as a junior member of her section involved her taking on simultaneously the role of fellow worker with the people in her section and of subordinate to her supervisors. Apart from the role-set at work, Susan had other roles. She was a daughter in her family, a member of the "gang" among the people who went to the same high school in her town, a participant in recreational activities and in groups at her church.

We have already introduced the concept of two kinds of status, achieved and ascribed. You may remember that an achieved status is one to which a person arrives by fulfilling some kind of obligation.

For example, Susan achieved the status of staff member of the newspaper by signing up and then by carrying out her duties. An ascribed status is one that goes along with a person's biological and social character in a predetermined way. Susan has ascribed status as a daughter; there is nothing she can do about gaining or losing this status. Both achieved and ascribed statuses carry with them certain kinds of expected behaviors. A person's activities and beliefs are shaped by the network of statuses, both ascribed and achieved.

One last concept that should be introduced is that of *reference individuals*. In Chapter 1, we talked briefly about the concepts of modeling and identification as reflected in the experimental work of Bandura and in the psychoanalytic concepts derived from Freud. The people with whom an individual identifies represent sources of affiliation to reference groups as well as important influences on behavior. These reference individuals are sometimes called *role models*. That is, they provide information about the way in which a person is supposed to carry out his or her roles.

Ginny provided a role model for Susan during the early phases of her new job. Susan probably liked the idea of being a warm, outgoing, and socially attractive person. Perhaps during this early stage of her life at work, Susan imitated Ginny's behavior. In fact, it might well have been comic to see Susan drinking coffee from a plastic cup, holding a cigarette in her lips in a certain way, looking harassed while getting out the newspaper at two in the morning, in precisely the way her idol did.

As time wore on, Susan became less and less attracted to the employee's association as a center for her life and more interested in the department in which she was working. Perhaps one of the important determinants of this shift was her growing identification with a new role model, the supervisor on whose research team she started working.

The operation of reference groups in shaping people's ideas is clearly shown in our story about Susan. Remember the way Susan gradually adopted the ideology of the women in the staff association? She probably found herself looking at the world in a different way than she had earlier, as was indicated by her prickly reaction to a supervisor's sexist remark. As time went on, however, conflicts began to emerge among the expectations set up by various roles in Susan's role-set. There were times when being a good friend to the women in her department was inconsistent with the point of view of the minority of workers who were active in the employees' association. The social activism characteristic of the employees' association was often incompatible with the commitment to advancement in the job and, possibly, to intellectual activity among the people who formed the core of the group working in the systems department.

In Susan's story, one of the most important events in the beginning of her working career was the development of a sense of identity as a member of the newspaper group. Being part of the warm, bustling activity of "makeup" night was probably one of the forces that most attracted her and led her to assume this identity. Unfortunately, the demands of this reference group conflicted with Susan's older patterns of independence of thought. This conflict made it difficult for her to submerge her identity, even though being a member of the newspaper crowd was very attractive. Perhaps this is what led her to switch affiliations, join the new reference group of the section in which she worked, and adopt a new way of life on the job. Some of the underlying causes of these events in Susan's life will emerge more clearly as we discuss group processes in the next section.

I think you can see how powerful are the concepts of reference group, role, and status as tools for the analysis of behavior. They represent the work of several generations of scientists in analyzing the way individuals form a part of social groups, are influenced by these social groups, and in turn influence others. Now, however, we must move on to a new kind of discussion. In this chapter we have been dealing with Susan as an individual and her interactions with other individuals. We will now change our focus from the individual to the group. One of the major emphases in the social sciences has been a study of group processes in themselves. This study has led to the development of theoretical models for groups and of a large body of information about the factors that determine the character of group activity.

On Your Own

1. Anything by Goffman (see references) is readable except his very latest books. I would start with his first, *Presentation of Self in Everyday Life.* Another good book of his is *Stigma,* which deals with our reactions to people who are deformed or otherwise

different. *Asylum* handles the adaptation of patients or prisoners to a closed social system. Unfortunately there are no good treatments for the general public of the developments in social psychology dealing with person perception and attribution theory. The brief approach to theories of personality in this chapter may have given you an appetite for more. If so, I would suggest the book by Cattell cited in the references or, even though it is very much a textbook, Calvin S. Hall and Gardner Lindzey's *Theories of Personality,* second edition.

2. Write a story about a transitional period in your own life in which you made new friends. It would be helpful if you remembered episodes when you had to choose sides in a conflict.

3. Analyze your story first by determining the factors in Table 1 that led to your liking or disliking someone. Does your story include a description of your forming an immediate impression of someone? What produced the impression? Was it something physical or behavioral? Was your liking based on shared experiences or values? What were the consequences of the impression?

4. Draw a diagram listing the important reference groups in your social environment. How do they affect you?

5. Next time you have to see someone on whom you depend (your boss if you are working, a senior member of your family if you are not), analyze the interaction using the system of contingencies in Fig. 1. Does the person with whom you are interacting pay attention to what you are saying, or is he or she merely attending to an internal program? How about you? Are you sensitive to the person with whom you are interacting?

6. Watch people in a public place like a shopping center or a supermarket. Do they exchange eye contact with people they do not know? What are the apparent limits to permissible interaction with strangers? Does it depend on the place? If you read some Goffman, apply his theatrical scheme to the people ahead of you in a checkout line, if you can eavesdrop on a couple who know each other. Are they acting as if they were alone?

8
The Study of Groups

The best way of studying the characteristics of groups is to observe some people in action. From such observations, one can begin to tease out the variables required to characterize group processes. The following anecdote should provide the raw material needed for this exercise.

Imagine yourself on a trolley car (we still have them in Philadelphia, where I live). You get on the car, pay your fare to the conductor, glance around at the people, choose a seat, and sit down. The car is rolling along towards the center of the city. After you've been on it for a few minutes, the trolley descends into a tunnel that leads under a river and into the city. Suddenly, the car stops, and the lights go out. An emergency light goes on. People become restless and uneasy. A baby starts crying. The trolley conductor stands up and says in a loud voice, "Don't try to get out. Sit in your seats." He then gets out and starts fussing with the overhead cables, trying to regain power. People start talking to each other. Several of the older people in the car are quite upset, and a young woman in a nurse's uniform tries to calm them down. She holds the crying baby and rocks it while the mother rummages through her bag for a bottle. A man with an authoritative manner, possibly an off-duty policeman, tries to soothe people by saying that everything will be all right. The light goes on, the trolley car begins to move, and people settle down into their seats.

The first question to ask is whether the collection of people sitting in the trolley as you entered it was a group in any sense. One could argue that it was not. True, the passengers shared a common goal, going to the center of the city. But they were not interacting to any degree. Clearly, something changed after the emergency began, since the passengers and the conductor were much more aware of each other than they had been, and the level of interaction rose.

But we could examine the situation before the emergency a little more closely, especially if we have been reading Goffman. Were there any interactions? Indeed there were. The passengers had to pay the driver. Each passenger who entered the trolley and walked down the aisle may have glanced fleetingly at those already seated, assessing them as possible seat companions. As Goffman points out, there are some clear rules about how overtly we can carry out such an assessment, how much eye contact is allowed. If the new passenger were young and male, he might be on the lookout for a pretty girl, even if he really did not intend to try to break the taboo against casual pickups. A woman might try to avoid a male seat partner, especially one whose attentions might be unwelcome.

When the emergency began, a tremendous change took place. The passengers wanted to draw closer: interaction helps reduce anxiety. Even without anxiety, an emergency reduces inhibition against talking with strangers. A recent example of the effect of festive occasions on the barriers between people was the friendliness and warmth among the individuals who crowded into New York City during the visit of the tall sailing ships on the Fourth of July, 1976. Everyone noted how the normally reserved New Yorkers and their out-of-town visitors all talked with strangers and offered help to those in need. It was a veritable explosion of good feeling.

In the trolley car, people responded to the emergency individually on the basis of their training and their temperament. The policeman took over and created a little island of security. The nurse helped, as she had been trained to do. The mother reacted to the child's crying by trying to soothe her. The conductor used his technical skill to cope with the failure of the equipment.

From the changes that took place during the emergency as well as from the situation before the lights went out, we can define a number of characteristics of groups. These characteristics may be considered a series of dimensions, equivalent in social analysis to the physical dimensions of height and weight. Just as you can describe an object as being so tall and so heavy, you can use appropriate dimensions to describe a group.

The first dimension is *group structure.* This can be characterized either in terms of patterns of communication or relative authority among the people in a group or as a network of roles and associated statuses. The second dimension is *cohesiveness,* the degree of attraction to or away from the group among the members. The third is the nature of *goal direction.* Since the establishment of goals and the focusing of energies towards their achievement are very often the function of leaders, we could almost say that the third dimension, goal direction, can be identified with *leadership.*

The group in the trolley obviously differed on each of these dimensions before and during the emergency. The preemergency group had a relatively undifferentiated structure: the only person whose role was clearly established was the conductor. The level of cohesiveness was extremely low; there was little reason for people in the trolley to be attracted towards each other. And the progress of the trolley towards the city, while it fulfilled the needs of the passengers, did not represent any action of the group as a group. One could say that the preemergency trolley car represents a group quite close to the zero point on each of the three dimensions. But the position was not quite at zero. To the extent to which there was any interaction, any differentiation of status, any common goal, there was a kind of minimal group character.

In this discussion we have been regarding a group as a kind of system, in the sense that the pond introduced in Chapter 2 was a system. As with the pond, a group of people is in a state of dynamic equilibrium. That is, it is bounded; the membership may be defined. The forces that act within the group are sufficiently in balance so that the group's integrity is maintained. However, the balance is created by the mutual interaction of forces and is therefore considered dynamic. If the forces (cohesiveness and goal direction in groups, consumption of food and oxygen in the pond) get out of balance, the result is change.[1]

For the remainder of this chapter, I will discuss each of the three

1. Many of the ideas presented in this chapter were first worked out by a German psychologist named Kurt Lewin, who left his homeland during the thirties and migrated to the United States. He brought together ideas from the Gestalt psychologists, who emphasized dynamic systems in perception, Freud, who focused on motivation, and the social psychology of small groups. It was his influence which stimulated the intensive development of group dynamics as an area of research during the forties and fifties. Many of the social psychologists mentioned in this chapter were his students.

dimensions described in the last several paragraphs. We will deal with small, face-to-face groups very much like the newspaper staff in which Susan functioned or the passengers in the trolley car. Analysis of larger social units is carried out in the following chapter.

Social Structure

As I said above, one can view a group as a kind of a system. It consists of a number of people who interact, i.e., do things together. The *boundary* of the system is an abstract notion. Presumably, it is a line that encircles all the people who interact among themselves. However, each member of a group has all kinds of relationships with other people who are not members of the group. Therefore, one has to define the boundary of a group in terms of the particular activities in which members are engaged. The boundary should be drawn so as to include all of the people who share a set of activities—for example, a ball team and its coach or the students and teacher in a class.

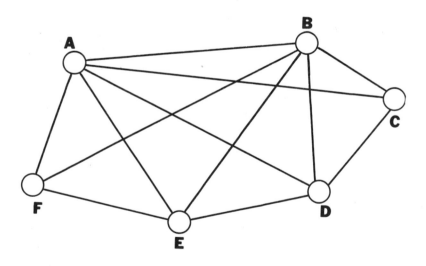

Fig. 8:1. A decentralized communication network: Folk song enthusiasts

As we noted earlier in the discussion of reference groups, the structure of a group is characterized by a series of positions in a network of communication. This means that people in a group have to talk with each other or affect each other in some way, and the structure is described in terms of the ways people can affect each other. Some groups are organized so that anybody in the group can work with any other member. In other groups, there is an arrangement of ranks (a hierarchy), and people must work through a defined chain of command. Figures 8.1 and 8.2 illustrate the two kinds of groups. The first permits people to interact freely. The second is hierarchical. All communication must go through the center.

The department in which Susan works is clearly hierarchical. The section head communicates primarily with the managers of the various projects, who, in turn, communicate with the people who do

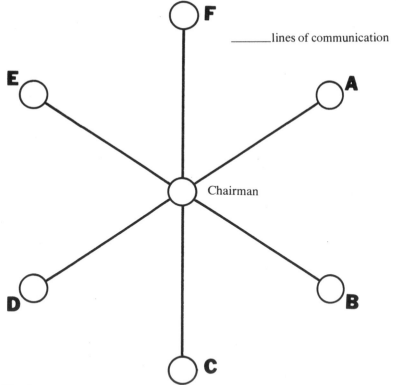

_____ lines of communication

Fig. 8:2. A centralized communication network

the legwork. It is true that someone at the bottom occasionally has some contact with the person at the top. But most of the interactions follow the chain of command.

The diagram of Susan's reference groups (Figure 7.3) includes a folk-song club. This is probably an informal collection of people who come together to play the guitar, sing, exchange new songs, and generally enjoy good fellowship. Communications probably do not follow any predetermined pattern. Everyone talks to everyone else and helps everyone else. The interactions probably flow in a manner determined by momentary characteristics of the situation.

Psychologists and sociologists have done a great deal of research on how the pattern of communication affects the behavior of people in groups. The best-known studies have come to some conclusions that, while fairly obvious, are helpful to those who have to organize group activity. A group that channels all information through a central person, as in Figure 8.2, is efficient in solving relatively routine problems, as long as the central person is an efficient processor of data. On the other hand, the people on the periphery may be unhappy with the arrangement especially if they have strong needs for achievement. Their low morale may very well affect the quality of their work. In addition, a group of this kind loses the contributions that would come from free interaction among all of its members. And so, a centralized group has advantages and disadvantages, depending on the kind of task and on the character of the members.

A decentralized group of the sort described in Figure 8.1 may be less efficient in handling routine tasks but certainly permits people to solve complex problems with a high level of creativity. The members feel closer to the center of things and have much higher morale than those in the group in Figure 8.2.

We have already mentioned the fact that each status carries with it associated roles. That is, the group has a set of expectations of the behavior required by the position that each member occupies. These expectations provide a framework of norms controlling the behavior of members towards each other and towards outsiders.

Formal and Informal Structures

Groups actually have two kinds of structure—*formal* and *informal*. A formal structure is one that is carefully organized follow-

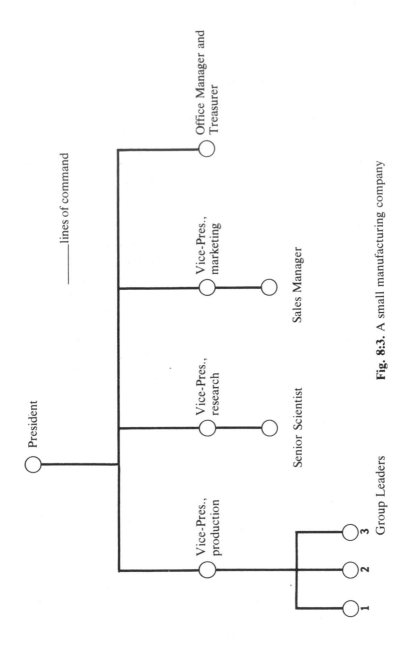

—— lines of command

President

Vice-Pres., production

Vice-Pres., research

Vice-Pres., marketing

Office Manager and Treasurer

Senior Scientist

Sales Manager

Group Leaders

1 2 3

Fig. 8:3. A small manufacturing company

ing some predetermined plan. It can usually be described in terms of a table of organization like the one in Figure 8.3. Informal structure concerns interactions outside official channels. I'm sure you have participated in social organizations in which the officially designated authorities are not always the people you turn to for help. For example, everybody who has watched World War II movies on TV knows that the weather-beaten old soldier who has been busted five times is a much better source of information on how to get by in the army than the bright new second lieutenant who has just come from officer candidate school or ROTC.

Mention of the old soldier and the second lieutenant points up the possible coexistence of two kinds of social structures. The same people who are organized in a formal group also form informal groups with their own structures. In these informal structures, roles and statuses are different from those in the coexisting formal structure. For example, during the Tuesday night sessions of the newspaper, the people officially in charge were probably not the most important sources of help for newcomers to the staff. Somebody like Ginny, who was not very high in the hierarchy, was actually a major force in guiding the people who were just starting on the newspaper. One might call her an *informal leader*.

The study of informal structures is vital to an understanding of how any social group works, for such structures are likely to develop powerful norms that determine the behavior of their members more than do the norms enforced by the formal structure. One of the first investigations of this difference was carried out near Chicago at the Hawthorne plant of the Western Electric Company during the late 1920s. In a study of men involved in wiring banks of switches for telephone exchanges, a team of social scientists discovered the existence of an informal social structure outside the formal system of foremen, supervisors, and time-study engineers. The ideas about a "fair day's work for a fair day's pay" that arose from the norms of the informal group had a major influence on the pace at which the men produced. Men who worked too hard were punished by being frozen out; they made others look bad and even gave management a chance to reduce the incentive pay offered under a piecework system. On the other hand, unless there were very good reasons for it, men who did not work hard enough ("slackers") were also held in low regard since they tended to harm the reputation of the group. You can see that social norms which define the proper behavior of people in various positions, in both informal and formal structures, determine the expectations that people bring to their interactions within a group. These expectations are among the most important influences on a group's activities. When the norms of the formal and informal groups conflict, a great deal of emotional difficulty may result.

Conflicting Roles

The different roles people play often conflict. Think of the difficulty faced by a teacher who is the parent of a pupil in trouble over delinquent behavior. Is the teacher to be stern and disciplinary, as required by the academic role, or supportive, as required by the role of parent? Sometimes a single role includes the seeds of conflict. A school superintendent is the representative of a community board, with the mandate to hold costs down; he is also the leader of the faculty, with a commitment to excellence. The resolution of such conflicts is of the greatest importance to the effectiveness of the group and the happiness and productivity of the individual.

Individuality and Role

Does each of us have a "real self" buried under the textured pattern of social roles? It would certainly be possible to postulate a "true self" as one of the elements of a mix that includes the various social roles we have to play. At this point it is not clear whether one should *add* the person's idea of the true self to the pattern of roles, or whether a complex interaction among the expectations and values associated with socially determined roles *determines* each person's self-concept. The issue is a complex one.

There is one phenomenon that offers a way of differentiating role-determined behavior and actions that may indicate a person's perception of his or her real self. People often feel distant from the social roles they are required to carry out. Goffman describes the projection of "role distance" as behavior that informs a spectator that a person is not really in sympathy with what he or she is doing but is merely carrying out the demands of a role. I remember the difficult time I had when, at the age of twenty-one, I took a job as a salesman in a second-hand-music store. My idea of myself as a knowledgeable amateur musician required that I recommend the best possible choices to prospective customers. But my role as a salesman required me to promote the music that was hardest to move. The owner of the shop was very unsympathetic to my acting the expert; needless to say I did not last long at the job. The creation of role distance was hardly compatible with success as a salesman. In some ways, this incident illustrates a kind of role conflict; I was faced with the incompatibility between my self-selected role as musical expert and the required role as salesman. My display of role distance argues that I felt "musical expert" closer to my self-concept than "salesman."

Sociometry

The last area to be covered in this discussion of social structure deals with a widely used technique for describing the structure of a group. This technique, *sociometry,* was developed by a Rumanian-born American sociologist named J. L. Moreno, who is also noted for his development of psychodrama as a way of helping people with emotional problems.

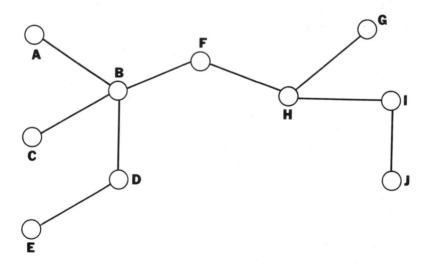

Fig. 8:4. Choices of work partners in a group of construction workers

In sociometry, members of a group are asked to pick other members with whom they would like to share an activity. For example, the students in a chemistry class could be asked to indicate their choices of lab partners. Or the men in a factory where work is done in teams could be asked to name the people with whom they would like to work. To produce a valid representation of the group, sociometric procedures have to insure that people believe that their choices will be honored and choose others with whom they actually could interact. A *sociogram* is a diagram that describes these choices. Each person is represented by a circle, and the choices are shown by the lines connecting the circles. Figure 8.4 is an example of such a diagram.

The shape of the sociometric diagram enables an investigator to discover the nature of subgroups. A leader can use such a pattern to assign people to activity groups so as to minimize friction and promote cooperation. Work teams set up through the use of sociometry have fewer accidents and less absenteeism than those assembled without consultation with the members. Of course, the pattern of choices depends on the nature of the activity. In one study, naval recruits made very different choices when they were asked to pick the sailor with whom they wanted to share shore leave and with whom they wanted to work in a difficult watch.

Summary

Analysis of the structure of groups enables us to understand how position in a group affects an individual's behavior. The nature of group structure influences the performance of tasks as well as the morale or happiness of individuals in a group. An understanding of structure also permits us to define the way in which the interactions of the group promote a sense of identity and belongingness. We now go on to consider emotional aspects of group behavior.

Cohesiveness

Some Definitions

The term cohesiveness, as defined above, refers to the sum total of the forces attracting people to a group and those tending to push them out of it. When people belong to a highly cohesive group, they generally value their membership; membership in a noncohesive group is seldom valued.

It would seem a simple task to assess the cohesiveness of groups. Unfortunately, this has not turned out to be straightforward. A number of different techniques have been used. One strategy is to estimate the level of cohesiveness from the frequency with which members leave a group. Another is the use of projective tests: group members are asked to tell stories about pictures depicting groups. The stories are analyzed for indications of cohesiveness. A third involves asking members to indicate their willingness to leave a particular group for another with different membership but equivalent function. In one study, five different methods were used to measure cohesiveness in the same groups. The correlation among the results of the different methods was extremely low. At the moment, although cohesiveness is a theoretically useful concept, the problems of measurement do not seem to have been solved.

The Effects of Cohesiveness

As was implied in one of the measures of cohesiveness, a group that is highly cohesive can maintain itself more successfully than one that is not. The level of cohesiveness of a group also has a powerful impact on the degree to which it controls its members' activities. In a number of studies conducted among industrial work groups and groups assembled in the laboratory on a one-shot basis, investigators have found that a group that is cohesive can "police" its members more effectively than one that is not.

This does not mean that cohesive groups always work more effectively than noncohesive groups. In fact, in a study of teams of industrial workers, a psychologist at the University of Michigan named Stanley Seashore discovered that cohesive groups produced more than average only if their members shared the values and goals of the company. In fact, cohesive groups produced much *less* than average if they failed to share company values and goals. Similar findings were established in laboratory studies. Cohesiveness is thus a double-edged sword. It can lead to a high level of creative and fruitful work, or it can cause a group to withdraw in a body from its assigned activities.

Highly cohesive groups are harder on deviants than groups low in cohesiveness. For example, in one experiment, Stanley Schachter assembled college students into thirty-two clubs. The groups had a variety of reasons for existence and differed considerably in cohesiveness. At some point, each club met to discuss a case study of a delinquent boy. At each meeting, three members who were actually confederates of the experimenter expressed opinions about the disposition of the case that were very different from those of the majority. Schachter reported that the more cohesive clubs tried vigorously to persuade the members who expressed deviant opinions. When the deviants did not yield, the result was a great deal of hostility. In contrast, the noncohesive clubs did not make much effort to convert the deviants, nor were they hostile.

Our story about Susan illustrates the effect of the cohesiveness of groups on their treatment of deviants. You may remember that she found it very hard going in the group of newspaper staff members because she was skeptical of their position on the issue of a lawsuit over discrimination against women. If the newspaper staff had not been the tightly organized, highly cohesive group that it was, it is likely that Susan's unorthodox point of view would not have attracted so much attention. It is also likely that she would not have been put on the spot to give up her disagreement or leave the newspaper.

The influence of cohesiveness on social control is well known to many dictatorships. They make great efforts to set up small, self-policing groups that root out deviant opinions and punish them severely. In some ways, the issue of cohesiveness poses one of the most complex problems in social organization, one to which we shall address ourselves in the last section of the book. If you never participate in highly cohesive groups, you may have a sense of loneliness or lack of affiliation. On the other hand, if all of your contacts are with cohesive groups, you may find your life stifling. The trade-off between a sense of affiliation and a sense of freedom to hold your own opinions is often extremely difficult.

Goal Orientation and Leadership Style

Research on variation in the style of leadership and in a group's focus on goals leads to yet another important distinction among different kinds of groups. Or, rather, it defines another dimension on which groups may vary. In some groups, the most important factor engaging the participants is some kind of externally oriented task.

The key to the group's activities is a *product*. In other groups, the most important factor is the delight that people have in being together.

I'm sure that you know many people who engage in a hobby—the basketball team at the YMCA, an amateur string quartet or church chorus, or a bridge club. To what extent are these groups really focused on turning out a finished kind of product? Is it important for them to play really good basketball, to sing expressively and in tune, to win at the card table? Or do the members get together because they enjoy one another's company and find as much pleasure in the casual conversation that accompanies the meetings as they do in the actual activities of the group?

The distinction that social scientists have made is that between *task* and *process* orientation. The former deals with orientation towards the output of the group, the latter with orientation towards the maintenance of the group itself as a social organization. Many of the above-mentioned considerations about groups are relevant primarily for task-oriented groups. For example, it has been found that there is more differentiation of status and role in task-oriented than in process-oriented groups. Similarly, the effects of cohesiveness are probably greater in task-oriented than in process-oriented groups.

Task and process orientation may be viewed either as descriptions of types of groups or as a set of dimensions. I lean towards the latter since it seems likely that no groups are completely lacking in process orientation, in the sense that people have no stake in the continued survival of the group and no pleasure in being together. Similarly, almost any group has to have some kind of task as an excuse for existence. So I would prefer to think of task and process orientation as two dimensions like height and weight along which any group can be placed. Some groups may be high on both—for example, a basketball team that functions as a smoothly oiled machine and in which the members are very close friends. Others are strongly task-oriented but basically do not like each other. There is a famous picture of the Budapest String Quartet in which the four members, who had worked together intensively for many years, are seated on a railroad platform facing away from each other and obviously finding no joy in each other's company. Still other groups meet primarily to enjoy social interchange but have little interest in their tasks.

Task and process orientation each require different kinds of leadership. Obviously, a task-oriented group must have a leader who is able to initiate action, plan, make sure tnat the group has the resources to carry out its task, integrate, and organize its activities. On the other hand, a group that is primarily process-oriented must have a leader who is capable of smoothing out friction, developing social ties among the members, projecting a sense of interest in and affection for the members. Unhappily, the results of some early investigations by social scientists have led to a kind of myth that the only factors that are important in leadership are the factors related to process orientation. It is widely believed that social scientists think "people-oriented" leadership is the only effective kind. In a widely quoted study by Kurt Lewin and his colleagues, leaders of groups of boys in a social club created three different kinds of social climate. In the first, a laissez-faire climate, the leader was cool and permissive. In the second, which featured authoritarian or *autocratic* leadership, the leader told the boys what to do at every stage of their activities. In the third, the *democratic* leader permitted the boys to participate in decisions about the group's activities and showed relatively little directiveness towards the group. Lewin and his colleagues found that the democratic leader was by far the most effective both in maintaining the integrity of the group and in promoting its activities.

Unfortunately, the kind of groups with which Lewin worked were almost entirely process-oriented. They were not faced by the necessity for carrying out a particular task in an efficient manner. Attempts to replicate Lewin's studies in an industrial context have shown that purely process-oriented leadership is rarely effective. On the other hand, there is no question that the sort of leader who is highly directive and has a distant and hostile manner is also very ineffective. The most successful leaders are probably those who manage to combine the skills of task orientation with the personal warmth of process orientation. It is probably also true that the involvement of individuals in group decision making has a very positive effect on their willingness to participate in the activities of the group and on the eventual success of the group as a social unit. The ways participation in decisions affects the behavior of groups will be discussed intensively as we examine some novel social systems in Chapter 13.

We have so far demonstrated how a social system in miniature may function. We next go on to discuss larger social systems. Much of our discussion in this chapter has dealt with small, face-to-face groups whose activities cover a relatively short span of time. Larger systems are also affected by interpersonal perception, patterns of interaction, and structural variables. The city, the state, the nation share many of the characteristics of the small group as we have just discussed it. However, the process of decision making in the community as a whole has some unique characteristics, and it is to these that we now address ourselves.

On Your Own

1. For the study of small groups, two books by sociologists are cited in the references, Mills and Olmstead. Neither is exactly exciting, but both are thorough.

2. An old but very interesting application of social science to the real world may be found in J. A. C. Brown's *The Social Psychology of Industry*.

3. One of the most important consequences of the growing study of social groups since World War II has been the development of group dynamics as an area of application. The insights of Kurt Lewin and his followers, as well as those of sociologist G. C. Homans, have been used to train industrial managers, teachers, social workers, and government leaders in the art of navigating within social groups. An organization called National Training Laboratories, of Bethel, Maine, and Washington, D.C., has been especially active in this field. The concepts derived from research on groups have also been applied to the treatment in groups of patients suffering from a variety of behavioral disorders. An expansion of group therapy to include many people who wish to enlarge their personal horizons and solve their problems of adjustment, but who are not labeled "mentally ill," has taken place under the aegis of the human potential movement. While many people involved in these movements have been helped in an unexceptionable manner, there has been an unmistakable odor of quackery about the fringes. The history of these developments is admirably summarized by Kurt W. Back in *Beyond Words*.

4. Write an analysis of a group to which you belong using the three dimensions discussed in the text—structure, cohesiveness, and goal direction or leadership. Is the group growing or shrinking? Can you say why on the basis of your analysis of dimensions? If the group is declining, can you suggest ways in which it could be salvaged?

9
The Elements
of a Functioning
Community

The early chapters of this book have concentrated on individuals, their motives, the determinants of their decisions, and the character of their interactions. It was only in the discussion of culture that we dealt with large-scale communities. In this chapter the focus will be on the structure and function of such broad social organizations as cities, states, and nations.

In order to create a bridge between the study of individuals and of communities, I shall relate a day in the life of a person I shall call James Miller. I hesitate to call him an "average" man, since there really is no such thing. James Miller's life is characteristic of an urban middle-class existence in an advanced industrial country. Impinging on him are many social organizations, both formal and informal. He is affected by government, by the economic system, by informal associations. Following him from waking to bedtime through a typical day provides an opportunity to delineate these social organizations, examine their interrelationships, and study the way they provide a framework for his life.

A Day in the Life of James Miller

James Miller is an assistant curator at the natural history museum of a large city in the northeastern part of the United States. He lives in an old but pleasant residential neighborhood not far from the downtown section of the city in which his museum is located.

Waking

Miller's alarm clock wakes him at 6:45. Although he hardly thinks about it, the operation of his alarm clock is dependent upon electricity that comes to his house courtesy of the local electric company, a private organization "owned" by fifty thousand shareholders. Several governmental agencies are concerned with the electricity that powers Miller's alarm clock. The rates for electricity are set by a public utility commission of the state government. This commission is composed of members appointed by the governor with the consent of the state legislature. The Federal Power Commission, a body appointed by the president of the United States with the approval of the Senate, is also involved in regulation of power companies if their business activities cross state lines.

Miller's alarm clock also provides ties to that network of non-governmental activities called the private sector. The clock was bought in a retail store. Most of the store's activities are determined by the play of supply and demand rather than by governmental regulation, but the establishment does face some governmental controls. It cannot stay open on Sunday, it must maintain separate washrooms for its male and female employees, and it must act as a collection agency for sales and wage taxes that help support the local, state, and federal governments. If the shop wants to alter its physical plant substantially, it has to get a building permit from a city department and submit the alteration to inspection (a procedure much open to corruption). It cannot hire a stock boy who is underage. But it can, barring price controls imposed in national emergencies, sell the clock at any price a buyer is willing to pay.

Washing Up

Miller's first step when he wakes is to wash. The water he uses comes from a local river through a system controlled by the city. It is treated with large doses of chemicals to make it safe to drink, if not exactly a delight to taste. The waterworks, unlike the electric power company, is a department of the city government run by technically competent employees hired through competitive examination, i.e., a civil service. The mayor appoints the head of the department that operates the waterworks. This person does not have a permanent appointment in the civil service, but rather serves at the pleasure of the mayor.

The city also maintains a department of health whose function is to provide a variety of preventive and protective services. This department supervises the safety of the water supply; Miller can brush his teeth without fearing disease. In this particular city the water department, under guidance from the health department, adds a substance called fluoride to the water to prevent dental caries. Many people consider this an invasion of the rights of citizens, forcing them to ingest a food additive against their will. The issue of fluoridation has generated a great deal of controversy in the past, although the best scientific evidence is that addition of fluoride is an inexpensive and safe way of improving health. At the moment, except for a few crusaders, no one in the city is much concerned one way or another about fluoridation. Still, the practice raises profound questions about the limits of governmental responsibility for the welfare of the population.

Breakfast

James enjoys a hearty breakfast. The food, which his wife bought at a local supermarket, was brought to the city on roads and railroads that are part of a network of transportation supervised by the federal government, through the Interstate Commerce Commission, and by state highway departments. The food was first sold in a wholesale food market maintained by the city government for the convenience of food wholesalers. From the wholesaler it was shipped to a retail shop where it was sold to the public.

Several agencies watch over the safety of food. The health department of the city inspects both wholesale and retail vendors. If James eats bacon that was processed in the Midwest and transported across state lines, it is likely that the bacon was packed in a plant inspected by the U.S. Department of Agriculture. This department, one of the major components of the federal government, is headed by a cabinet member, the secretary of agriculture, who is a political appointee of the president and must be approved by the Senate. However, the bulk of the department's work is carried out by career civil servants who serve until retirement, barring misconduct, and are selected and promoted by means of competitive examinations.

The process by which the bacon was cured was evaluated by another arm of the federal government, the Food and Drug Administration (FDA). The bacon probably does not have as pleasantly pink a color as bacon once had because the FDA has recently banned the use of a dye, Red #2, which had been widely used to impart an attractive hue to meat and other foods. Laboratory research, carried out in government laboratories or under contract to university researchers, has suggested that Red #2 may cause cancer.

Getting to Work

After breakfast, James takes a bus to the museum. The bus is operated by a "public" corporation controlled by the city government. Such agencies, usually called authorities, permit the government to run activities that have some of the character of a private business. The authority that operates the bus system can sell bonds—that is, it can borrow money to pay for the cost of improvements in service. The bonds are redeemed—i.e., the loan is repaid—out of the money obtained from passengers. The authority derives some of its support from the city and neighboring counties and can turn to the city for help should it go into the red.

The orderly progress of the bus to the center of the city is made possible by several arms of the city government. The police department furnishes patrolmen who regulate traffic at important intersections. It also operates a computer-based system that controls the traffic lights so that lines of traffic move smoothly and efficiently in the direction of maximum travel during rush hours. The lights themselves and the road signs are under the jurisdiction of another agency, the streets department, which contracts their maintenance to a private company. The streets department is also responsible for repairing the streets, filling the innumerable potholes created by the rigors of winter. Much of the irritation felt by citizens towards government is probably due to the inadequacy with which this function is often carried out.

Some of the roads on which the bus travels are maintained by the city. Some, however, are parts of through roads that link up to highways between the city and other parts of the state. These roads are maintained by the state government through its highway department. If James were curious, he might note that one of the main streets on which the bus takes him to work has a marker indicating that it is a state highway.

Work

The museum is a municipal institution. It is run by a board of trustees appointed by the mayor. The board consists of citizens from various walks of life, mostly people of high status who serve on the board as a community service. Although they spend a great deal of time on the affairs of the museum, they do not get paid. The museum director, the curators, and other professional officers are full-time employees and do get paid for their work. They are supposed to be appointed by the trustees, although only the director has direct contact with the board.

James and his colleagues are members of a variety of organizations. They belong to a union that negotiates with the administration and with the board of trustees over working conditions and salaries. Many also belong to professional organizations appropriate to their fields. For example, James is not only a member of the union but also belongs to a group called the American Anthropological Association, which publishes journals, holds meetings, and operates a kind of clearinghouse to help its members locate jobs.

The museum building is cleaned and guarded by a small army of blue-collar workers. These men and women are employees of the museum and, indirectly, of the city. They too are members of a trade union. They have profited by the recent improvement in the financial position of civil servants; wages have increased markedly. This development has, however, had unfortunate effects on the museum. A number of the galleries have had to be closed because of lack of adequate funds for guards.

The museum's funds come from various sources. One is the city, another is the state. In addition, it receives grants from various arms of the federal government and from private foundations. Since the museum has active educational programs for both school children and adults, it has been able to attract additional support from governmental agencies. Some of its educational programs are funded by the Office of Education, a branch of the Department of Health, Education, and Welfare (HEW). To the extent that Miller's work is affected by these grants, he is under the control of governmental officials appointed by the secretary of HEW who, like the secretary of agriculture, is appointed by the president and confirmed by the Senate.

HEW funding of the museum is also affected by the overall federal appropriations to educational activities. This part of the national budget, like all others, originates in appropriate committees of the House and Senate, is reviewed by the President's Office of Management and Budget, and is confirmed by legislation that has to be passed by both houses of Congress and signed by the president.

In the last analysis, much of the museum's support is the result of politics. Elected representatives to legislatures and elected executives at all levels—city, state, and national—evaluate the needs of the community for education and allot money to meet these needs. Some of the decisions to support specific programs are based on recommendations from the permanent civil service; others are based on formal appeals by experts or interested citizens in appearances before committees. The decisions are also affected by pressures from many groups and individuals on both legislators and members of the executive. The museum, for example, profits from the influence of voluntary associations and private citizens interested in natural history, the environment, the study of man. These groups exert what influence they can in an effort to increase appropriations for the museum's activities.

The Rest of the Day

After work, James takes the bus home and has his supper. I don't think we need repeat the list of community agencies that are involved in this phase of his life. Shortly after supper, James reads the evening paper. The paper is printed by members of an aggregate of six craft unions. The editorial material is provided by members of the Newspaper Guild. The people who own the publication belong to an association of newspaper editors and owners. The newspaper James reads gets a large part of its news from an organization called the Associated Press. This agency collects news stories from all over the country and, indeed, all over the world and transmits them to each newspaper that buys its services. The newsprint is probably made from logs cut in the forests of Maine or Canada. These forests are maintained by a small number of companies, which harvest the lumber, manufacture the paper, and send huge rolls of newsprint by truck to dozens of cities.

James watches TV briefly before he goes to bed. The local station that he watches is owned by a network with headquarters in New

York City. The airwaves are, of course, the property of the whole nation. However, only this station and the network that owns it can use a particular set of wavelengths called a channel. The channel was assigned to the station by a federal agency, the Federal Communications Commission. The rules for this commission were set up by the Congress in the Federal Communications Act, which was passed in 1934 and signed by Franklin Roosevelt, who was then president.

If James watches an entertainment program, he is probably enjoying the artistry of people who belong to a trade union called the American Guild of Variety Artists. The commercials on the program were subject to review by another federal agency, the Federal Trade Commission, one of whose functions is to make sure that business organizations tell something approximating the truth when they advertise.

And so James goes to bed. I suspect that he might be a bit startled by the recital we have just given about his life. He rarely thinks about the intricate network of social institutions that makes it possible for him to be fed, to travel, to go to work, and to enjoy his comfortable and rewarding life.

Summary

You may remember that in Chapter 2 we defined a system as an interrelated set of forces in a state of balance. The community we described is a good example of such a system. Like the pond in Chapter 1, the social system as a whole stays in something approaching a state of equilibrium. Although it may seem a bit insulting to compare a human being to a water bug, the even progress of James Miller's life within the great social system of his city and country is similar to the life of a water bug skating on the surface of the pond. Just as the combination of forces in the pond provides the water bug with food, oxygen, a place to breed, and some safety from predators, so does the combination of forces in the community provide the circumstances within which James Miller can live and function.

The Components of the Social System

At this point I would like to present a more organized picture of the social system than was possible as we surveyed James Miller's day. The various institutions that play a role in his community may be classified and placed in the overall social system. At least three kinds of institutions can be identified in the social network around James Miller. One kind is the formal governmental apparatus. The next is the private sector, which is composed of commercial and industrial organizations that provide some of the goods and services James Miller needs. Lastly, there are the voluntary associations and other organizations of citizens in which people living within the social system come together to influence its operation. In the next sections of this chapter we shall take a general look at each of these components. The following chapter uses a single problem to illustrate the roles of all three kinds of institutions in the making and carrying out of decisions.

The Formal Governmental System

At one point or another, almost every aspect of government has some impact on Miller's life. The local level of government runs the city in which he lives. This government consists of an executive, the mayor; a legislative body, the city council; and (although this did not come into the story) a group of judges and the courts. A similar set of components is found in the state government, with its governor, legislature, and courts, and the federal government, with the president, the Congress, and the federal courts.

Since each level of government has three centers of authority—executive, legislative, and judicial—one of the most pressing social necessities is a scheme for ensuring that they work well together. In many parts of the world, the despotism of an executive has made the operation of a free community impossible. Elsewhere, as in contemporary Italy, government is so dominated by a disorderly legislature that the nation's affairs are bogged down in continual disputation. In one of the most successful inventions of the constitutional convention of 1787, each of the three main components of government in the United States was given an independent area of function. This is the concept of "separation of powers." Under such a system, the executive is not rendered so powerless that the community is unable to function, but the existence of an independent legislature and judiciary limits the tendency of executives to become dictators.

The formal governmental apparatus, however, consists not only of executive, legislature, and judges but also of a large number of regulatory agencies. Typically these are appointed by the executive with the approval of the legislature. Each has an independent area of operation. Examples in our story include the Federal Power Commission, the Federal Trade Commission, and the Federal Communications Commission. Such agencies affect James in all sorts of ways, from setting the price of electricity to licensing the people who broadcast his favorite TV show. A high proportion of the actual conduct of government is in the hands of such regulatory agencies.

The Provision of Goods and Services

Most of the *things* James Miller buys come from private businesses. His automobile, for example, was manufactured by a branch of a multinational corporation whose annual income is larger than that of most governments. The gasoline to run it also originated in such a multinational corporation. However, both the car and the gas were sold through small businesses that depend on the parent companies for merchandise. There is a bit of give and take in the prices asked, depending on the level of competition in the local community. But in general, prices are controlled by the parent company. Miller's food, as we noted, also comes to him through private business, and his house was built many years ago by a local builder. General economic conditions affect Miller as they do everyone else. He lives on a fixed salary, but the prices of the things he buys have been rising rapidly for the past six or eight years. In fact, one of the most upsetting things about his life is the sense of being perpetually cheated; almost everything he buys and almost all the services for which he pays are far more expensive than he thinks they ought to be.

Miller probably does not differentiate too clearly between the aspects of his life dominated by the private and public sectors. As we have seen in the story of his day, the water he used for washing, the bus he took to work, and the cooking gas with which he brewed his morning coffee all were furnished by semipublic agencies. If Miller is like many Americans, he thinks he pays overly high taxes, regards money that goes to the government as in some sense wasted, and takes for granted most of the benefits his taxes provide.

Voluntary Associations

The social system in which James lives includes a large number of formal and informal organizations that serve as vehicles for expressing the needs of their members. Although the Constitution of the United States nowhere mentions political parties, these have become a most important aspect of the social system. In each city and state, groups of people organized more or less formally into political associations select candidates and raise money for their campaigns. Between elections, the parties act as a bridge between officeholders and the voters and so provide the ordinary citizen with a kind of voice in governmental operations. The national parties, which are loose confederations of these local groups, come to life every four years when a president is to be elected.

James's story mentioned several other kinds of voluntary associations. One was the professional organization to which he belongs. Like similar associations of doctors, lawyers, grocers, and master plumbers, the American Anthropological Association represents its members in the community and also provides a variety of services to them. It acts as a representative when, for example, it lobbies for appropriations for anthropological research by meeting with congressmen and senators influential in setting the budget for social science in the National Science Foundation's appropriation. It provides services when it publishes a journal or runs a meeting. Another kind of voluntary association is the trade union. In addition to bargaining for improved wages and working conditions for its members, unions often maintain educational programs and health and welfare facilities.

How Does the System Function?

There are two ways in which social systems can function. The first is an arrangement by which one person or party is boss. In the second, no one person or group has total authority. Instead, individuals or groups each committed to their own interests engage in bargaining. When people work for their own benefit they may be called *partisans.*

The first scheme permits authoritative individuals to exert control. After evaluating the consequences of various choices, they come to decisions and issue orders. A system of this kind may seem extremely attractive. It permits the efficient gathering of the information needed for making decisions and allows for the unquestioned assumption of responsibility and authority. However, there is always the danger that an individual who has complete authority may be less than ideally committed to the good of the community as a whole; he or she may make decisions intended for personal profit or for advantage to a few.

The second way a system can function is through mutual adjustment, or bargaining by partisans. It is conceivable that in an ideal world there would be no partisanship because people would discover that they all shared the same long-range ends. In actuality, however, there are usually differences in goals, and most people fight for their own interests. Although this process can lead to stalemate, the process of bargaining by many groups and individuals with limited power is often a good way to achieve a balanced system.

Some components of American society are clearly based on the concept of chain of command; others are democratic and operate through mutual or partisan adjustment—that is, by bargaining among roughly equal forces. Business, the civil service, the military all run on authoritarian lines, with responsibility and authority at the top. On the other hand, most functions of government are based by tradition and constitutional law on the concept of mutual partisan adjustment. In our system, the voters delegate authority to legislators and executives but do not give them overwhelming and unchallengeable power. The balance of power is intended to lead to a system in which negotiation by partisans results in the best possible decisions for the community.

In actuality, as we shall see in the next chapter, the balance of power is subtle and complex. Business organizations, voluntary associations, political groups all try to bring to bear as much persuasive force as they can in presenting their own needs to those who actually run things. It is not always clear what combination of influences leads to a particular outcome. Historians have been known to quarrel for years over the way a war began or a major legislative program like the New Deal was enacted.

There is a real difference of opinion among political scientists as to whether the American social system permits genuine mutual adjustment among equals or whether it is sham. Many political scientists view our society as truly open and responsive. In an opposing viewpoint, sociologist C. Wright Mills has proposed that a "power elite" dominates almost every segment of American society. This position is attractive to almost all critics of American society; it may be found on the extreme left and on the extreme right. It is amusing to find followers of Chairman Mao and the John Birch Society agreeing that the country is run by a single center of conspiracy. The conspiratorial view of American society is not easily attacked or defended on rational grounds; accepting or rejecting it seems more a matter of temperament than of hard evidence, as you may have discovered yourself if you have ever tried to argue with an extremist of either the radical left or right.

How Good Are Decisions?

We have contrasted two ways in which people in a social organization arrive at decisions. These two ways represent two arrangements of authority. But no matter what the structure of a social organization, it still has to deal with information, choose goals, decide on ways of reaching those goals. The ideal way of arriving at a decision would be to first identify all possible outcomes of all possible courses of action. You would determine the costs and benefits of each of these outcomes. The comparison of costs and benefits would lead to a choice of the route that provides the greatest benefit at the least cost. This process is equivalent to the assessment of values and expectations described in Chapter 4 as the basis for individual decisions. Such a procedure may be ideal, but it is hardly practicable for complex social decisions. Firstly, it is virtually impossible to forecast all possible outcomes of various choices. Secondly, it is often very difficult to measure the costs and benefits precisely. Lastly, even if it were possible to gather such a vast amount of information about all possible decisions, it is doubtful that even the most powerful computer would be able to sort and treat all this material.

A political scientist named Herbert Simon has proposed that, instead of aiming at the impossible ideal of examining all conceivable outcomes of all alternatives, people should look at a *sample* of possible outcomes of some of the most obvious alternatives and choose one that is, if not ideal, at least *good enough.* Simon invented the term "satisficing" for this procedure. He has developed a rather elaborate scheme that would permit those responsible for decisions to arrive at criteria for what is "good enough." Simon's idea of "satisficing" sounds makeshift. But it may be that it really is the best people can do in an imperfect world. The trouble is, as we shall see in the next chapter in a discussion of the interstate highway system, that what looks good enough now may turn out to be a disaster a decade later if some of the alternatives we choose not to examine are actually the ones we should take into account.

Summary

Political scientists and economists have tended to view the operation of the social system as one in which competing groups arrive at decisions by negotiating on the basis of their self-interests. The balance of forces that this creates is supposed to lead to an overall process of decision making that yields long-range benefits to the whole community. In order to see how such a system operates, we will turn our attention to a particular area in which some important decisions were made, decisions that have had an enormous impact on our country. It may be that, through the analysis of such an instance, we will be able to get a feeling not only for the way the community arrives at decisions but also for the wisdom of the choices.

On Your Own

1. The best source for insight into the operations of the social system is a good daily newspaper. Newsmagazines are a fair substitute, but they tend to be superficial. One exercise you can carry out is to mark up a copy of the best newspaper of record available in your part of the country (or the Sunday *New York Times*). Trace any one story over a period of weeks and identify the interrelated activities of public and private agencies, governmental regulatory groups, legislative committees, quasi-public institutions that furnish services, and voluntary associations.

2. Again using newspaper articles, determine the procedure by which a governmental decision was taken. Examples could be the planning of a new power source such as an atomic energy plant, the location of a new school, the reaction to foreign competition considered dangerous to American economic interests. Was the decision arrived at through action by an authority or through bargaining by partisans? If the latter, were the partisans equal in power? What were the sources of their bargaining power? Were all parties satisfied with the outcome? What were the criteria used for the final decision? Were all alternatives exhaustively considered or was this decision resolved by "satisficing"?

10

The Interstate Highway System: A Study of Community Decision

Now that the elements of the social system have been defined, the next step is to examine the way they actually function. I have said that the lives of people like James Miller depend on the successful activity of a large number of organizations operating in an intricate network of interacting systems. The story of James's day should have given you some notion of the day-in-and-day-out activity of the network. But it provided no insight into the way society reacts to the major challenges it must surmount in order to survive. In the remaining section of the book, I will attempt some generalizations about the problem of reaction to challenge. Before I do this, however, it is necessary to understand the way our own society, as it functions today, makes major decisions. And we have to look at the way these decisions create radiating effects whose impact reaches every corner of the community. If a beaver builds a dam that changes the water level in a pond, no aspect of the pond's life will remain unaffected—neither the chemical details of oxygen concentration and acid/base balance nor the survival of algae, waterbugs, frogs, and fish. Similarly, no part of our great national pond is unaffected by decisions about taxes, monetary policy, or conservation, not to mention decisions about war and peace.

The problem I have chosen for us to examine is the development of what President Dwight D. Eisenhower called the greatest public works project in the history of mankind—the interstate highway system. People who are under twenty-five may not be able to remember a time when this country was not covered by an interlacing network of superhighways and cloverleaf intersections. When I was growing up in the 1920s there were no superhighways. A road was a narrow ribbon of indifferent quality that led from town to town through scores of villages. An automobile journey was a long progress from traffic jam to traffic jam through the centers of countless towns, punctuated by endless waits at rivers for the ferries. Today, one can practically drive from the Atlantic to the Pacific without stopping at a traffic light.

A Brief History of Transport in the United States

National support for the building of roads and canals was a controversial issue during the early history of the country. Henry Clay and other leaders who were committed not only to the development of the West but also to a major national role in that development argued for public subsidy to the construction of highways. It was one of their triumphs that projects like the Cumberland Road, which crossed the Appalachians, were accepted as a federal responsibility on the basis of a section of the Constitution that authorized federal aid to the promotion of commerce.

By the middle of the nineteenth century, interest shifted to the expansion of the rail network. Public highways were no longer considered necessary. Instead, an enormous network of railroads was built, in part with money invested by British and American capitalists. The federal government encouraged this development with vast donations of land to the new railroads.

When the automobile age began in the first part of the twentieth century, the condition of roadways was grim. There were few paved roads in the country, and those that existed were not joined in a continuous network. The period between the two world wars saw a considerable development of hard-surfaced motor roads between major communities. However World War II found the system of roads quite inadequate for the needs of an economy gearing up for the production and transport of goods for the military effort. Although the crowded roads were heavily used, their poor condition and the need to conserve gasoline and rubber for use in combat zones meant that the bulk of war materiel was moved by rail and water. Similarly, civilians and military personnel traveling any distance also used the railroads.

The end of the war saw an enormous boom in the ownership of private automobiles. The desire for personal vehicles was prompted in part by wartime memories of crowded and uncomfortable trains and buses. The capacity of Detroit automobile plants, expanded during the war to build tanks and planes, was adequate to the increased demand for private vehicles. In fact, the boom in private automobiles was one of the factors that prevented the postwar depression that was expected to follow the demobilization of twenty million men. The industrial establishment, straining the capacity of a railroad system that had barely been adequate for wartime needs, also turned to ever larger trucks. Unfortunately, the system of roads was generally inadequate. Except for a handful of such toll roads as the Pennsylvania Turnpike, virtually no new roads had been built since the twenties.

By the early fifties, it was widely accepted that some kind of massive national effort would be necessary to provide the system of highways that the country seemed to want and need. The only problems were how the roads were to be financed and who would decide on their locations and set the standards for construction.

The executive branch was the first to respond to this need. It is important to remember at this point that the president is the only official who has a mandate from the entire country. It is his unique responsibility to consider national needs as a whole, rather than the particular problems of individual states or congressional districts. In 1953, President Eisenhower appointed a commission headed by Gen. Lucius D. Clay, a banker and former American High Commissioner in occupied Germany after World War II. It was entrusted with the task of gathering information about the need for roads and the ways in which they could be financed.

The reports of the Clay Commission give a most instructive picture of the kinds of witnesses who appeared and argued for various points of view. One group of witnesses consisted of government officials from the bureau in charge of public roads. They urged a federally built and federally financed highway system. Witnesses from the state governments wanted the states to maintain control but presented arguments for massive federal funds. Lastly, there were appeals from organizations associated with highway use. These included truckers, the trade unions to which truck drivers belong, the oil industry, and the automobile industry. All these groups argued for a great expansion of road building.

In the record of the public discussion, it is hard to find any voice arguing for alternative ways of meeting the country's transportation needs. The sole plea presented by the railroads was a request for financing new highways out of specific taxes on highway use rather than out of general taxes. As long as the railroads did not have to contribute to the cost of building the new highways, they were delighted to have the community pour its resources into roads as a means of creating new transportation capabilities. Thus, there was virtually no conflict over the need for the highways, merely a question about who was to pay. In view of later developments, the decisions taken represent an abysmal lack of foresight. Hardly anybody anticipated the problems that would be posed by an enormous expansion of motor transport and a simultaneous decay of other means of moving goods and people.

The Clay Commission proposed a huge program, $100 billion worth of construction over a ten-year period. This was to be paid for by bond issues guaranteed by the revenues from federal taxes on gasoline, tires, and similar products. There was some conflict between the Republican minority and the Democratic majority in the 1954 session of Congress over the proposal that the government borrow money to pay for this huge program of public works. The advantages of financing the system of roads from long-term bonds would be that the money could be made available when it was needed without an annual appropriation from Congress. This was essential because roads must be planned over a long period of time. The disadvantage was that the interest on the bonds would add greatly to the cost and the repayment would be a burden on future generations. Although the Democratic party under Franklin D. Roosevelt had been more than willing to build public works through borrowing and delayed expenditures during the thirties, the Democrats in Congress during the fifties were opposed to bond issues as a way of financing highways. As a result, the proposal for a system of interstate highways was temporarily defeated.

The following year, however, the Democrats came up with a social invention designed to provide long-range stability of financing without putting the country into debt. This was to set up a highway trust fund that would receive all the revenues from taxes on gasoline, tires, and other automotive products as well as from taxes on trucks and their users. Thus the interstate highway system would have a stable and continuing financial base and would be freed from the necessity of coming to Congress for funds every year.

In 1956, consensus was achieved on the details of the system. Maps were prepared showing the approximate locations of the new roads. The planners were aware of the danger that the interstate system would drain off so much federal money that the supporting network of roads would decay. To counteract this danger, sizable funds were guaranteed to feeder roads, the so-called A B C system of rural and urban secondary roads. The feeder roads would get 50 percent of their support from the federal treasury. In contrast, the interstate highway system would receive ninety percent of its support from the federal government; only ten percent would come from the states. The building of the interstate roads would be in the hands of the state highway departments and thus under some measure of local control. Towns that were afraid of being bypassed and losing business were assured that there would be no restaurants or service stations on the roads themselves.

The early proposals had called for concentration of planning in Washington, but in the end, it was left to the state governments through their highway departments to decide where the roads would be placed. But federal standards *were* set for the quality of the roads. For example, all were required to consist of at least four lanes with a wide median strip separating opposing streams of traffic.

Each of these features of the new program was arrived at by intense bargaining. Congressmen and senators, especially those on key committees, were the focus of pressure by innumerable interested groups. (If you don't like representatives of such groups, you call them lobbyists. If you do, you call them advocates.) The whole story illustrates nicely the process of mutual adjustment by partisans described in the last chapter. The progress of the interstate highway system from idea to reality may be traced from committee hearings through the drafting of bills by congressmen and their assistants to the enactment of bills by the House and Senate. Where the two houses differed, as they did in some details of the highway program, a joint committee of the House and Senate had to come up with a compromise version which was then passed by each body.

After the president signed the bill, he directed the Bureau of Public Roads and other appropriate agencies of the executive to carry out the requirements of the program. Tax monies had to be moved into a highway trust fund. Criteria for roads had to be drafted and publicized. State governments had to be alerted to the details of the new programs so that local plans could be made. As the law required, public hearings were held in each locality before final routes were confirmed. Concerned citizens could appear at these meetings to try to protect their interests from the disruption caused by highway construction. They could also press for routes that would favor the economic or social development of their areas. Finally, routes were approved, contracts were made with local businessmen, workers were hired, and the bulldozers began to move. Years later, the network of roads began to stretch across fields and forests and into the outskirts of cities.

The Consequences of the Interstate Highway System

The network of roads had vast consequences. The new highways were safer by far than the old two-lane or three-lane roads. People living in previously isolated communities gained ready access to metropolitan areas. On the other hand, the ease with which people could travel to the city or to the new suburban shopping centers led to the decay of many small towns and the loss of commercial and recreational facilities in previously vital if small-scaled centers of population.

As the new roads spread out, an enormous growth of industrial and commercial activity took place along their paths and, even more, at their intersections. The landscape was transformed by the development of industrial parks, elaborate shopping centers with roofed-over malls, huge parking lots. The new suburbs, with their widely spread subdivisions, developed a way of life based on the automobile: there were few facilities within walking distance of people's homes. Work, recreation, the purchase of necessities all depended on travel by automobile.

Lastly, there was a massive shift in the overall national pattern of transportation. As the use of rail and water diminished, the trucking industry mushroomed. And the character of the new highways encouraged a new technology in which ever larger trucks are powered by ever more potent engines to travel at higher and higher speeds.

The first hints of trouble came from stories of local corruption. It was inevitable that road builders, land developers, and politicians should try to profit from private information about the location of the new roads and that the traditional American practice of awarding construction contracts to the friends of politicians would emerge. The newspapers of the period provide a number of stories of legislative hearings in which corruption was uncovered. But the extent of this petty thievery seems to have been relatively small. The building of the roads provided a tremendous amount of work to many and enriched a goodly number of entrepreneurs.

Rather more serious, from a social point of view, was conflict over the placing of the roads. There was little outcry over the location of the rural sections of the interstate highway system, since these went mainly through relatively unpopulated areas. However, whenever the system intruded on the urban scene, there was a wave of destruction in its wake. And sometimes the citizenry rose in rebellion against the prospect of that destruction. For example, the people of New Orleans fought a battle through the courts to prevent highway builders from destroying the most beautiful old square in the famous Latin Quarter of that city. Similarly, the people of San Francisco, organized in citizens' groups, fought to prevent their famous waterfront from being covered by an elevated highway. The major north-south highway for the East Coast, I-95, has still not been completed because Philadelphia resisted for a long time the invasion of its Society Hill, one of its primary areas of urban renewal, by a road that would not only generate noise and pollution but would also shut off this area from the riverfront.

In this whole discussion, we have said relatively little about the role of the courts. Most of us think of a court as a place where judges and juries attempt to give a fair trial to people who are accused of breaking the law and establish their guilt or innocence. We also know that people who feel that they have been injured by others, even if no law has been broken, can appear with their lawyers and, in actions called civil suits, demand fair compensation. But the courts have another role to play. Citizens can ask judges to determine whether either of the other two branches of the government, the executive or the legislative, has engaged in action that runs counter to the basic rules set down in the state or federal constitution. Similarly, the executive branch can be challenged if a citizen or citizens believe that its actions run counter to the law. Judges have the power to order public officials or private citizens to refrain from activities that are considered unconstitutional, illegal, or unfair. This power, the power of *injunction,* is almost always, if not universally, obeyed.

During the course of the interstate highway project, concerned groups of citizens often formed informal organizations to fight road-building projects and, through the judicial process, succeeded in stopping the builders from carrying out their plans. In many communities, however, the citizens' committees were unsuccessful, or there was no organized outcry. And so, many urban communities have been ringed by highways that displaced large numbers of people and generated slums in formerly livable areas.

Energy and Pollution

A problem that was almost entirely unforeseen in 1956 but that vitally concerns us now is the depletion of natural resources as a result of the expansion of motor transport. The United States now faces the necessity for importing ever increasing amounts of oil. Native sources of fuel cannot keep up with the tremendous demand generated by our almost complete dependence on the internal combustion engine for transportation. And even if we could pump enough oil from offshore waters and the North Slope of Alaska to meet our needs, the potential for damage to the continental shelf and the beaches and the enormous increase in pollution would be additional consequences of the highway system.

The result of dependence on foreign oil has been an imbalance in the economy as dollars flow out. While other factors have also promoted an unfavorable balance of trade, the continual drain of our resources to pay for the import of oil has certainly contributed. It is probable that all of these trends would have led to an eventual crisis even without the shock of the Arab oil boycott in 1973 and the subsequent increase in the price of oil.

Automobile-related pollution is another problem unforeseen in 1956. In fact, if someone had set out purposely to find the mode of transportation that would have the most destructive effect on the environment, the internal combustion engine would have been ideal. The interstate highway system encouraged not only the building of ever larger and heavier automobiles and trucks but also the use of huge engines to move these vehicles at high rates of speed. These vehicles use enormous quantities of fuel, and they use it very inefficiently. As a result, large amounts of polluting material are expelled into the atmosphere. To the burden created by unburnt gases from engines must be added the pulverized rubber from tires and asbestos from brake linings—which together make the American environment a fit subject for black humor.

Impact on Other Modes of Transportation

Lastly, the growth of the highway system had an inevitable impact on other components of the transportation system. As automobiles and trucks handled an increasing proportion of shipping and travel, other forms of transport lost business. It was almost inevitable that, with the tremendous focus on the automobile, the public attention paid to railroads would diminish. By 1960, the railroads had just about given up on the possibility of maintaining passenger travel. All through the 1960s, the railroads continued to drop passenger lines with the blessing of the Interstate Commerce Commission, whose mission it is to regulate land transport in the public interest. Finally, in 1970, Congress set up a National Railroad Passenger Corporation (later called Amtrak) to take over financial responsibility for passenger service on the railroads. In 1975, a large part of the freight service in the Northeast was merged into a new semipublic corporation called Conrail.

Although almost everyone pays lip service to the need for mass transit, advocates of this service have had little effective power in Congress. Contrast the $40 million allotted to support Amtrak for its first year with the $600 million appropriated for the development of a supersonic airplane (a project later scrapped), not to speak of the billions for roads. The Congress has made a tentative gesture to permit a small part of the highway trust fund to be used for mass transit where a local government wishes to do so. But the funds available for mass transit are still minute in comparison to the money spent on roads. The net result has been to reduce rather than increase the rail facilities available to most citizens.

Some increased service has been made available in one area, the Northeast Corridor from Washington to Boston. The success of that service has demonstrated that people will use the railroads rather than private automobiles or airplanes if rail travel is comfortable, convenient, and not overly expensive.

While the movement of goods by rail has not fallen off in absolute terms, the proportion of freight carried by rail continues to diminish. This drop in the use of rail was unnecessary. The most tragic mistake was the failure of government to encourage the development of the so-called piggyback system of long-range freight transportation. There is no question that trucks are an efficient way of getting goods from one place to another over short distances. However, economic analyses show that the most efficient method for transport over long distances is to load truck trailers onto flatcars and transport them on the rails—thus the term piggyback. If you want to move your furniture from San Francisco to New York, you can load it into a trailer, use a truck tractor to take the trailer to the railhead in Oakland, put the trailer on a flatcar, and then send the flatcar by rail to New York. You can then transfer the trailer to the roads and haul it with a tractor to its destination.

Using individual gasoline or oil-burning tractors to haul individual trailers from one side of the continent to the other creates massive waste of raw materials and unnecessary pollution of the environment. The political power of the teamsters' union and the trucking industry and the indifference of the railroads played a part in making the shift from rail to road possible. But it was the choice of the interstate highway system as an important national effort that made the shift inevitable during the expansion of American industry in the fifties and sixties.

Not the least of the effects of the highway system has been its consequences for the pattern of development of metropolitan communities. When cities grew along bus, trolley, or rail lines, the new areas were compact. Housing developments were planned so that transit was readily available. Community facilities grew up about stations or transfer points. In the new world of the interstates, and with the stimulation offered by government support for mortgages, developments could sprawl over huge areas of land. This was not only wasteful of arable land, an important resource, but it also prevented the formation of genuine communities. Instead, the pseudo-community of the suburban shopping center filled the need for places to buy essentials. The shopping center also provides movie theaters, restaurants, and even art galleries, but it is not a real town. The people who frequent it are usually anonymous; it does not give them the kind of focus for human association that is found in the neighborhoods of a city or in a small town. Will we ever know how much the lack of community contributed to the increase of drug use, abuse of alcohol, delinquency, and family instability among middle-class people in the new suburbs during the 1960s and 1970s?

Along with the growth of the new world of subdivisions and shopping centers, the shift of population drained vitality from the inner cities, leaving a void to be filled by migrants from rural areas who had been made redundant by mechanization of agriculture. True, the migrants would have come anyway. But if cities had maintained their original populations, they might have been able to absorb the newcomers with less disruption than actually occurred. American cities will not recover from this series of blows for a long time, if ever.

Summary

The decision to concentrate an enormous national effort on the building of an interstate highway system was taken in reaction to a real emergency, the need for adequate transportation in the booming United States of the post–World War II era. The process by which the decision was taken illustrates the roles of national and state executive, legislature, and judiciary in the formation and implementation of national policy. It also illustrates how business, interest groups, and voluntary organizations play a part in the initiation and execution of public programs. Lastly, it shows how decisions arise out of the bargaining process as individuals and organizations fight for their own interests.

The story certainly fits Simon's concept of "satisficing" as a goal; no attempt was made to survey all possible outcomes of all choices, and the final decision was based on an expectation of an outcome that, so far as anyone could see, was good enough, if not ideal. The most powerful voices in the discussions that led to the decision were the manufacturers of trucks and cars, the trucking companies, the truck drivers, and various local and state agencies, whose perspectives were quite limited. The agencies responsible for transportation, which should have been able to approach the problems in a disinterested way, were dominated by officials who maintained close contacts with highway lobbyists and often moved back and forth between government jobs and jobs in the transportation industry. Even some of the key congressmen who shaped the program had very close contacts with organizations of highway builders or truckers and received lecture fees and campaign contributions from these interested parties. As a result, the examination of alternatives to highway building was perfunctory at best, and the evaluation of possible negative consequences of the interstate program totally inadequate. Hindsight tells us that the decision was a poor one and that its overall effect on the country was little short of a disaster. Perhaps by analyzing the way it was reached, we can gain some insights that may help prevent similar decisions in the future.

An Analysis of the Decision to Build the Interstate Highway System

This section reexamines the history of the decisions that led to the interstate highway system in order to evaluate the role of the various actors who participated in the evolution of that decision.

The Executive

Executives play two kinds of roles. In the first, they plan and initiate action. In the second, they implement decisions. In the history of the highway system President Eisenhower played both roles. It was his initiative in appointing a commission that led to the first gathering of information and the earliest planning. Similarly, a meeting of the governors of states led to the establishment of a kind of pressure group, the Conference of State Governors, which played a considerable part in moving the Congress towards adopting the legislation. These events illustrate the importance of the executive in our social system in acting as a leader, mobilizing public opinion, and providing a sense of direction.

The executive's other role is to appoint and supervise the individuals who carry out plans once they are adopted. In the national government, the president was responsible not only for the cabinet departments that planned and funded the interstates, but also for the agencies that supervised motor transport and thus oversaw the operation of the system.

The president should have been able to rise above the private concerns of the partisans who bargained for a solution to the problem of a national system of transportation. Ideally, an executive transcends local and particular concerns and represents the interests of the community at large. In the real world, alas, many executives act as agents of special interests or carry out their own ideas in a way that runs counter to the general good. Undoubtedly, each president of the United States has viewed himself as representing the national interest in the development of transportation. One president after another has issued calls for the development of a balanced transportation system that would include mass transit as well as highways. However, they have often been less successful in selling the idea of support for mass transit than they have in forwarding the development of the system of roads. Why this should be so is not entirely clear, although some thoughts on the matter will be suggested below. It may be that an executive, like most leaders, is successful in leading only where his followers wish to go.

The Legislature

Many aspects of the functioning of the legislature are illustrated by the story of the highway system. Although a presidential commission began the search for solutions to the problem of a national transportation policy, the work of gathering information to permit the Congress to evaluate the Clay report was carried out by congressional committees. They invited interested and expert parties to come and talk about the needs of the community and to advance appropriate solutions.

The power of congressional committees is enormous. They usually consist of congressmen with a particular interest in the kinds of legislation the committee handles. At the time the highway decisions were taken, the committee chairmen were chosen by seniority. That is, the majority party member with the longest service automatically became chairman. Unfortunately, committee heads sometimes represent Special interests as well as the constituency of their districts or states. Characteristically, the heads of the congressional committees that planned the interstate highway system had strong ties with trade associations and unions in transportation and often profited personally from their association with the interest groups that were pressing for the new highways.

It would be easy to regard the combination of businessmen, union leaders, and legislators as a conspiracy. But that would be an oversimplification. The businessmen and union leaders were engaged in furthering what they saw as their legitimate interests. The fact that the chairmen of committees responsible for highways received fees for speaking at trade association meetings need not be construed as bribery; it is perfectly reasonable that congressmen with expertise in a field should be asked to participate in the work of voluntary associations in that field. Are we suspicious when senators or congressmen who have drafted health legislation appear before groups concerned with health, or when legislators who have promoted aid to schools lecture to educators? The association between the congressmen who took the lead in planning and supporting the highway system and the users was a natural outgrowth of their common interests. The fact that both sides profited is certainly not against the rules in our competitive society.

Somewhat less innocuous is the fact that many civil servants responsible for supervision of highway construction moved into jobs with highway users or truck manufacturers. Even here, one would need proof that their decisions as regulators, which were often highly favorable to their eventual employers, involved venality. It may very well be that their decisions were proper and that their subsequent employment by the industry they had been regulating was based only on a natural tendency to recruit men and women with appropriate backgrounds. Let us say that the whole question of conspiracy must be given a Scottish verdict of "not proven."

Whether there was a conspiracy or not, the central problem was the lack of leaders and experts who could speak for the long-range needs of the country by assessing all the alternative ways of meeting its requirements for transportation. Neither the legislative leaders nor the highway users were able to respond to the problem as a whole by evaluating all the possibilities in a disinterested way. The result was a one-sided examination of the issues.

We are not likely to repeat the particular mistakes of the last generation. A strong lobby now speaks for the environment, and it has found many allies in the Congress. While there is still controversy over many aspects of transportation, a limited national consensus has developed in favor of some expansion of mass transit. This has not as yet been translated into full support, but the direction of the next decade will probably be towards the increased use of rail and waterways and the decreased use of roads.

But new decisions with consequences for the future are yet to be made. It is worrisome to contemplate the possibility that some of these decisions will produce terrible problems in 1990 or 2000 because the processes of mutual adjustment by partisans and the goal of "satisficing" do not permit an adequate look at many of the possible consequences or at all of the alternatives. We are deciding now whether to expand the use of nuclear energy. If we do, we will burden future generations with the care of an ever growing mass of radioactive waste products. We are "mining" the soil to grow food for the entire world. The consequence is damage to the ecosystem from the effects of fertilizers, herbicides, and insecticides. Our crops often consist of large stands of single species of hybrid plants. These are particularly vulnerable to disease and insect pests. And this vulnerability increases the need for herbicides and pesticides. We continue to tolerate a social system in which a sizable proportion of the population has no meaningful social role; the consequence in social disorder continues to grow. A generation ago, people were worried by the proliferation of atomic weapons. Now, with more and more countries possessing the basic technology for nuclear weapons, we seem to have settled for a world in which the bomb continues to be stockpiled. We have no real assurance that it will never be used. Almost all of these decisions have been taken because the immediate consequences are tolerable, if not positively rewarding. It almost seems as if the entire human race is engaged in taking an extra drink for the road, stepping into a fast sports car, and roaring off down the highway on a mad joy ride.

Politics. The role of political parties in a story like that of the highway system is not too clear. When the interstate highway system was first being discussed, the Republican and Democratic parties disagreed over the method of financing the system. However, the conflict does not seem to have been related to ideology. It is usually said that the Democratic party in this country is a "populist" party that expresses the needs and aspirations of the masses of middle-class and poor people. The Republican party is usually described as the party of business and industry. There may be no necessary connection between these broad, rather vague positions and the two ways of financing the interstate highway system. Possibly the bankers would have profited considerably from money lending if the interstate highway system had been financed by borrowing. On the other hand, the "pay as you go" procedure, finally adopted through the efforts of the Democratic majority in Congress, does not seem to have any particularly "populist" connotations since, as I noted above, the Democrats have often favored massive borrowing to carry out public works.

Apart from political parties and their positions, there is another way in which politics entered into the evolution of the highway system. A congressman is beholden to individuals in his district for money and influence. In small towns and rural areas, such small businessmen as garage and motel owners and small construction contractors are often powerful far beyond their numbers. They have the time, the interest in public affairs, and the money to participate vigorously in politics. In contrast, the relation between a congressman and his or her constituents is far less direct in large urban centers, where most people tend to be fairly remote from politics. In addition, large urban centers were seriously underrepresented in Congress during the fifties and early sixties. The number of people represented by an urban congressman was much larger than the number represented by a rural congressman. It was not until the mid-sixties that the Supreme Court, in its "one man, one vote" decision, forced a more equitable representation of large centers of population. In addition, many rural and small-town congressmen, especially the midwesterners and southerners, had constituencies in which the same party dominated politics year in and year out. Such congressmen tended to be reelected many times. As a result, they gained seniority and committee chairmanships. Even today, when chairmanships are not assigned by seniority, congressmen who have been reelected term after term rise on a ladder that brings them eventually to domination of the committees in which the most important work of the Congress is carried out. Therefore, for many reasons, small-town and rural congressmen have been the most powerful voices in the Congress, and their influence continues today. Their interests were reflected in the final shape of the interstate highway system.

Patterns of Administration

In the United States, the system of relations between the states and the central government is, in some ways, unique. In most other advanced countries, the central government dominates the political and social scene almost entirely, no matter what the formal language of the constitution. In the United States, for all sorts of historical reasons, the individual states jealously guard a measure of independence. Each state regards itself as a "sovereign" community with an area of power specifically reserved to it by the Constitution which states quite clearly that all powers not expressly given to the federal government are to be held by the states. Local governments—cities and counties—do not have any such independence. We do not have the concept of a "free city" in the United States. The powers of cities and counties are almost completely determined by charters or other documents issued by the states.

As we saw, important roles in the development of the highway system were played by both the federal government and the states. It was the states, usually through bureaus of highway construction, that prepared the plans for local segments of the highway system, following general guidelines from Washington. The states did the work of surveying, let the contracts to local companies, and, after the roads were built, kept them functioning and in repair. The chief role of the federal government was to provide the overall plan for the location of the roads, set the standards by which they would be built, and to furnish ninety percent of the money. The power of the purse did enable the federal government to enforce its standards, but the influence of state governments was very great.

Once the highways were built, the federal government played a part in regulating their use. Of course, the states all have police forces that enforce speed limits and patrol the roads to assist travelers in trouble. However, the Interstate Commerce Commission, a federal agency, has the specific responsibility of supervising truck traffic. The agency makes rules for the use of trucks, and, indeed, sets the rates that may be charged by the trucking industry.

In a "free market," someone who sells goods or services can charge whatever the buyers are willing to pay. Presumably, competition among those who offer goods and services prevents them from exploiting their position. Only someone in a position to offer something unique can charge as much as he likes, and even he must find someone who wants his wares. The idea of the free market is traditionally rooted very strongly in the beliefs and values of most Americans. But reality and ideology often conflict. Although some small businessmen may compete in a way that approaches a free market, most areas of the American economy are dominated by large corporations that compete in advertising slogans but rarely in either the quality or the prices of their products.

One important area in which competition is generally not even expected is that of public utilities. In electricity, telephone, and rails, one company may control an entire market, and the government must regulate such monopolies to keep services adequate and prices fair. In other areas, transportation by truck, for example, the government sets rates even though there is no monopoly. The rationale for fixing rates is that the industry would be put into a state of total confusion if free competition were allowed.

Unfortunately, different federal agencies regulate the various modes of transportation. The lack of a broad general policy for controlling the costs of moving goods and people from one place to another leads to a great deal of confusion. While it is true that there is "machinery" by which the regulating agencies—the Interstate Commerce Commission, the Federal Aeronautics Authority, and the Federal Maritime Commission—can communicate about relative rates, the procedures are cumbersome and rarely used.

One problem with regulative and administrative agencies is that they are not quite as impartial as they are supposed to be. It is notorious that many of the people who are appointed to these commissions have ties with the industries they regulate before they join the commission and almost always go back to these same industries after their term of office. While an occasional brave representative of the public appears at hearings, the testimony of such individuals has little impact on regulatory decisions. Typically, the regulated industry and the regulating agency operate in a cozy partnership. This was true both for the planning and building of the roads and for the operation

NATIONAL HIGHWAY USERS CONFERENCE, INC.

BOARD OF GOVERNORS

Alfred P. Sloan, Jr., Chairman Emeritus

OFFICERS

Chairman

Albert Bradley, Exec. Vice President
General Motors Corporation

Vice-Chairman

Herschel D. Newsom, Master
NATIONAL GRANGE

Secretary-Treasurer

Louis J. Taber
President, Farmers &
Traders Life Insurance Co.

Vice-Chairman

Arthur M. Hill, Chairman, Executive Committee
The Greyhound Corporation
President, NATIONAL ASSOCIATION OF
MOTOR BUS OPERATORS

J. N. Bauman, Vice President
White Motor Company
Assistant Chairman
Motor Truck Committee
AUTOMOBILE MFRS. ASSOCIATION

Warren Bledsoe, President
NATIONAL RURAL LETTER
CARRIERS' ASSOCIATION

Benjamin F. Castle
Executive Vice President
MILK INDUSTRY FOUNDATION

Walter B. Cooper, Director
NATIONAL AUTOMOBILE DEALERS
ASSOCIATION

C. S. Decker, General Traffic Manager
The Borden Company
Chairman, Transportation Committee
INTERNATIONAL ASSN. OF ICE
CREAM MANUFACTURERS

Raymond C. Firestone
Executive Vice President
THE FIRESTONE TIRE & RUBBER CO.

Shelton Fisher, Publisher
"Fleet Owner" and "Bus Transportation"
McGRAW-HILL PUBLISHING CO., INC.

A. B. Gorman
Manager, Marketing Department
Automotive Division
Esso Standard Oil Company
President
PRIVATE TRUCK COUNCIL OF
AMERICA

Sam C. Hyatt, President
AMERICAN NATIONAL CATTLEMEN'S
ASSN.

Rowland Jones, Jr., President
AMERICAN RETAIL FEDERATION

Thomas F. Mansfield
Member, Executive Board
AMERICAN BOTTLERS OF
CARBONATED BEVERAGES

R. R. Ormsby, President
THE RUBBER MFRS. ASSOCIATION

Emery Rice
President, Rice's Bakery
AMERICAN BAKERS ASSOCIATION

Ted V. Rodgers
Rodgers Motor Lines
Honorary Chrmn. of the Board
AMERICAN TRUCKING
ASSOCIATIONS, INC.

Fletcher R. Smith, Vice President
A. L. Siegler Fruit and Produce, Inc.
Member, Advisory Board
UNITED FRESH FRUIT AND
VEGETABLE ASSOCIATION

H. N. Snyder
Vice President and Treasurer
Buffalo Slag Company
Past President
NATL. SAND & GRAVEL
ASSOCIATION

Ralph Veenema, President
Veenema and Wiegers, Inc.
TRUCK-TRAILER MFRS.
ASSOCIATION

L. S. Wescoat
Chrmn., Exec. Committee of the Board
The Pure Oil Company
AMERICAN PETROLEUM INSTITUTE

Walker A. Williams
Vice President
Sales and Advertising
FORD MOTOR COMPANY

Fig. 10:1 Members of a Highway Users Conference and the organizations they represented. From the files of the Center for the Study of Federalism, Temple University.

213

of the highway system. The one group consistently underrepresented was the general public.

The Client Groups

Figure 10.1 gives an interesting picture of the membership of one of the highway users associations. Note that there are representatives of trade unions, truckers, highway builders, and public agencies. These groups may disagree violently over some issues, but, where highway building is concerned, their interests tend to converge. For example, the trade union that represents the truck drivers engages in the most vigorous conflict with the organizations of truck owners when it comes to setting the wages of truck drivers. In fact, there have been violent and brutal strikes over issues of wages and working conditions. However, both groups have joined forces to lobby *for* extensions of highways and *against* diversion of funds from highways to mass transit.

In the 1960s, however, a new kind of client group emerged, the advocate of the public interest. In community after community, groups of interested citizens came together to protest the disruption that would be caused by planned new highways. In addition, as the problems of pollution and depletion of natural resources have become more acute, interest groups focused on ecology have become increasingly vocal. While there was little or no sign of such groups in the mid-fifties when the original program was planned, any hearing in the seventies would be sure to attract representatives who claim to speak for the community at large—for example, the Sierra Club and Ralph Nader's Public Interest Research Group. Similarly, organizations devoted to preserving the character of American cities as livable communities have pressed legislatures and regulatory agencies to develop mass transit rather than roads.

Who Pays?

As the interstate highway system was finally financed, the money came primarily from taxes on the use of trucks and automobiles. By far the largest proportion of the money came from the users of private automobiles. And yet, only a small proportion of travel in private autos actually takes place on the interstate highway system. Every time you drive from your house to the local shopping center to buy a quart of milk, the taxes on the gas you use help pay for the building of a new highway. It could be proposed that the benefits tend to even out. We all profit from the use of the roads by truckers who bring us things we buy. Most of us have used at least one of the new highways, either on a vacation trip or in some kind of travel connected with our work or study. But the average person's benefits from the system probably do not equal the cost in taxes.

A final assessment of the highway system should calculate the total cost of the system and its benefits. A purely economic analysis *might* find that the payoff from the system to the economy as a whole exceeds its cost. The payoff in such an analysis might be the total contribution towards movement of goods and services. The cost is the money spent to build the roads and the possible return we might have had from alternate use of the land. Some of the references at the end of the chapter include such detailed economic analyses. The consensus is that the system was worth more than it cost if the analysis is restricted to narrow economic terms. But these terms do not include all the costs. They do not assess the damage to the environment caused by cementing over such a large amount of land and the consequent runoff of water that would otherwise soak into the soil. The result has been an increase in floods and a lowering of the water table. The costs should also include the loss of vegetation and the purifying and oxygen-producing effect of this green cover. Lastly, they should weigh the disruption of urban communities that we described earlier and the decay in the quality of life, in both city and suburb, associated with the new culture of subdivisions and shopping centers. If all these costs were taken into account, it is likely that even an economic analysis of the highway system would show that it leads to serious deficits in the balance sheet of the national economy.

Could We Have Done Better?

In retrospect, it is hard to avoid the conclusion that it was a mistake to emphasize road building and motor transport at the expense of mass transit in the cities and of railroads to move goods and people across the country. For moving goods over long distances, rail is both cheaper and less polluting than truck transport. The movement of people in and out of big cities by rail or other forms of mass transit would certainly have been less disruptive of the ecology than commuter travel by car. To analyze some of the reasons the road system was built, we must try to identify the values and expectations that entered into the decision. (For a framework for this discussion, see Chapters 4 and 5.) Freedom and personal autonomy are among the most important values in American culture. If there is one thing that Americans prize, it is the ability to function without restrictions. In the back of almost every American's mind is a vision of his ideal: the clear-eyed frontiersman setting out on his horse for the beckoning unknown. Even though the realities of our expansion westward were far more complex than that, the myth of the frontiersman still pervades our national consciousness. It was, therefore, almost inevitable that we should opt for a system of transportation that gives maximum freedom to individuals to do what they want when they want to do it in the most flexible possible manner. The motorcar for individuals and the truck for businesses are extensions of the horse on which the frontiersman traveled the endless plains.

Complementing the influence of the values of autonomy on the decision to build highways, we have a set of expectations based on many aspects of American history. The railroads were universally welcomed when they first appeared on the scene. But very soon, the lavish land grants, the speculative manipulations by robber barons like Commodore Vanderbilt and Jim Fiske, and the huge size of the rail systems they built combined to give the railroads a negative image. Most people still find it hard, even after decades of bankruptcies and governmental assumptions of control, to think of the rail systems as anything other than corrupt and overbearing monopolies squeezing huge profits out of the helpless people. Lastly, years of deteriorating service, added to memories of wartime crowding, have produced an expectation that rail travel will be inconvenient, slow, and uncomfortable. The combination of these values and expectations made it unlikely that railroads or other forms of mass transit would capture the imagination of Americans sufficiently to win genuine national support.

Even if there had been popular support for alternative modes of transport, there was no one to speak for them. The consumer advocates, the groups focused on ecology, the scientists concerned with the balance of nature may have been waiting in the wings in 1956, but they could barely be heard.

With the highway system, as with so many other decisions, long-range interests suffered in the face of short-range advantage. However, this has not always happened. We have, indeed, devoted enormous amounts of time and treasure to distant goals. The two "public works" that have absorbed the largest proportion of the American economy in the past twenty years have been the defense and space programs. While each of these includes many components that act to the immediate advantage of many individuals, the primary support for the projects does not come from such advantaged individuals. It is probably true that neither the space program nor the defense program resulted from a conspiracy of self-interested businessmen engaged in a hunt for profits. Both programs were based on genuine cultural values and expectations. For defense, it was the fear of a communist enemy. For space, it was the sheer excitement of escape from the planet. It would be valuable for future decision making to try to determine why these three huge programs—highways, the military, and space—succeeded in commanding the resources and energy of the American community despite the fact that they contributed so little to the solution of our most pressing social problems.

It is one of the clichés of European and Asian political thought that Americans are too little concerned with "planning." Much of the rest of the world calls itself socialist and is devoted to central coordination and planning rather than to the kind of mutual accommodation characteristic of the American social system. Is it possible that we went astray because we did not have planners who could order the community to do what was good? It is beyond the scope of this book to evaluate fully the experience of the communities that have tried the centralist approach. If one were to attempt this, one would have to ask whether the citizens of socialist countries are freer, happier, more fulfilled than people in our own. The fence that keeps their population from leaving argues that they are not. What is more to the point in the context of this discussion, however, is to ask whether socialist countries, with their emphasis on planning, have avoided our mistakes. The best evidence seems to be that they have not. The socialist countries too have poured their treasure into armaments and heavy industry. They have not done too well in their attempts to solve the problems of housing and food production. More seriously, their tendency to wreck the ecology is not as subject to social control as is ours, since their closed social system makes it difficult for people to protest national policy.

Could we, then, do better than we have? In the next section, we shall turn to the question of whether one could devise novel forms of social organization that would be more successful in solving the problems uncovered in the course of our inquiry into community decision.

On Your Own

1. One of the areas we have really neglected is the study of attitudes. Several books on attitudes which might be useful are: Dawes, Robyn M., *Fundamentals of Attitude Measurement*. Triandis, Harry, *Attitude and Attitude Change*. Campbell, A.; Converse, P. E.; Miller, W. E.; and Stoyes, D. E., *The American Voter: An Abridgement*.

2. C. Wright Mills, cited in the references, is hard for most Americans to take since he really doesn't much like the social scheme in this country. But it might be healthy to try to understand the point of view of a genuine American radical.

3. Since much of the chapter is about decision you could try Miller, David W. and Starr, Martin K., *The Structure of Human Decisions*. This would also be useful for Chapter 5. A good summary of the problems of transportation (but with a strong anti-auto and pro-mass-transit position) is Buel, Ronald A., *Dead End*.

4. A city of 750,000 has been electing the fifteen members of its governing council at large for many years. That is, the entire city votes for all the candidates and the top fifteen get elected. A move is underway for a change in this procedure. Under the proposed new scheme the city will be divided into fifteen districts (dare they be called wards?), each to elect its own representative. Discuss the pros and cons of the change. Hints: (1.) How close or remote will people feel from government under the new system compared with the old? (2.) Use ideas from the previous chapters on social stratification, groups, etc., to suggest some of the changes the new scheme might bring about. (3.) Under which system is there more likely to be bribery and corruption?

Section V
Progress to a
Better Life

11

Criteria for a Good Society

Our inquiry into the social sciences has come a long way. We first looked at the relation of human behavior to the biological nature of man. We then developed methods of studying the motives of individuals. From this focus on individuals, we shifted to analysis of the organization of society and the processes of decision making. At each stage, I have tried to give some sense of the everyday world. Now, I want to shift to an examination of how the social sciences might be applied in an attempt to better the condition of the human race. In order to do this, I will first present some basic ideas about the fundamental needs that must be met by any organized society. I will then discuss some proposals for new societies, the literary and philosophical utopias. Lastly, I will review briefly some actual attempts to develop new ways of living together.

Why Think About a Good Society?

People have always had dreams of a better kind of life. Almost every country has a myth of a "golden age" in the distant past; many also have ideas about a heaven on earth that could be achieved if only man would follow the ideals of his religious or ethical system.

Nowadays, people tend to think of themselves as "conservative" or "liberal." Conservatives wish we could go back to a better world that used to be. Liberals and radicals would like to have the world advance to a new golden age.

219

But aren't we now living in a kind of golden age? As one looks around the United States in the late twentieth century, it certainly seems as if the lot of the majority of Americans is far better than that of any other group of people in the history of the world. We can extend this even further and say that the fortunate people living in Western Europe, in the socialist countries of Eastern Europe, and in Japan also enjoy a kind of prosperity that the human race has never known. Food is plentiful, except for occasional local shortages. Mass-produced clothing is wonderfully decorative and easily available. Individuals are free to move around in their cars; the relatively inexpensive long-distance transportation provided by jet airplanes has led to a tremendous expansion of travel. It certainly does seem as if for many people the world is about as close to paradise as one could imagine.

And yet—almost everybody is oppressed with a sense of uneasiness. The ring of bombed-out slums around the centers of American cities is a daily reminder that all is not well in paradise. Although the majority of the people living in the "advanced" countries are prosperous, debilitating poverty continues, not only among their minorities but also among the enormous number of people living in the poorer lands at, around, and south of the equator. Occasional stories on TV or in the newspapers remind us of the millions starving in the gutters of Calcutta or the squatters' shacks outside Rio de Janeiro.

Things are not perfect even for the majority of prosperous citizens in the developed countries. We have found it hard to cope with the problem of violent crime; as a result, many of us fear to walk outside after dark. Something must be wrong in a community in which so many need the chemical escape afforded by the legitimate drugs—tranquilizers, alcohol, and tobacco—or the illegitimate ones—marijuana and heroin. And in the background are the nagging realization of the explosive growth in the world's population and the daily reminder that we are slowly choking ourselves to death as we pour garbage from our factories and automobiles into the sky and dump industrial wastes and raw sewage into the waters.

It does seem worthwhile, therefore, to develop some ideas about the overall character of the social system required to provide a good life for its members. The rules should be based on the theories and data of the social sciences as well as on philosophical and ethical considerations. While ethics and philosophy may provide goals, the social sciences ought to furnish some ideas about the ways the goals can be reached. This chapter is devoted to some basic ideas about new social systems. In the next two chapters, these ideas will be applied to philosophical and literary proposals for good societies and to actual experiments in new social forms.

Requirements for a Good Society

The Nature of Humanity

Chapter 3 should have generated some skepticism about broad general statements on the fundamental nature of man. The burden of our argument there was that humanity is variable and that its character is greatly influenced by the nature of society. However, the last couple of decades of research in psychology have produced some evidence that these *are* universal human motives. These might provide a good working basis for evaluating proposals for the organization of a social order.

There is good evidence that two kinds of motives are universal to all advanced organisms, rats and monkeys as well as people. The first is a desire for comfort, for relief from tension, and for sensory gratification. People, like cats, tend to purr when they are stroked in the right places. And they tend to exert effort and to learn when they anticipate reduction of tension as a consequence of effort and of learning. The second kind of motive is quite different. There seems to be an almost universal desire for novelty, stimulation, relief from boredom. The work of one psychologist at the University of Wisconsin, Harry Harlow, indicates that even nonhuman primates will put forth considerable effort to win a chance to look at novel displays or to put simple puzzles together. It hardly needs proving that people, too, will subject themselves to incredible stresses to satisfy the urge to explore, to overcome obstacles, to penetrate the unknown.

If one tries to satisfy either of these kinds of needs, there is a danger that the other kind will go unmet. So, for example, if people enjoy a great deal of security in an environment almost entirely free of anxiety, there develops a serious danger of boredom. On the other hand, if people are overwhelmed with novel experiences, this generates too much tension and a need for a sense of peace and security.

The need for security in a society implies controls over individual impulses, the subordination of individuals to social requirements. The need for stimulation can be met only in a society that affords some degree of individual freedom. It is these two needs, social control and individual freedom, that are so often contradictory. Somehow a successful society must reconcile these divergent needs.

The Need for Social Controls

I should like to begin this discussion by summarizing an article by the ecologist Garrett Hardin, entitled "The Tragedy of the Commons." Hardin describes a situation in which the villagers in a rural area have the right to graze their animals on a commons. Each family is tempted to increase the number of animals in its own herd because adding animals increases the supply of food. Unfortunately, if every household in the village added even one animal, the commons would be overgrazed. As a result, the animals, and eventually their owners, would all starve.

The tragedy of the commons illustrates a universal situation. Each individual gains when he fulfills his short-term needs. But if everyone operates purely in terms of short-term needs, in the long run everybody loses. Hardin has no solution to this problem other than to point out that each society must develop some sort of social control that forces its members to give up some of their individual satisfactions in order to promote the general good. He has only the most general ideas about the ways in which individuals can be required to submit to the general good. His article seems to end with a thinly disguised plea for an autocracy run by "experts."

The Need for Individual Freedom

The problem with social controls is that they tend to stifle people and thus reduce the likelihood that individuals will lead productive lives. It has been a universal experience that slaves tend to be extremely inefficient workers. This has happened whether the slaves were serfs in the Ukraine, factory workers in nineteenth-century England, black field hands in the South of the United States, or, indeed, workers bound to collectivized farms in "socialist" states. A society that wants to flourish must give its members individual freedom, or at least the illusion of individual freedom. It may indeed be that freedom is an illusion. We will discuss this issue at great length a little later on when we examine the ideas of B. F. Skinner. However, illusion or not, the society that does not provide a sense of freedom for many of its members survives only if it is never exposed to danger. In the discussion of McClelland's work on achievement motive in Chapter 5, I commented on the economic expansion and the flowering of the arts in Periclean Athens, Elizabethan England, and seventeenth-century Holland. It may be no accident that these were, on the whole, societies that permitted freedom of expression to their citizens.

In summary, then, the basic requirement for a good society is that of a balance between social control and freedom from constraint. The more successfully that balance is maintained, the more productive will be the society.

Mechanisms of Responsiveness to Danger

A further requirement for a good society is that it be responsive to internal decay and external threat. Societies that do not have built-in mechanisms for detecting danger and reacting to it quickly and efficiently do not survive. They may fall to external invaders or die of internal rot. In one way or another, mechanisms of responsiveness must be developed. Think about the elements of a social system that make the work of a Ralph Nader possible. We are all familiar with Nader's many crusades against unsafe cars, polluted air and water, venal politicians and businessmen. It is the essence of a responsive society that men and women like Nader who see the decay in the social fabric are free to speak, have access to a free press, and so can be heard by the whole community. Other essential ingredients in responsiveness are courts in which a Nader can press his suits, a legislature in which his citizens' lobbies can exert influence, and a government that reacts to such challenges by constructive action rather than repression. True, an autocracy *can* be responsive. Legend has it that the Caliph Harun al-Rashid walked in the bazaars of Baghdad in disguise, heard the complaints of the people, and righted their wrongs. It is hard to know how consistent he was in reacting to the ills of his kingdom or how many of them he encountered. Contemporary autocracies also react to their citizens. It took bloody riots to make the Polish government rescind unpopular price increases in the spring of 1976. The mechanism of response seems both costly and unreliable.

In looking at proposals for utopia from writers and philosophers and at the attempts to create new societies, we will apply the criteria we have just reviewed. We will try to determine not only the degree to which each society has adequate measures of social control but also the level of freedom of expression afforded its members. And we will ask about the society's devices for reacting to danger.

Some Reactions of Social Scientists on the Problems of Improving Society

Three major issues have been discussed by social scientists in their treatments of the fundamental requirements for a good society. The first is the question of the best size for a social unit. Next is the impact of technology on human happiness. Last is the problem of social control, the reconciliation of the need for order and direction with individual freedom.

The Proper Size of a Unit for a Social System

One of the most destructive effects of modern industrial society is that it creates a sense of anonymity, a feeling of being nothing but an index number in a giant list or a set of marks on a computer tape. In the famous motion picture *Modern Times,* Charlie Chaplin was a tragicomic figure not only because his job was trivial and meaningless but also because he was a cog in a wheel in a huge machine. Many of us often feel like Chaplin, going through the rounds of our daily lives enmeshed in big business, big government, big unions. The implication of the Chaplin film is that the sheer size of our social units dehumanizes us; if you have no identity beyond a number, no one will care what happens to you, and you too will be indifferent to the fate of others. The implied contrast is with a village or small town where everyone has identity and people really care about what happens to their neighbors.

The vague feeling that the units of society are too large has led to some fairly specific investigations into the optimal size for a social unit. As we shall see later, Plato defined the ideal community as one that could be addressed by a single speaker. In his day, without amplification, that meant about five thousand people. Unhappily, that criterion no longer applies. Today, with the advances in technology with which we are all so familiar, a single individual speaking over radio or television could conceivably talk to the entire population of the planet.

In a sophisticated little book entitled *After the Revolution,* Robert Dahl suggests that a social system that would permit the "human dimension" to emerge must consist of units small enough that everyone in them *knows* everyone else. Since Dahl is realistic about the fact that we cannot get rid of huge cities, he would like to see the city reduced to an aggregate of neighborhoods, each a relatively independent unit consisting of around five hundred people. In fact, he proposes that we dispense with the city as a political unit and have each neighborhood governed by its own inhabitants. He would promote each citizen's sense of affiliation and responsibility to this tiny unit by having the people who govern the neighborhood selected by lot rather than by election as the governing council was chosen in fifteenth-century Florence. Everybody would stand an equal chance of participating in the government. He is aware that there would have to be interrelations among these tiny units, but he feels that a network of such interrelations could be set up to cope with specific needs.

A city planner who has had enormous influence on our thinking about the future of cities was a Greek philosopher–social scientist named Constantinos Doxiadis. He devised a way of looking at the organization of urban society and entitled his method *ekistics.* Unlike Dahl, Doxiadis did not want to get rid of the city as an organized unit. However, he would have liked to rebuild the cities so that, as in Dahl's scheme, they would consist of neighborhoods small enough that people could walk easily from one part to another. Doxiadis would also have liked to bring the country into the city with parks laid out in long fingers of green so that everyone would have access to some open space. Doxiadis, like Dahl, would make the unit for organizing our lives small enough that everybody within the unit could be personally known to everyone else.

The daydream of a society organized in village-sized units has been approached in some places. We are told that one of the reasons London "works" as a modern city is its structure of relatively small, self-governing boroughs. Many of the utopias we will discuss in the next chapter express the yearning for a human scale in society. I shall return later to some critical comments on the possibility that this yearning really could be satisfied.

The Proper Role of Technology in Society

From the beginning of the Industrial Revolution, people have had mixed feelings about technology. New inventions bring many benefits, but they also throw people out of work and change the face of the country, producing ugly cities where once there were green fields. You may remember the myth of the sorcerer's apprentice who stole one of his master's spells and used it to order a broom to bring water for his cleaning. This was fine except that he had forgotten to learn how to turn the broom off. The broom kept bringing bucket after bucket of water until the apprentice was over his head in it. Many social critics see technology as having created a spell on mankind, bringing us floods of good things but drowning us in them.

Characteristic of this kind of thinking is the work of a French savant named Jacques Ellul, whose book *The Technological Society* is a powerful indictment of the contemporary social order. He defines technique broadly as a "standardized means for attaining predetermined results." While technique includes the use of machines, it also refers to any rigid, stereotyped way of doing things. The outcome of reliance on technique is a loss of spontaneity. The rule of technique means inevitably that people focus on means and become careless of ends. In fact, technique becomes an end in itself. In such a world, efficiency is more important than justice, progress is dehumanizing as humanity focuses ever more on the ways of doing things rather than the reasons for doing them. Social systems become increasingly centralized since technology requires central planning. This is not due to a conspiracy; to Ellul, it is an inevitable outgrowth of the technological society. As life becomes increasingly rigid and structured, all of the grace and warmth may depart. Men and women, slaves of the machines and of the rituals developed to serve them, may resemble robots.

But we must be careful to discuss this question realistically. We have become so accustomed to the easy living made possible by technology that it seems difficult if not impossible to give up our conveniences now. Very few people are willing to dispense with the delights of modern plumbing and motorized transportation. More than that, it becomes increasingly apparent that the brute problems of feeding and housing the huge population of the earth would be impossible to solve without the use of complex technology.

One solution that has been advanced is the adoption of small-scale technology. There are two aspects to this proposal. The first calls for a reduction in the level of human wants. People living in advanced societies have become used to an overabundance of really wasteful things. The huge automobiles, the lavish houses, the eight-lane roads, the elimination of every trace of effort by machinery that does everything from opening our cans and brushing our teeth to polishing our shoes—all these do not seem necessary to a good life. Presumably, some of the needs for technology could be eliminated if people were willing to give up some of these luxuries.

No one has thought of a practicable political means for making people give up a luxurious way of life short of military conquest. But the change may be forced by the increasing depletion of resources and by environmental deterioration. However, the second aspect of the proposal for small-scale technology may provide an answer. Advances in the recent technology of miniaturization raise the possibility that we could devise a technology that would actually be more efficient in small units than the current giants. For example, the old-fashioned ways of manufacturing steel by means of open-hearth furnaces or Bessemer mills require huge factories because they are impossible to operate on a small scale. However, it is now possible to manufacture small quantities of steel very efficiently in small workshops.

If one thinks of the way Skylab, the satellite that remained in orbit for weeks, was fitted up to serve as living quarters and workshop, one can see that it is certainly feasible to create a rich and complex environment in very small units. What it takes is a change in orientation—away from bigness and towards a human scale. The designers of Skylab knew they would have to cram everything necessary for survival into a tiny space because of the limitations on the size of a body that could be ejected from earth's gravity and placed into orbit. If the tremendous ingenuity that has been directed towards the space program could be turned towards the problems of human survival on spaceship Earth, then conceivably a similar kind of miniaturization could be applied to the scale of manufacture needed for the things we require in everyday life.

A parallel possibility is that both agriculture and industry could be revised so as to fit more easily and with less disruption into the ecology of the planet. Think about Earth as a giant Skylab; there is no such thing as "garbage" since everything has to go somewhere. And you can manage very nicely by using air, water, and other supplies over and over. Writers on ecological problems, such as Barry Commoner, have long been urging that we shift over from ecologically disrupting to ecologically sound methods of solving technological problems. For example, in traditional agriculture, animals were pastured on grasslands. Their wastes enriched the soil as manure. And since people cannot eat grass or hay, the animals did not compete with man for food. They provided needed supplements of protein and fat to a grain-based diet. Today, animals are fattened by being fed grain in huge feedlots. The grain is grown with massive applications of fertilizer and insecticides. Animal wastes are treated as sewage and discarded. True, the meat from grain-fed animals is more tender than that of animals fed on grass. But our tender steaks are obtained at the cost of an agricultural system that disrupts the ecology by generating widespread pollution and exhausting rather than maintaining the soil. Similarly, we now depend largely on synthetic fiber for clothing rather than using such naturally grown fibers as wool, silk, and cotton. Natural fibers are grown by the energy of the sun, but the manufacture of synthetics depends on the use of our ever diminishing supplies of fossil fuel.

In summary, the writers whose work we have been discussing urge us to reduce our demands on the environment in order to limit the destructive impact of technology on the earth's resources. They propose a radical shift in the nature of technology, away from large scale installations and a wasteful use of energy and materials towards small, highly efficient productive systems that fit with a minimum of disruption into the tightly organized environment of the earth.

Means of Social Control

One of the major controversies in the design of social systems has concerned the means and extent of social control over individuals. One side tends to argue that a social group in which people are left in complete freedom would work out its own ways of running things so that a good society would result. This point of view has been presented forcefully by such radicals as Paul Goodman *(Growing Up Absurd)* and A. S. Neill *(Summerhill)*, whose pictures of the virtues of freedom and the horrors of autocracy have been so convincing to the last several generations of young people. Interestingly, arguments against governmental control also can be found among such extreme conservatives as William Buckley, author and editor of *National Review.*

Their argument basically is that a self-regulating, homeostatic system will emerge if each individual is totally free of constraints except for the absolute minimum of rules required to keep people from harming each other. One could label their point as "anarchist" if the word were not associated with bewhiskered bomb throwers. On the other side of the spectrum, one finds writers who feel strongly that the rigorous exercise of authority by a knowledgeable elite is essential to the running of a society. Again, this "conservative" point of view is also found among the supporters and leaders of the Communist states of Eastern Europe and Asia. One way of describing this point of view is to call it "authoritarian."

In the following chapters, we will explore the conflict between the needs for social control and the rights of individuals in analyzing several attempts at new social systems. At this point, I would like to call your attention to the work of one social scientist who has made what I believe are some particularly interesting contributions to the discussion of this question.

B. F. Skinner, a psychologist whose work has attracted much attention recently, is neither an anarchist nor an authoritarian. He proposes that the concept of freedom is an illusion. According to Skinner, people are shaped by their experiences and learn to behave in ways that are determined by their histories of reward and punishment. He also notes that, in any given instance, people operate on the basis of the rewards anticipated from one or another choice. The anticipations are, of course, based on past learning. Thus, to the extent that no one is free of his or her own past, freedom is indeed an illusion.

However, Skinner differs from the authoritarians on the proper way of running a social system. He is strongly opposed to the use of power or compulsion in organizing social activity. Instead, he suggests a system in which everyone is able to reward everyone else. Thus, by mutual reward people "shape" each other towards behavior that is not only individually pleasurable but also socially beneficial. He feels that one of the worst ways of "shaping" an organism is to use punishment. Punishment merely suppresses behavior; it not only does not train in new behavior, but it also creates harmful emotions that disrupt organized patterns of action. I will discuss Skinner's ideas in greater detail in the next chapter when we talk about his literary utopia, *Walden II*.

The questions we raised in the last chapter on community decision remind us that, in the large-scale units of contemporary society, individuals can lose contact with the actual business of running the community. The formality of voting for an often meaningless choice of candidates is no substitute for close participation in the government. In a reaction to the depersonalization of representative government, radicals of the New Left in the 1960s often favored a system they called participatory democracy. In this, government would be based on consensus among members of small, face-to-face groups. The organized system of voting on choices of opposing positions characteristic of groups run according to *Robert's Rules of Order* would give way to free and open interchange. In essence, the call for participatory democracy is a demand for a return to the sort of involvement that characterized the Society of Friends or the New England town meeting. This would require marked reduction in the size of social units unless new techniques of mass communication (the radio phone-in talk show, for example) made it possible for communities larger than a town of five hundred to govern themselves by direct rather than representative democracy.

One last point. I have been talking about individual freedom. But there are really two kinds of freedom. One is the freedom to create, to think, to talk. The other is the freedom to consume. The first could conceivably be without limit. The latter, given the limited quantity of goods, must always be constrained. Unhappily, the abstract distinction is often not easy to apply. As the Supreme Court put it, no one has the right to shout "fire" in a crowded theater where there is no fire. The Russian or Chinese censor who refuses a dissident poet the right to publish his poetry, or the American court that bans pornography, sees no question of freedom to *create;* to the censor, the poet or pornographer is *consuming* in the sense that the interference his poems or pictures create in the lives of others takes something intangible from these people. It is only through such a rationalization that dogmatic libertarians can justify censorship. The conflicting demands of nonconformists for freedom and of society for the enforcement of social norms create a genuine dilemma. Any model for a good society will have to develop rules for the solution of this apparently unsolvable dilemma.

In summary, the ideas that we have examined suggest that an ideal society should consist of small units in which people can have a strong sense of identity and can deal personally with all the people with whom they have to interact. A society of this kind would develop small-scale technologies that would permit it to cope with the problems of subsistence and also to provide enough surplus goods so that the people would not have to spend all their time working merely to survive. And, lastly, a society of this kind would have to work out a solution for the problem of balancing off individual freedom and social authority.

Now let us take a look at some proposals for utopias and analyze the degree to which they meet the various demands we have just outlined.

On Your Own

1. One of the most popular recent presentations of the case for small-scale technology is found in a book by E. F. Schumacher, *Small is Beautiful,* which is available in paperback. This has become a best seller and has influenced a number of political figures. Schumacher advocates "Buddhist economics," a system essentially equivalent to those proposed by the writers we cited in this chapter who favor the prepotency of ends over means and therefore call for technical systems that are as little disruptive as possible.

2. A book by Barry Commoner, *The Poverty of Power: Energy and the Economic Crisis,* provides a marvelous lesson in the basic physics needed to understand the problem of energy shortage. Commoner also offers a devastatingly critical discussion of the possibility of a good society based on a system in which profit rather than utility is the basis for decision. You may not accept Commoner's social philosophy, but his exposition of the meaning of the first law of thermodynamics for energy use is something every citizen should understand.

3. One of the foremost exponents of the concept of the planet as a single ecosystem is R. Buckminster Fuller. His book *Operating Manual for Spaceship Earth* is most thought-provoking.

12
Utopias

Why consider people's ideas about utopia? There are a number of reasons. Letting our imagination run gives us freedom to explore alternatives unhampered by the demands of practicality. Industry calls this brainstorming. While there is no good evidence that brainstorming provides really good solutions to problems, it is certainly fun, and it may be worthwhile to get people started. If, for a while, we do not have to worry about actually applying our wild ideas, we may be able to come up with some useful concepts that might not otherwise have occurred to us. But outrageous ideas may not always be impracticable. The utopian proposals of one age very often become the workable solutions that the next age applies to its problems. In my own youth, social programs like social security and medicare, technical advances like atomic energy, space travel, and computers were all the stuff of science fiction. It seems worthwhile, therefore, to examine the fantasies of the writers and philosophers who have dreamt of a better way of life.

A plan for a utopia has to fulfill several requirements. First, there must be a stated or implied set of notions about the basic nature of man. For example, some writers about utopias think of man as basically good, cooperative, but often pressured into evil by sick societies. Others see man as basically greedy, hostile, mastered by needs, requiring strong social controls. These two views of mankind would certainly lead to very different plans for utopia. The view of the nature of man leads to the second requirement, a specification of

the human needs that must be fulfilled by society. The third requirement is the daydream, the scheme that is advanced as a way of fulfilling the needs the author has implied or stated openly.

The definition of the nature of man and the specification of the
needs he brings to organized society are clearly within the province
of the social sciences. Much of this book has dealt with the question
of human needs. In the previous chapter, we looked at the way some
social scientists have spelled out the relation of social forms to human
needs. Now we can evaluate some of the better-known utopias, identifying the underlying concepts of "human nature" on which they are
based and the programs they propose to solve the problems faced by
the human race. Finally, we will discuss the question of transition,
the steps to be taken in achieving utopia. A statement of the means to
an end helps define the character of that end itself. Violent means
often lead to a violent and repressive end, no matter how well-
meaning the overall plan. Even though utopian thinkers tend to
ignore problems of transition, we should analyze the events that accompany attempts to develop new social forms.

In looking at these utopias, we will apply some of the ideas developed in the previous chapter. We shall characterize the size of the
unit they require and the ways in which the writer proposes to maintain social order. Especially for the more modern plans, we will
evaluate the attitudes toward technology and the awareness of
ecological problems. And, lastly, we will look at the writer's resolution of the conflict between individual freedom and social control,
placing each utopia on a scale ranging from extreme emphasis on the
needs of society, which we might characterize as "authoritarian," to
an extreme reliance on the ability of people to achieve a balanced
society without any external social controls, which might be labeled
"anarchist."

Was Utopia Ever a Reality?

Utopian writing and thinking go back almost to the beginning
of history. Almost every primitive and most classical societies have a
myth of a "golden age" in which mankind lived in peace and enjoyed
freedom from turmoil and want. There may have been such golden
ages. The ancient Greeks, for example, may have had dim memories
of the beautiful civilization of Minoan Crete, which led to the myth

of Atlantis. The fact that the last in the series of Minoan eras ended with a great tidal wave may have been responsible for the story of the foundering beneath the seas of the earthly paradise of Atlantis.

The great American urbanologist Lewis Mumford suggests that all the myths of the golden age have their foundation in the New Stone Age or Neolithic period. At that time, most members of the human race lived in small, peaceful villages on the bountiful soil, carrying on a form of agriculture well attuned to the local ecosystem. The series of discoveries that created the Neolithic culture included the domestication of animals, the development of grains and garden crops, and the utilization of polished stone for tools. All of these signaled a shift from the earlier Paleolithic period in which man, as a hunter and food gatherer, exploited nature by drawing resources from the environment but replacing very little. In Neolithic times, man lived off *renewable* resources, soil that could be kept fertile by rotation of crops, flocks of animals that were continuously maintained. It may be surprising to think of the Stone Age as a golden time, but the way Stone Age people fitted into the environment, as exemplified by the most successful of Native American societies (at least successful until the coming of Europeans) should furnish important lessons to our presumably advanced society. In many ways, then, Neolithic culture does furnish a model of utopia in its small scale, its close relation to nature, and the supportive social structure of its villages. Whether this model is really useful when population is numbered in the billions rather than thousands is a question to which we shall have to return.

Some Literary Utopias

The balance of this chapter is devoted to an examination of several literary utopias and some of the problems they raise. Those selected are only a few of the many fascinating attempts at descriptions of ideal societies, but they were chosen because they are well known and also because they lend themselves to discussion of the basic issues raised at the beginning of the chapter.

Plato's Republic

The first of the utopias, apart from the primitive myths of Eden or a golden age, is, of course, the society described by Plato in *The*

Republic. Plato's ideal is a small city-state similar to the communities in the Greece of his time. It is situated in an area where nature provides enough bounty so that no one suffers real want. The community is divided into three groups. At the bottom are laborers, who cultivate the land and carry out what manufacture of goods is needed. In the middle are a group of military men, whose function is to defend the state. At the top are the leaders, who govern the community. These leaders are selected by merit and trained in philosophy. Their only goal is the search for truth. Plato gave them absolute and complete authority over the city. In order to guard against corruption and a resulting accumulation of personal wealth, Plato required that no one own property or work for personal profit.

In its concentration on a search for something called "truth," Plato's community has no room for the idle and subversive luxuries of art. Plato's utopia is rather warlike; he found it impossible to visualize a world in which there would not be almost constant conflict. And the constant warfare leads to a perpetual state of emergency. The philosopher-rulers are given such total authority that they are even permitted to lie in order to protect the state.

Plato's dream of an ideal community has often been seen as a model for the dictatorships of both the extreme right and the extreme left in the twentieth century. Plato's city, like the fascist and communist states, is one in which the leaders, a self-selected elite, know what is good for the community and bend all energies towards achieving those good ends. On the continuum from individual freedom to social control, one would have to place Plato's community almost all the way on the side of social control. The social unit he describes is small; scholars have surmised that the Republic would have about five thousand citizens, the number who could gather in its central meeting place to hear an orator speak. Technology was not, of course, of much interest to educated Greeks in Plato's day, and so the Republic is patterned after the Athens of his time in its dependence on human and animal labor and its use of only simple tools.

Would Plato's dream provide a useful model for today? As I have suggested, the idea of a governing group of unselfish, truth-seeking people who are given total power is part of the theory of fascism and is implied in the practice, if not the theory, of such contemporary "socialist" states as the Soviet Union and the People's Republic of China. The almost complete sacrifice of individual freedom under such systems seems abhorrent to most Americans. And the descent from philosopher-rulers to a hereditary caste of selfish aristocrats that Plato cynically forecast as a likely fate for his Republic seems to be happening in the Soviet Union today. We shall consider the merits of the Platonic ideal further in the next chapter.

Sir Thomas More's Utopia

The first work in which the word *utopia* appeared was that of Sir Thomas More, a scholar who lived in England in the time of King Henry VIII (the monarch with the many wives). More was steeped in the new learning of Renaissance Europe; he was most certainly familiar with Plato. In More's time, explorers were beginning to bring back reports of new lands beyond the sea in the Americas and in the Far East. More's hero is a man who comes back from travel across the oceans to describe a wonderful place in which the disorders and miseries of contemporary Europe are unknown. This island is called *Utopia,* a play on words, since the name in Greek means "no place." The island is a thinly disguised copy of More's England with its one large city and its miles of prosperous farms. The governmental pattern is, however, very different from the hereditary monarchy under which More worked. The inhabitants of Utopia are divided into small groups, each of which elects a leader. The elected leaders then assemble to choose a prince who rules for life over the entire community.

There is a close connection between the countryside and the city. Everyone is a member of an extended family that is based in both the city and the country. People who live in the city all have an attachment to farms and spend a part of the year working in the fields. In addition, almost everybody has a skilled trade and participates in the production of goods. The population eats together in communal dining rooms that sound something like the dining halls of an Oxford college.

Virtue is found by living according to nature and refraining from passion. More believed that a good life comes when people have modest needs. There is a general feeling of joy in work, with great status placed not only on cultivating the soil but also in making beautiful objects. In that respect, More differed from Plato, who allotted agriculture and craftsmanship to the lowest levels of society and considered those occupations fit only for slaves.

Like Plato, More could not imagine people at peace. And so he saw the Utopians carrying out military forays, not only to win scarce raw materials, but also to extend their power over neighboring lands.

The most important of More's values are the downgrading of the possession of material things and the emphasis on craftsmanship, learning, and the joys of communal life. More was less concerned than Plato with abstract truth; his ideal world shows the wonder at nature and beauty that characterized that expansive period in Europe when a vital people burst its boundaries, explored half the globe, built great cities, and developed the institution of the national state. But More, perhaps anticipating the troubles that this explosive expansion would bring, urged modesty, a small scale of social organization, and a sense of dignity for the individual.

Many of the particulars of More's Utopia make it appear less than ideal for a twentieth-century American. His view of human nature stresses the creative, seeking drives rather than the need for relief of tension. However, the constraints in his society are as external as those in Plato's ideal community. Given the zeitgeist of Renaissance Europe, it would have been unlikely for More to feel a strong attraction towards a democratic, internally controlled form of social organization. The Utopia is full of evidence that More expected his society to need a great deal of compulsion in order to function smoothly.

Within the framework of an autocracy, More's world has small social units, a stress on craftmanship and search for knowledge, and a potential for smooth integration of human activities into the balance of nature. All these suggest that this social order might promote human happiness and provide a sound basis for the good life. One reservation is based on the apparent inflexibility of the social organization. The ruler is elected for life. There are means for tapping the opinions of the population, but it does not seem likely that More's scheme would lend itself to rapid and flexible responses to stress. In summary, one concludes that More's Utopia would be a difficult place for nonconformists or for those whose creative bent was overly individual, and that it might not survive either external attack or internal forces of decay. But, for most of its inhabitants, it would provide a far better life than they could have found in the Europe of More's time.

News from Nowhere: A Socialist Utopia

In this necessarily brief survey of utopian writing, I shall pass over the many attempts to describe an ideal society written between the sixteenth century, when More worked, and the nineteenth century. You will remember that during this time Europe went through the evolution of national states, the establishment of industry and commerce on a large scale during the industrial revolution, and the enormous increase of wealth consequent on the exploitation of new lands beyond the sea.

That Europe became extremely wealthy is without question. However, this wealth was unequally distributed. The life of eighteenth- and nineteenth-century Europe was one of enormous luxury for a tiny proportion of the population and extreme misery for the remainder. During the first part of the nineteenth century, a number of thinkers decided that the force responsible for this maldistribution was private property. They began to imagine a world in which the goods of the earth would be owned by people in common. The general name for these writers and thinkers is "socialist." A number of socialist writers in the first part of the nineteenth century were responsible for attempts to found actual communities based on their ideas.

Of course the best known of the socialist writers of this period was Karl Marx. His devastating criticism of society created a movement whose impact is still felt today. Marx was opposed to utopias and to attempts to found small communities in isolation from the world. He felt that energy should not be diverted from the task of rebuilding society as a whole by revolutionary means. However, people who were influenced by Marx during the latter part of the century did write utopian books. Some of the best known of these are Edward Bellamy's *Looking Backward* and Samuel Butler's *Erewhon*. The socialist utopia I would like to discuss in some detail is the society described by English author William Morris in *News from Nowhere*.

Morris's ideal world is very different from that of Plato or More. It is democratic, almost anarchist rather than authoritarian. Morris describes an imaginary England in which private property has been abolished. The great cities of the late nineteenth century, their skies blackened by smoke belching from factory chimneys, have vanished. Instead, the entire population lives in small, peaceful villages spread over the entire countryside. People live very close to the soil. The arts of handicraft, which Morris saw in decline during his time, have revived. There is no unpleasant labor, since almost any task can be left to someone who will find it rewarding. There is complete freedom of social movement. The absence of private property and the muting of greed and aggression mean that there are virtually no crimes, and therefore no need for compulsion or law. Morris did see a need for some activities that crossed the boundaries of his little villages, primarily maintenance of a network of transportation. But transportation in Morris's terms is a pleasant glide down the Thames on a small steamer, not the noisy and dirty railways of his time.

Interestingly enough, unlike most other utopians, Morris did pay some attention to the transition from his contemporary world to utopia. In his book, he predicted that there would be a general strike, and a riot in Trafalger Square, which would lead to an almost complete destruction of society. The people, primarily the workers led by intellectuals and artists, would slowly evolve a new social order. Morris thus proposed that a peaceful, communal mode of society could arise out of disorder and chaos. His account of the disorders that would begin the transition to Utopia was written in the 1880s, and it formed a remarkable anticipation of the events of the Russian Revolution of 1917. But the free society he pictured arising from that disorder certainly bears little resemblance to the grim reality of the U.S.S.R. Morris's pastoral daydream combines the beauties of the English landscape and the delights of medieval craftsmanship with freedom under democratic socialism. Many people might find it dull; but the contrast with the crowded, dirty world of today certainly makes Morris's dream attractive.

In terms of the criteria proposed in the last chapter, Morris' Utopia deserves a favorable evaluation. The inhabitant of his society is little concerned with relief from discomfort; Morris's concept of the nature of the human species falls clearly on the side of creativity, stimulation seeking, and self-fulfillment. His world would get very high marks from such modern humanistic psychologists as Carl Rogers, Abraham Maslow, and Rollo May. Needs are so fully met that little external constraint is required. Constant interaction among the citizens ensures a rapid and flexible response to danger. Technology is minimized; what there is disrupts the environment very little.

Many of Morris's ideas fit beautifully into the framework of contemporary thinking about novel social forms. Some of these ideas are discussed in greater detail in the following chapter, where social experiments in Yugoslavia, Israel, China, and Sweden are presented.

Skinner's Walden II

One of the few utopias constructed by a working social scientist is found in the novel by B. F. Skinner entitled *Walden II*. Skinner's ideal community is a self-sufficient group of about a thousand people. The group engages in small-scale agriculture and handicraft, but is dependent on the outside world for some food and manufactured products.

Work is carried out in exchange for work credits to the community. The more unpleasant and undesirable a job is, the larger the number of work credits it earns. And so people who want to do as little work as possible in order to free themselves for private activities that do not earn credits can do so by carrying out tough and demanding but unattractive subsistence jobs. Almost everybody in the community has a good bit of leisure for art, scientific investigation, or just plain loafing and sociability. The community is a very convivial place in which people are described as happy, in a mild sort of way.

The most novel aspect of *Walden II* lies in its program for bringing up children. Children are raised according to Skinner's concept of positive reinforcement as the best source of learning. Thus the behaviors that are ideally suited to a cooperative community are encouraged by being rewarded; undesirable behaviors are discouraged, not by punishment, but by lack of reward. In a concept that has been widely criticized, children are taught to tolerate a certain amount of frustration by a game in which they refrain from eating when hungry or resting when tired for short periods of time in order to teach themselves how to moderate their wants.

The community is run by people called "planners" who happen to be good at the task of coordinating activity. Skinner did not expect these planners to enjoy higher status or prestige than anyone else, although it is hard to escape the idea that in a real community they actually would command more than average respect. Skinner proposed that planning is a technical skill whose exercise does not involve power over others. In Skinner's community, no one has the ability to force anyone else to do anything, except through the indirect compulsion arising from the offer of rewards for a desired act. Even the planners cannot *compel;* it is assumed that the desirability of their plans will be self-evident.

Evaluating Skinner's utopia is easier than one would expect, since he was explicit about its character. Even so, there are areas open to controversy. For example, Skinner's psychological theory demands that organisms be viewed exclusively as entities responding to external events or to changes in internal biological states. And his utopia does put great emphasis on the manipulation of people through the environment. Skinner's notorious book *Beyond Freedom and Dignity,* written many years after *Walden II,* claims that no organism is free in any meaningful sense since all behavior is the product of an interaction between the biological state of the organism and stimulation from the environment. The book's notoriety as a supposed attack on humanistic values is probably due to misunderstanding. Skinner does not require that people be under the control of other people; his rejection of the concept of freedom is based on the notion that we are never free of our own natures or of the pressures of the environment. Thus, his utopia is not an autocracy, except for the control exercised by adults over children. The managers cannot force anyone to do anything. They offer choices that are rewarded differentially. And people are "free" to adopt the options which are not highly rewarded. The community exercises social control through the manipulation of rewards and through the training system, which leads people to want options that favor the continued peaceful and prosperous life of the group.

The paradox is that Skinner's people act as if they did have inner creative urges. Nothing in the social engineering prepares one for the concentration of the inhabitants of Walden II on chamber music, gardening, or philosophical meditation. In fact, these activities are *not* specifically rewarded with work credits. It is the dreary labor of subsistence that wins large numbers of credits and frees the time of the laborer for music or meditation. Skinner's overt theorizing describes man as manipulated; his unstated model of humanity is as creative and self-actualizing as that of any humanist.

The formal side of Skinner's utopia is not dissimilar to that of Morris's. The social unit is small; all its members are acquainted with each other. Technology is ingenious but nonintrusive. One flaw is the concentration of social control in the hands of a small group of managers not unlike Plato's philosophical governors. While these are people suited by temperament and training to administer, the fact that responsiveness to threat is localized in a small group probably robs the society of some of the interchange among citizens that promotes creative reactions to danger. The pattern of communication in Skinner's society is more like that of a wheel than a circle. As we noted in Chapter 8, the wheel works well for the solution of routine problems as long as the person in the center is an efficient coordinator. But the circle, with its free and equal interchange among all participants, is more effective in searching out creative solutions to complex problems.

In summary, Skinner's *Walden II* holds out promise of a form of social organization in which knowledge of a psychological technology permits the group to shape its own behavior so that the problem of social control is no longer pressing. The system of rewards also enables the group to assign the necessities of subsistence so that all those who desire the creative life may earn the opportunity for it. The only problem Skinner does not pretend to deal with is that of transition. He is opposed to compulsion, to power in the hands of those who profit from its exercise. He is certain that the punitive, power-ridden society in which we now live is doomed to ever increasing social pathology. But he has no idea of how to move towards his human paradise.

The Antiutopias

Starting with the early part of the twentieth century, a kind of quasi-utopian writing that emphasizes the horrors rather than the benefits of attempts to construct new societies has become more and more common. If the twentieth century is to be judged by its writing about the future of man, then our world must indeed be a nightmare. Starting with a book called *We* by a Russian named Eugene I. Zamiatin, and progressing through Aldous Huxley's *Brave New World,* George Orwell's *1984,* and Kurt Vonnegut's *Player Piano,* anti-utopian writers have constructed pictures of a future world in which people become ants in a managed society. The managed society controls its citizens sometimes by bribery, sometimes by force.

In Huxley's *Brave New World,* people are bred in incubators and biologically manipulated so that they form classes ranging from unskilled workers to intellectuals. By a combination of luxurious living, drug-induced euphoria, and social pressure, everyone is bribed into leading a socially approved life. Huxley showed this world through the eyes of a primitive who somehow has grown up in a wild reservation set aside as a kind of zoo. Huxley's vision certainly seems nightmarish to anyone who values human individuality.

In *1984,* Orwell described a society in which brute force and perpetual spying by a superpowerful secret police keep people in line in a kind of parody of the Platonic Republic. The leaders of Orwell's state have the same freedom to lie and cheat that Plato's philosophers do, but instead of using this freedom for the sake of a search for truth, they use it in order to perpetuate their own power.

Vonnegut's negative utopia, or *dystopia,* is a society in which the need for individual workers has been reduced enormously. The work of skilled craftsmen has been recorded into a kind of player piano tape that is used to run machines. Most of the population, supported in idleness, is slowly going mad from boredom. Only a tiny handful can achieve the luxury of a real job.

The dystopias represent a revulsion on the part of intellectuals against the soured dream of the fascist and communist states whose replicas of Plato's Republic have created so much misery in this century. But they reflect disenchantment with the liberal West as well. Their writers feared that the concentration on sensuality and self-indulgence inherent in the prosperous world of England and the United States would lead to the kind of moral decay so clearly described by Huxley and Vonnegut. In recent years there have been relatively few hopeful utopias. Only Skinner and his followers seem to be able to maintain the dream of an ideal world. But among students, there is a growing interest in the utopias of the past, and this phenomenon argues that hope for the future has not been lost and that people are still ready to dream.

Can Utopias Be Realized?

Virtually none of the literary utopias, with the possible exception of Morris's, pays any attention to the problem of transition. In each, the ideal or feared society is presented as a fait accompli, springing full grown from the imagination of the author. The failure to deal with transitions, in fact, was one˙of the reasons that Marx and his followers were so impatient with utopian writing and of the utopian experiments, which they saw as diversions from the real business of improving the lot of the human race.

A recent book on the problem of transitions by a psychologist named Seymour Sarason has some interesting thoughts on the likelihood that we can ever achieve new social forms. They may be worth discussing at this point as a bridge from the study of dreams in this chapter to an analysis of social experiments in the next. Sarason discussed the creation of new settings for various kinds of human activity. These new settings range from a marriage, in which two people try to create a way of life together, through the establishment of a new social agency, university department, or school, to attempts to build an entire new society.

Sarason saw a common series of stages in the history of all kinds of new settings. In the first stage, there is a kind of "honeymoon." Usually under the impact of a forceful leader, the initial period in the establishment of a new setting is filled with enthusiasm. Everybody who joins the leader feels like a member of an elite. Personal interests are subordinated to the needs of the new community. Enthusiasm is high, but a sense of realism is low. During this first phase, it is difficult for people to imagine that things could go wrong. There is a sense of boundless optimism, a lack of appreciation of limitations on the available resources and on the potential for growth.

The first, happy stage of the creation of any new setting tends to be followed by a period of disillusionment. The leader may get bored with his job, since the problems of beginnings are always more fascinating than the problems of maintaining a new setting. The difficulties of the new group are compounded by a continual necessity for facing up to shortages of goods, of facilities, of people. The outside world tends to interfere and may even negate the work of the new setting. And, most important, individuals who in the first phase had subordinated their personal needs to the needs of the group now shift focus to their own requirements. Cliques begin to develop. As a result, conflict within the group tends to destroy the rosy feeling that something wonderful and new is being created. If a group manages to surmount the second stage, it will be able to stabilize, develop routines, and go on as a living, if no longer exciting, institution.

The most important contribution that Sarason makes is his assessment of the requirements for avoiding the worst problems posed by loss of the initial enthusiasm of phase one in the discouragement and despair of stage two. He sees two things as critical. The first is that the people who are designing the new setting be conscious of the origins of the participants and of the institutions that go into the creation of the new setting. If one is unrealistic about the continuity from past to present, then well-nigh unsurmountable problems are sure to emerge. A new setting for highly educated people with a tradition of individual autonomy poses completely different problems from one that must work for semiliterate peasants with no experience of self-government. Secondly, the people designing the new setting must anticipate conflict. Lack of realism about the future, a sense that any obstacles can be overcome by superhuman effort and good will, is a sure precursor to failure.

Thirdly, in addition to anticipating conflict and thinking in terms of continuities, it is necessary to develop a clear set of rules about the operation of the new setting. Sarason points to the constitutional convention that set up the government of the United States as a prime example of a highly successful creation of a new setting. In this convention, fortunately carried out in secret, people were able to face up realistically to many of the problems that would be encountered by the struggling new republic. Since they were working in secret and did not have to respond to immediate pressures from their constituents, they were able to compromise and develop clearly defined ways of coping with these problems. They gave careful attention to the details of the operation of the proposed national government, anticipated conflicts, and even more importantly, provided ways to modify the system by amendment. The resulting governmental structures gave the new state stability. And, indeed, the United States has had the longest and most stable constitutional government in the entire world.

Of course, the writing of a constitution in itself is not a panacea. Constitutions can be remote from reality, as was true of the famous 1936 Constitution of the Soviet Union. The paper document described a never-never land of freedom and civil liberties that had virtually no resemblance to the real world of Stalinist Russia. It had little effect.

Lastly, Sarason places a great deal of emphasis on the role of leaders. He sees the leader as a galvanizing force for the group that is creating a new setting; the leader directs the group towards the achievement of its goals. In almost all the records of new settings cited by Sarason, there has been a leader whose realism or lack of it has been most important in determining the success of the group. This may, of course, not be a universal phenomenon. As we pointed out in Chapter 5, the emergence of a single leader is based on a kind of personality pattern that derived from the patriarchal family structure common to the advanced Western societies.

After this discussion of some ideal imaginary societies, we now turn to an evaluation of some actual experiments in new social orders.

On Your Own

1. Available in paperback and worth looking at are—Skinner's *Walden II*, Neill's *Summerhill*, and Chianese's *Peaceable Kingdoms*.
   A good scary discussion of the problems faced on spaceship Earth can be found in *Replenish the Earth: A Primer in Human Ecology* by B. Tyler Miller, Jr.

2. Write your own utopia. First use the rules presented in Chapter 11 to decide what mix of social control and individual freedom you yourself would find most necessary. Then try to draft a set of rules for a new society that would meet the needs described in that chapter.

3. Collect some material on some part of the world where social experimentation is going on. Analyze it using the criteria for a good society proposed in Chapter 11. A good place to work with is Holland. Another is Japan. A third is Cuba.

4. Read about a utopia other than the one analyzed in this chapter. Good choices might be those by H. G. Wells, Bellamy, or the Italian Renaissance philosopher who wrote *City of the Sun*, Campanella. Analyze the society using our criteria. Evaluate it as a place in which you might or might not want to live.

5. A hardy band of enthusiasts has tried to set up communes based on the model of

Skinner's *Walden II*. The first of these is described in K. Kinkade's *A Walden Two Experiment: The First Five Years of Twin Oaks Community*. The experimental community did not try to rear children, and it did require that its members work outside in order to earn enough money so that the group could survive. But they tried to work out the rest of Skinner's scheme complete with managers, work credits, and the rest. The history of Twin Oaks has not been an uninterrupted story of success. Many of the participants were ill-suited by temperament to its disciplined life. But there were many rewards to life in the commune. On the whole, however, this report does not encourage a belief that Skinner's scheme offers an immediate and universal remedy for the ills of a troubled world.

6. Is there an experiment in communal living in your area? If so, it probably would not discourage a serious-minded visitor. If you can spend some time with the group, analyze its successes and failures in the terms used in this chapter. That is, look at the nature of social controls and the success with which they are exercised. What view of human nature is implied in the social organization of the group? How does it respond to stress?

13
Some Attempts at New Social Forms

The human race has survived by adapting. It began as a hunting and food-gathering species. First of the major adaptations was the shift from this stage, the Paleolithic, to an age of agriculture, animal husbandry, and village life, called the Neolithic or New Stone Age because of the technological change to polished stone implements. This revolution was responsible for the emergence of the human race as a major species on earth; the availability of a stable food supply and fixed dwelling places meant that surpluses could be accumulated and complex social orders and an expanding population could be supported. There have been other adaptations, although few were so profound. The shift to urban life began early as a reaction to the need for trading places. Classical civilizations created a new kind of social organization that united towns and villages over a large area into kingdoms and empires. The massive remains of classical architecture still astound the visitor to Egypt, Crete, or Yucatan. More recently, the technological and social developments that led to the shift from the feudal system of the Middle Ages to the expanding economy of contemporary industrial Europe represent fundamental change on a great scale.

The implication of this discussion is that we *are* capable of adaptation; our species has shown the flexibility necessary to change its way of life in response to new circumstances. At the moment, the most important question before mankind is whether we will again be able to adapt to the changed environmental conditions created by the explosion of our numbers, the imminent exhaustion of our supplies of readily available energy, and the dangers posed by the destructiveness and pollution inherent in advanced technology.

Attempts at change are often called "experiments." In the loose sense in which an experiment is a trial of something new, this is appropriate. But in the sense in which scientists use the term, there are no genuine experiments in social orders. A real experiment requires that the outcome of a new procedure be compared with some control procedure so that the impact of the novel can be evaluated. Further, the scientific method requires that the entities—people or objects—with which the experiment is concerned be assigned randomly to experimental or control groups. This is necessary if the effects of the new (i.e., experimental) procedure are to be distinguishable from effects due to the nature of the group or to accident. There have been virtually no social "experiments" that have met these criteria. There are no control groups. In fact, in each of the four communities we shall discuss in this chapter, unique characteristics of the particular society may be as much responsible for the current state of the social system as is the new societal form. One cannot know how much the peculiar character of contemporary China, Sweden, Israel, or Yugoslavia is due, not to the new social forms, but to historical background or accidents of climate, geography, or culture. Nevertheless, these societies are worth looking at because they have tried novel approaches to social systems. An attempt at evaluation of these novel approaches by means of the criteria we have just applied to literary and philosophical utopias should yield useful suggestions for social decisions elsewhere.

Prerequisites for Social Adaptation

Conservative forces in most societies are sufficiently powerful that relatively little change takes place unless the need is great. As I suggested in discussing social change in Chapter 5, either external forces or internal evolution can generate such needs. It is not always easy to identify the determinants of adaptation; the ecological model suggests that no one factor by itself can make the evolution of new social forms inevitable.

However, we can identify a number of factors without which new social forms are unlikely to emerge. The first of these, as I have already suggested, is an emergent need, such as the pressure of an enemy, a change in climate, the exhaustion of resources, or the desperation of a segment of society that perceives its life as inadequate. The second is the accumulation of a surplus beyond the necessities required for subsistence. The third is sufficient openness in the society so that novel forms can be proposed and considered. This does not imply that change does not sometimes arise out of violence; obviously it often does. But a *totally* closed society cannot provide the breeding ground for the forces that lead to revolution. The next and final point deals, not with the general readiness of a society for experimentation, but with the direction of the experiment; as indicated in Chapter 5, change in a society is not likely to occur except along lines already implied in the culture of that society.

The accumulation of capital as a prerequisite for social experimentation requires some further comment. Usually, societies that operate at a level beyond the most primitive produce more than they require for subsistence. The resulting savings may be used for luxury or display, as in the accumulations of gems and gold by Indian rajahs. They may support specialists in warfare who protect their fellows or engage in foreign adventures. Savings may also provide the basis for the development of art and science. And lastly, savings may be invested in the training of technicians and the accumulation of land, raw materials, and productive machinery. All of these uses were enormously stimulated by the development of money, a medium of exchange that can be stored and then used later to call on resources of labor, skill, and materials.

Social experimentation of any kind is dependent on the availability of capital accumulations. If a community must spend virtually all its energies merely to survive, it has neither the ability nor the inclination to try new ways of organizing and carrying out its activities. Only where trained talent (which is a kind of capital) and some surplus are available is experimentation possible. Thus an evaluation of attempts at novel social forms must include an assessment of the techniques used by each community for the accumulation of capital.

The Nineteenth Century

Although one does not often think of it in these terms, the nineteenth century was one of the great transitional eras in human history.

In some ways, the changes introduced during that epoch match those in the shift from Paleolithic to Neolithic culture that we discussed earlier. Most impressive physically were the artifacts of the new industrial civilization—the factories, railroads, steamships, cities. But in some ways, a more profound change came in the attempt in much of Western Europe and North America to create a self-regulating economic and social system, one in which governmental and other societal controls would be minimal and in which the "invisible hand" (to use the term of the famous eighteenth-century British economist Adam Smith) of mutual self-interest operating in a market economy would promote universal happiness.

A school of economic and social thinkers in England called "Manchester liberals," followers of Smith and his fellow economic philosophers David Ricardo and James and John Stuart Mill, provided philosophical support for the concept of a self-regulating social order. Their ideal community had no place in it for the rigid controls over most aspects of life exercised by the rulers of the seventeenth- and eighteenth-century states whose *mercantile* system required governmental regulation of virtually all economic activity. To the liberals, the best government was the one that governed the least; their point of view can still be heard among present-day conservatives.

But these ideals did not survive the test of reality. From Bismarckian Germany to the post–Civil War United States, communities discovered that intervention in the free operation of society was necessary to meet social needs. Sometimes this intervention was directed towards mitigating the miseries suffered by the least-powerful elements of society, the mass of the poor, especially the helpless women and children. Laws regulating the conditions under which children could work were among the earliest limitations on the purely self-regulating character of nineteenth-century society. In other kinds of intervention government helped in the accumulation of capital by winning colonies, with their sources of cheap raw materials and labor, or by sealing off borders to foreign competition through tariffs and other restrictions on trade. One of the more comic aspects of these developments was the passion with which both social legislation and imperial or protectionist adventures were attacked in the name of liberalism by groups willing to support departures from ideological purity for their own benefit. Neither the businessmen who protested social reform nor the reformers who protested tariffs or governmental subsidies to business saw the incongruities in their positions.

Although the major social experiment of the nineteenth century was the attempt to create a liberal, self-regulating economic and social system, the costs of that attempt to the poor and powerless soon led to movements in the opposite direction. Some of these were limited to attempts to reform the existing system, others revolved around political action in which the "have nots" were organized to work for fundamental change. A few hardy souls attempted totally new social organizations in isolated settings. Followers of the Comte de Saint-Simon and François Fourier in France or of William Owen in Britain gathered their forces, bought or rented land, and tried to set up experiments in communal living. Other experiments, like those of an American religious community called the Shakers, built on the two thousand years of experience of the monastic orders; these groups combined religious and social motives in their undertakings. Almost all the communal groups expressed a profound rejection of the individualism of the larger society in the nineteenth century. Their members were moved by a yearning for cohesiveness, for the mutual support that can be obtained from a community of kindred spirits. Most of the communal experiments were unsuccessful. The experience of Brook Farm (the Transcendentalist community of Bronson Alcott and his friends from among the philosophers and writers of Concord, Massachusetts) showed that the hard work of subsistence agriculture was far less attractive than intellectual specu-lation. Where tight discipline was exerted, either by personally force-ful leaders or through shared religious enthusiasm, the communities lasted. However, even the most stable, such as the Shakers or the Oneida colony in New York State, did not survive far into the twenti-eth century in their original form.

Some Background for Twentieth-Century Experiments

The twentieth century has been marked by wide disorders and social disorganization. The sources of this disruption of the social fabric are undoubtedly complex. It would be an oversimplification to attribute them solely to the internal tensions created by the failure of industrial society to arrive at the perfect equilibrium that was the ideal of Adam Smith. But the two world wars, the incredible brutalities of the period, the procession of social disintegration, economic depression, revolution, and genocide make a pattern of almost apocalyptic scale. If the century has been characterized by disorder, however, it has also seen many attempts at new solutions of social problems. Many of these have come directly from the stimulus provided by the disasters. The economic depression of the thirties led to the Western European experiments in social democracy; we shall discuss the experience of Sweden as an example. The social disintegration that followed warfare made possible the socialist revolution; we shall discuss the Yugoslavian and Chinese experiences as examples. And it was the horror of genocide that stimulated the withdrawal of a tiny, talented group of women and men into the communal experiment of the Israeli kibbutz.

These "experiments" (let me repeat that they are not genuine experiments in the scientific sense) provide illustrations of a variety of potential solutions to the problems of mankind. In the discussion that follows, the kind of analysis used in the last chapter to evaluate utopias will be applied to actual social innovations. The size of the social unit and the relation of primary social units to the individual is of major concern. Equally important are the balance between individual freedom and social control and the methods used to enforce societal needs. The discussion also assesses the degree to which the society is responsive to internal and external danger, the uses of technology, and the relation of the community to the environment. In general, each experiment is evaluated as a potential model for the species.

Sweden: Social Democracy in Action

Sweden is a country of dark forests and numerous lakes, stretching past the Arctic Circle. Her people have a history of poverty, of a tightly controlled class system, of isolation from the main currents of the Western world. Except for a brief period during the Thirty Years' War, Sweden was not involved in the dynastic and national conflicts that form the history of post-Renaissance Europe.

She was also little concerned with the explorations that carried European power over the globe; the only trace of early Swedish settlement in the United States is a faint memory of the arrival of Swedes on the shores of Delaware Bay in the seventeenth century.

Despite some industrialization, achieved mainly through the exploitation of forest products and the mining of steel, Sweden continued to be a depressed area during the nineteenth century. Poverty and oppression combined to drive almost a quarter of its population into emigration to the New World. Even though Sweden did not participate in World War 1, she was not immune to the postwar depression that brought unemployment and misery to so much of the Continent. By 1933, forty percent of the working population was without jobs. At that time, after the shock of a massacre of strikers, the Social Democratic party came to power and maintained stable rule into the mid-1970s.

The Sweden of the time before 1933 was characterized not only by extreme poverty but also by an enormous gap between the mass of poor workers and farmers and a tiny handful of wealthy families. Except for emigration, there was virtually no opportunity for social mobility. The contrast between the Sweden of today and that of earlier times is marked. As in Britain and other Western European countries, the economic gap between rich and poor has been considerably narrowed, but the social system of class and caste survives in differences in tastes, linguistic practice, and manners.

The Basic Organization of Society

Although Sweden in the mid-1970s had a Social Democratic government, it is not a socialist country. That is, all but a small minority of Swedish enterprises are privately owned. Still, the social system would be barely recognizable to a nineteenth-century liberal or, indeed, to an American businessman. There are a number of ways in which the independence of private enterprise is severely limited by the community. Each of these controls has developed independently; this makes the Swedish experience an ideal example of change through internal evolution.

Historically, the first major change was the creation of a system of social welfare in response to the effects of the Depression. There were many models for such a system; some of them date back to late nineteenth-century Germany, where Prime Minister Otto von Bismarck initiated unemployment and health insurance as a response to the attacks of his socialist opponents. In the years since 1933, Sweden has erected an all-encompassing structure that literally wraps each citizen in a blanket of security from cradle to grave. No person need ever fear hunger, lack of shelter, or lack of care in illness or old age.

There is a price for the system of social welfare. Each person must expend enormous effort to deal with rules, regulations, waiting lists—all the traps laid by a bureaucratic society. Even here, however, Sweden cares for the individual. The institution of the *ombudsman,* now worldwide, originated in Sweden and bears a Swedish name. The ombudsman is an official dedicated to the rights of private citizens. He or she is independent of normal governmental lines of control, although the salaries and expenses of the office are paid out of government funds. It is the ombudsman's job to investigate all complaints by individuals or groups of individuals against governmental offices or officials. The independence of the ombudsman is the most important aspect of the institution. It provides the assurance that a citizen who tangles with bureaucracy can count on having someone with power who is "neutral on his side."

A vivid picture of life in modern Sweden is given by Sture Källberg in a collection of brief life histories of ordinary people entitled *Off the Middle Way.* Although all now live in urban settings, most of Källberg's subjects have ties to the countryside. The older ones were born and brought up in small towns, the younger have grandparents or aunts and uncles there whom they visit regularly. Their needs for livelihood, housing, and health care are all met. Many live in a perpetual tangle with government bureaus, but none seems to lead a really unhappy life. For most, the year is a somewhat tedious procession of work days broken only by visits to the country or, in many instances, by vacations in the sun in the Canary Islands or Italy.

In many ways, the record of labor-management cooperation is one of the most impressive aspects of Sweden's way of life. Since 1939, negotiation of disputes between unions and management has been compulsory. One gets the feeling that the atmosphere of such negotiations is marked by a willingness on both sides to listen and understand. This is not a matter of governmental intervention; rather, it is the result of bargaining by equally strong and responsible groups.

The Role of Government

Aside from running comprehensive health and housing schemes, the government plays a major part in directing the growth of the economy by virtually controlling capital investment. The level of taxation is so high that neither individuals nor corporations can accumulate much surplus. Much of the money raised by taxation is put into governmental funds used for investments into private industry. The government also makes investments from massive pension funds that represent one of the major accumulations of capital in the country. Sweden does not seem to fear cartels or monopolies. In fact, much of Swedish industry and commerce is organized into large, privately owned combines that control one field or another. A number of these combines are parts of multinational corporations. The community controls them, however, by keeping a tight rein on sources of credit.

Just as government controls industry, it also monitors trends in manpower. There is a national labor market board that watches the employment situation carefully. When early warning signals of possible unemployment are noted, the government attempts to abort this trend by using its power over the expansion of industry through the extension of credit. The government also sets up retraining programs and gives individuals training allowances and funds for resettlement in order to achieve a goal of total employment. In this way, the adjustments and transitions that are inevitable in any dynamic society are handled with a minimal amount of social damage. For example, during the period from the close of World War II to the end of the sixties, the proportion of the population engaged in agriculture fell from twenty-five percent to about eight percent. Yet virtually no social dislocation resulted from this change.

The worldwide economic boom of the sixties found Sweden in an ideal position to provide technological services and manufactured goods to fill the ever increasing needs of both advanced and developing countries. However, there was a real shortage of manpower. As a result a large number of workers came to Sweden from Italy, Yugoslavia, Turkey, and other less-developed countries. This great influx of foreign workers was handled by an outpouring of social services, subsidized housing, and language classes. The new workers were given all the rights and privileges of Swedes, including the right of political participation. In many ways, Sweden provided a better way of life for its migrant workers than any other European country; the contrast with the shantytowns outside French cities or the cheerless barracks in Germany is marked.

Worker Participation

The best-known aspect of the Swedish "experiment," aside from the all-enveloping system of social security, is the attempt to move towards industrial democracy. Beginning in the early sixties, a number of Swedish companies, manufácturing everything from steel to office furniture, initiated administrative arrangements in which those doing the work assumed increasing control over the planning and direction of their efforts.

The Kalmar plant of the Volvo Company provides a good example of these changes. In this factory, a small number of workers, about six hundred, assemble the famous Volvo automobiles. They are organized into relatively autonomous work groups whose responsibility is to create an entire automobile. The groups control the pacing of their work and rest, the arrangement of their work spaces, the timing of operations, the supply of materials. They carry out their own inspections to assure the quality of their product. In consultation with the workers, the factory was designed to minimize noise and make available attractive rest areas. One cannot imagine a greater contrast with the inferno of an American assembly line plant.

The workers at Kalmar and other Volvo plants and at the factories of such companies as Orrefors, the makers of the famous crystals, are increasingly empowered to make the day-to-day decisions that control their lives at work. However, their power over the fundamental decisions that lead to profit or loss, to choice of technical processes, and to selection of personnel is still severely limited. In 1975 and 1976, legislation was considered that would mandate greater participation by workers in the overall planning and direction of their companies. If the proposed laws are implemented, workers' representatives will sit on the governing boards of all companies and, eventually, exercise a controlling voice. At that point, the distinction between the limited social democracy of Sweden and the full-fledged socialism of Yugoslavia will be greatly lessened. Of course, in Sweden these changes are taking place within a totally democratic framework, as are similar moves towards worker participation in plants in West Germany, Great Britain, and other European countries. It remains to be seen whether the current holders of power will yield it without protest. The next decade should provide a critical test of the possibility of democratic evolution towards a socialist state.

An Evaluation of the Swedish Experiment

What follows is, of course, mostly speculation. No truly meaningful evaluation is possible without extensive data directed towards the tests implied in the criteria for a good society. Therefore, this discussion will raise more questions than it answers. However, the criteria proposed in Chapter 11 do provide a beginning for evaluative discussion.

The Size of Units and the Scale of Life. We proposed that one of the major sources of misery in contemporary society is the enormous scale on which most activities are conducted. At work and in our neighborhoods, most of us have to operate as part of a mass of anonymous people. The result is a feeling of rootlessness and normlessness summarized in the term *anomie.*

Sweden is shifting towards a human scale of productivity in which small groups of people work together in carrying out satisfying tasks. But the transition is far from complete. In most of their interactions, Swedes operate in large social units that are far from the ideal of participatory democracy.

Probably as a compensation for the large scale of the units at work and elsewhere, Swedes tend to belong to a great many clubs. For many, the trade union provides a framework for social activity. However, reports from Sweden give the impression that many urban dwellers lead rather isolated lives. The hard winter tends to keep people indoors. Visitors comment on the lack of a bustling street life, on the absence of the cafes and restaurants that make other European countries so convivial. The people who inhabit the drab housing projects in featureless suburbs certainly do not have the kind of affiliative existence that promotes a sense of fellowship.

Freedom and Social Control. The second criterion dealt with the trade-off between individual liberty and social control. Sweden is a democratic country whose official ideology emphasizes individual freedom. The scope for individual liberty is probably greater there than in most places in the world. Swedes do drink a great deal, are notorious for a high rate of suicide, and accept a range of sexual activities that would shock a Puritan. Yet many commentators describe the Swedes as being excessively conformist.

If the country does not seem free, it may be because individuals are controlled by the subtle forces of the paternalistic community; the lines within which they act out their social roles are held firm by the system of care. In some ways, Sweden is a Skinnerian society; the individual is shaped by a generous society to behave in socially acceptable ways. Many Swedish individualists say that they would dispense with security in order to feel less stifled. At least, this is the position voiced by a fair number of the better-educated young people in contemporary Sweden.

Responsiveness. Since Sweden is a parliamentary democracy in which governmental power depends on maintaining a majority in the legislature, popular opinion can affect public policy directly. True, there was one-party rule for more than forty years. But the majority party can never ignore the public will. Indeed, in elections held in late 1976 the ruling party was ousted.

Even more important, the institution of the ombudsman provides a direct avenue of communication between the individual and social institutions. Unfortunately, many Swedes still feel the alienation and powerlessness that are so frequently described as an inevitable phenomenon of industrialized society. From the outside, Sweden looks like one of the most responsive communities in the world. It may not feel so from the inside.

Last is the question of response to signs of danger. The Swedes have brought social monitoring to a very high level. They are watching for signs of unemployment, ill health, social disruption. For the present, they seem to be able to react very flexibly, despite the built-in cumbersomeness of a democratic system.

Technology. So far as I can tell, Sweden has done relatively little to face the technological problems of industrial civilization. She is fortunate in having abundant space and natural resources and a fairly low population density. I found little evidence that Swedes are concerned with a search for new sources of energy, for ways of conquering pollution, or for reductions in the scale of industry. The work groups may be small, but Swedish industry, on the whole, is conventional in scale.

A Final Comment

As usual, it is hard to separate the characteristics that derive from social innovation from the traits that depend on Swedish culture, on the climate, on the richness of resources. If foreign workers feel a lack of warmth and caring among Swedes despite the generous provisions for social security and political rights, this may have little to do with the structural character of the social system. If Sweden does not seem to have developed much art, aside from the well-known films of Ingmar Bergman, this may be due to the national character rather than to any inhibiting effect of industrial democracy on artistic production. The issue is arguable. Some have said that the stifling effect of security does inhibit creativity. Surely one cannot prove or disprove the point with the available evidence. Many aspects of the Swedish system inspire respect. If the United States had been as careful in handling the shift of population from agriculture to the cities, we might have been spared the riots in the streets of Detroit! Sweden may not as yet be a certain model for the world, but her social innovations must assuredly be carefully watched.

The Israeli Kibbutz: A Socialist Island

The state of Israel had its origin in the aspirations of the Jewish community for a homeland. Traditionally, Jews in every part of the world have regarded themselves as originating in Palestine, the country in which the events of their holy Scriptures are set. The Jews' vague yearning for a return to their place of origin was kept alive by religious ritual; each year at the Passover celebration the phrase "next year in Jerusalem" was duly repeated. It is ironic that the realization of the dream of a return began during a period when Jews were beginning to be emancipated from the restrictions of ghetto life in Western Europe and the United States. Although many Austrian, German, and British Jews participated in the Zionist movement at the turn of the century despite the relatively favorable climate of their own countries, the major force behind the movement came from

Russian Jews, who were subject to bitter persecution not only because of the policies of the czarist government but also through random violence from the Russian people.

It was almost inevitable that a communal form of settlement should seem attractive to some of the first settlers in Palestine. They brought with them not only a sense of identity as Jews but also a moral commitment to a socialist ideal. Cooperative farming was an obvious solution to the problems of surviving on the malarial swamps or infertile deserts. At the beginning of World War I there were eleven communal groups, or kibbutzim; by 1918 there were twenty-nine. During the period of the British mandate between the two wars, the kibbutzim became centers of agricultural experimentation in ways of reclaiming the soil. The kibbutz also served as a kind of strong point, an armed camp in which the young people who came as pioneers could protect themselves from the growing hostility of the Arab population. During the disorders of World War II and its aftermath, the kibbutzim were centers for the underground defense force, the Haganah, which fought the British authorities and the Arabs and later became the nucleus of the army for the new state. After independence, the kibbutz movement expanded considerably as Jewish refugees from the Nazi terror were joined by migrants from Western countries and South Africa. The communal program was attractive to young, idealistic settlers from advanced countries; it had little appeal for the large number of migrants from the Muslim countries, who were expelled in the tragic exchange of populations that accompanied the founding of Israel.

By the beginning of the seventies, the kibbutz movement included over 86,000 people organized into 229 settlements. This represented from three to four percent of the population of the country. The members of the kibbutzim form a kind of aristocracy. They provide leadership to the country far out of proportion to their numbers. In 1973, 20 of the 120 members of the Israeli parliament, the Knesset, were from the kibbutz. Over the past ten years, one-third of the cabinet members have held membership in a kibbutz. Men from the communes move easily into positions of leadership in the army, the diplomatic corps, the government. There is a tradition of noblesse oblige: this tiny minority bore twenty-five percent of the casualties in the 1967 war! The kibbutz is something of a hothouse growth, cherished not only by Israel but, indeed, by the worldwide community of Jews. Its favored position does seem to be well earned. The kibbutz symbolizes the fierce urge for survival of the Jewish people. It provides not only political but also moral leadership.

The Organization of Life in the Kibbutz

The typical kibbutz has three hundred to five hundred members. Most communes today operate both farms and small industrial plants, although originally the major activity was agriculture. A newcomer to membership surrenders his or her personal assets, keeping only personal effects. Members have small apartments, most of which are tastefully if sparingly furnished. Most meals are taken in a communal dining hall. The food is prepared by individuals permanently assigned to the task, but serving, clearing, and dishwashing are rotated among the members. Visitors are impressed by an occasional cabinet member or general back for the weekend taking his turn at clearing tables. The members also take turns at the necessary task of standing watch.

Administration of the kibbutz is in the hands of a general meeting of all members, who gather weekly to make decisions about matters of policy. The meeting also elects the general secretary, who is the chairman of the gathering and represents the kibbutz in all but economic matters. A most responsible officer, the economic manager, is in charge of the business affairs of the community. Day-in-and-day-out management is conducted by committees that deal with economic matters, including long-term planning, education, cultural activities, and social welfare. These committees work with a secretariat consisting of elected representatives who organize the work of the farms and factories, assign tasks to individuals, and report to the committees and the general meeting on the affairs of the group. These arrangements are typical of most kibbutzim, but there are some differences among groups, depending on the degree of commitment to "pure" socialism. Some of the communes permit more private activities than others.

Many of the kibbutzim are among the most attractive places in the country. They are characterized by a profusion of flowers and lawns surrounded by orange groves. The pace of life is leisurely and the atmosphere peaceful, in contrast with the crowded, hectic air of

Israel's cities. The older settlements have recreational facilities—swimming pools, tennis courts, and playing fields—that are far more luxurious than those available to most Israelis. It is only on the frontier that barbed wire, weapons, and shelters are reminders of the history of the kibbutz as a beleaguered outpost.

Members and Outside Workers

Originally the value of manual labor was a central element of the ideology of the kibbutzim. In the earlier days, all the work in fields and workshops was carried out by the members. However, as the needs of the community for the products of the kibbutz expanded and as offers of external investment in the operations of the kibbutz increased, the pressure to hire outside workers grew irresistible. Despite the fact that the kibbutzim still maintain a socialist stance and are still officially completely egalitarian, second-class citizens who perform menial labor are almost universally employed. More often than not, these are Arabs or Oriental Jews whose level of education and technical skill is far beneath that of the members of the kibbutz. The hiring of these workers was not accomplished without agonized discussion. But in the end, ideology yielded to necessity. While the ritual clearing of dishes persists, most members are either in administrative or technical jobs or leave the kibbutz during the week for work in a university, the government, or the armed forces.

Among members, the division of labor between the sexes has changed since the early days. When the kibbutz was a frontier outpost, women carried guns, did productive work, and participated in leadership. More recently, they have retreated into more traditional women's occupations. Virtually none of the general secretaries or economic managers are women. But most of the individuals in the category defined by the kibbutz as "nonproductive work" are female. These women care for the children, handle service work in laundries and kitchens, carry out the clerical tasks. In comparison with the women among the founders, present-day women in the kibbutz perceive themselves as having little status. This is not entirely due to a conspiracy on the part of men; the glorification of child bearing and child rearing in a society whose hope for the future rests in its children has made many women welcome the traditional roles. It may be because of this system of values that women prefer to concentrate on traditional activities rather than to serve on important committees with power to make economic and social decisions.

The Rearing of Children

Of all the social innovations in the kibbutz, the methods of rearing children have received the greatest attention. Shortly after birth, the child is taken over by a communal facility in which responsibility for its nurture is in the hands of full-time child-care workers. Mothers return to their full-time jobs. Unlike the situation in Alor (see Chapter 5) this does not imply any emotional rejection by the parents. Quite the contrary—kibbutz parents are proud and loving. They spend much of their free time with their children, some of it during daily visits by the child to the family home. But the child sleeps and takes most meals away. The parents are far less important as socializing agents than as a source of affection. The job of socialization is taken over by the child-care workers and by the peer group. As the children grow up, they continue to spend some time with their families, but their fellows form a second family in which emotional ties are very close.

The central norm of kibbutz socialization is cooperation. In one experimental study, children reared in a kibbutz, when offered the opportunity to play a game cooperatively or competitively, rejected the competitive rules. In other studies, children raised in the kibbutz were found to dislike those who excelled too obviously.

Somehow, many of the products of this system of bringing up children evolve into effective army officers and industrial and governmental leaders. But it is interesting that few have become entrepreneurs in a country in which enriching oneself is far from taboo. It has been noted by many observers that the children of the kibbutz present to the world a personality characterized by emotional flatness. They seem to reject the flamboyant, outgoing temperament so typical of their parents' generation. Bruno Bettelheim, a child psychoanalyst who spent some time observing children in the kibbutz, has commented that never have there been two generations as different as these parents and children.

The value placed on cooperation and morality has both positive and negative effects. When children from the kibbutz were compared with middle-class children raised in the city, they showed a fairly high *average* level of performance on tests of academic achievement. But few of the kibbutz children were in the uppermost group. However, when children reared in a kibbutz were asked, in another study, about the attractiveness of a mildly unethical but gratifying act, they rejected the unethical act even when they did not expect to be observed. Comparable groups of children in Israeli cities, and even more, children from Russian schools, tended to give socially acceptable responses only when they thought that their behavior would be public.

In summary, the kibbutz produces highly moral young people with a strong sense of affiliation to their own group and a tendency to reject individual achievement. They have a strong love of the land and a powerful sense of obligation to the community. They also seem brusque and somewhat cold to outsiders, a manner that may hide a certain uneasiness in social interaction with unfamiliar people. Of course, no one can say, for lack of control groups, to what extent these characteristics are due to the communal method of rearing children and to what extent they are due to the fact that the children of the kibbutz are raised as members of an elite majority in a small farming community but have parents who were shaped by the experience of the ghetto, of the Holocaust, and of migration.

Evaluation

Unit Size and Social Scale. In some ways, the Israeli kibbutz is an almost perfect reflection of the utopian thinking discussed in Chapter 12. The number of members is small enough so that all can share a feeling of kinship. Almost all the activities of the kibbutz take place within a system of direct democracy. In contrast with people who live in large cities, no one need feel alienated. Yet surely some members of the kibbutz must feel oppressed by the confined social atmosphere. It is characteristic that the most talented young people leave to get advanced education. They maintain an affiliation with the kibbutz but return only for occasional visits on religious or secular holidays.

Furthermore, the kibbutz seems to require the space of the countryside; there are no urban kibbutzim. And it is doubtful whether they could have developed as they did without massive infusions of capital in the form of money for the purchase of land, machinery, and raw materials, and without the large number of trained and talented people who joined their ranks. All of these considerations argue that the kibbutz as an institution is not a practicable model for the entire world. However, it is certainly possible that some aspects of the Israeli experience of communal living might provide useful models for others. And, indeed, many people have come to Israel to participate in the life of the kibbutz in order to evaluate the possibilities of this institution in their own countries.

Forms of Control. The kibbutz, as I have indicated, is a direct democracy. Unfortunately, as with the Athenian democrary, control is in the hand of the elite who are members. The hired worker comes and goes, contributes his labor, is well paid and properly treated. But he or she takes orders. Except for that anomaly, the formal system is as free as can be imagined. The informal culture, however, is less free. As with the Swedes, members of the kibbutz conform because of an inner need to be accepted by their groups. Israeli society as a whole is lively and disorderly; it tolerates a vast range of opinions. The contrast in constraint between Tel Aviv and the kibbutz is striking; nonconformists tend to gravitate towards the former. One could argue that the kibbutz still maintains a frontier, guardpost-oriented frame of mind. If so, the conclusion would be that, within the kibbutz, despite the direct democracy and the ideology of freedom, social needs tend to outweigh individual expression.

Responsiveness. The general meeting of the kibbutz is, one is told, an extremely lively forum for debate. The institution is small enough and the members sufficiently informed and sufficiently alert so that signs of danger are readily perceived. It is hard to determine from the reports of students of the kibbutz, however, to what extent the responses to these signs of danger are flexible. Certainly, individual problems are freely aired and, within the framework of the system, receive careful attention. But some observers have suggested that the kibbutzim as a whole are rather rigid in their adherence to ideological stands that may be out of date. True, they did, with much discussion, accept the necessity for hired workers. And there is some move towards altering the child-rearing arrangements·and permitting children to sleep and eat with their parents for part of the time. Israel, one would hope, will survive the current state of hostility with its neighbors and evolve towards a state different from the garrison. It remains to be seen whether the kibbutz will be able to adapt to such a change.

Technology. The kibbutzim have been extremely ingenious in adapting sophisticated technology to minimal resources and small scales of operation. For example, their patterns of irrigation, which save water wasted in many systems, are widely imitated. Economic studies have shown that kibbutz industries are much more efficient than those in Israel as a whole, a country noted for its efficiency. If the kibbutz does provide a model, this is the area in which it lies. Actually, technicians from the kibbutzim have participated actively in Israel's program of foreign technical aid. They were welcomed by many of the less-developed countries until the events of 1973—the Yom Kippur War, the Arab oil boycott, and the growth of Arab political power—made the Israeli presence unacceptable in many areas.

A Final Comment

The Israeli kibbutz is the child of nineteenth-century idealism married to twentieth-century pragmatism. As the generation of founders dies, it is being replaced by a second generation who are products of the communal education, but who are also the result of an upbringing in a small, relatively isolated farming community. Many of the characteristics of the present generation may be typical of farmers—the conservatism, the inward turning, the love of the land, the sense of obligation that leads them to sacrifice themselves in war and to serve the community in peace. True, the growth and survival of the kibbutz have been dependent on external support. But if the future salvation of mankind depends on the revival of the social forms and technological systems of the Neolithic village, we have a great deal to learn from these disciplined, inner-directed, and abstemious people.

Yugoslavia: Self-government at the Grass Roots

A visit to Yugoslavia provides a mass of contradictory impressions. A neat, small, modern airport. Great stone walls in the Adriatic sun surrounding ancient Dubrovnik. A huge automobile assembly plant in old Serbia with miles of dreary shacks in its shadow. Shining plastic hotels on the seacoast reminiscent of Miami Beach. A road in Šumadja with few cars or trucks, a procession of men and women on foot, the woman, leading a laden donkey, a few steps behind the man. Women in traditional peasant costume working in the fields with wooden hand tools. A fashionably dressed crowd chattering in the lounges of the Belgrade Opera during intermission. School children walking miles to and from school, neatly dressed in uniforms, carrying little briefcases.

A young Muslim craftsman showing off his little place in the street of shops near the old Turkish bridge in Mostar, proud of the jewelry he makes, anxious to practice his English at the dinner table in an outdoor cafe on the banks of the river in sight of the lit-up bridge. His wife is at home, as a good Muslim wife should be. Two charming girls, just graduated from high school, elegantly clothed, hitchhiking to the family vacation place before they go off to the university to study medicine and art history. A young apprentice, thumbing a ride to a town several hundred miles away, carrying no luggage, speaking not a word of a Western language, but telling in the few words of Serbian or Russian his hearer could understand of his plans to become a skilled machinist.

The graves of Partisans, each marked by a picture of the martyred young man or woman, lining the roads. A migrant worker back from Germany, planning to open a small auto repair shop in Belgrade with his earnings at Mercedes Benz, pumping the foreign visitor for information about the cost of things in America. A huge crowd gathered on the ancient steps of a walled city on the Adriatic to celebrate Tito's birthday, listening to the chorus of children singing the songs of the revolution, to the speakers repeating the formulas, walking about indifferently. A group of highly trained medical scientists and practitioners discussing the organization of the system of health care that brings medicine at little or no cost to each citizen. In a soft-drink bar, a conversation with an acquaintance about student protest suddenly breaks off when a man in a belted trenchcoat pauses behind the seats. An interview with the profoundly scholarly dean of a public health school about the serious problems of alcoholism and smoking, about the difficulty of controlling air pollution when the cost of control is a decrease in production or employment.

And always, a memory of crowded streets, carefully tended fields, traffic jams, magnificent views of mountains, waterfalls, riverbanks, seaside. In every way a fascinating country.

Some Historical Background

The part of the Balkan Peninsula that is now Yugoslavia has been settled since the earliest times of human habitation in Europe. The native Illyrians were conquered by Rome and integrated into the Roman Empire. During the invasions by the barbarians, Slavic-speaking peoples settled in most of the area, although remnants of the original natives probably remained. The latter spoke both a form of Latin and an even older tongue that may be the ancestor of contemporary Albanian. During medieval times, some sections of the peninsula were ruled by Serbian or Croatian monarchs, and others were dominated by Venice, Hungary, or Austria. By the end of the fourteenth century, however, the southeastern part of the area, Serbia and Macedonia, had been overrun by Turkish power. This area had been culturally affiliated with Byzantium; the dominant religion was Eastern Orthodox. The four hundred years of Turkish rule that followed left the people in a primitive state. Except for a few graceful bridges and public buildings, a group of converts to Islam, and a heritage of torture and exploitation, the Turks contributed little.

The northwest of the area, Slovenia and Croatia, had a very different history. The cultural affiliation was with Central Europe and Italy, and the religious affiliation with Rome. Political power was at first held by native dynasties of Slavic-speaking rulers, then taken over in the interior by Hungary and Austria, on the Adriatic coast by Venice. Although the inhabitants of these areas felt a sense of political oppression, Venetian and Austrian rulers were far less destructive than the Turks. During the course of the nineteenth century, some of the various elements of what was later to become Yugoslavia won their freedom; Montenegro, a small mountainous area in the southeast, had always maintained its independence. The origins of World War I, or at least the igniting forces, were in the attempts of Slavic-speaking peoples to break away from the Austro-Hungarian Empire. A result of that war was the assembly of a diverse group of peoples who shared little—not even a common language—into the country of Yugoslavia under a Serbian dynasty.

After World War I, the new country moved from parliamentary democracy to dictatorship and back again. The union of socially advanced Slovenes and Croats with the less-advanced Serbs and the backward Macedonians and Albanians was an uneasy one. In both Croatia and Macedonia, separatists kept agitating for independence. At the same time, the beginnings of industrialization led to the growth of a class of industrial workers among whom a small but active Communist movement maintained a revolutionary drive.

The invasions by Germany and Italy at the start of World War II led to internal dissension. A large part of Catholic Croatia collaborated with the Germans in setting up a fascist state. The armed forces of that state, the Ustashi, carried out a horribly brutal slaughter of Serbs; the reports of death and devastation are almost too hideous to believe. Two resistance movements arose in Serbia. One, headed by Gen. Mihailovic, was tied to the monarchy and was primarily Serbian in composition. The other, the Partisans led by Tito, brought together elements of all the nationalities in the country and was built around a nucleus of prewar Communists. The Partisans accused the royalist faction of collaborating with the Germans; whether this was true or not, the royalists were unable to obtain significant support from the Western allies. The war ended in a struggle of epic character that imparted an almost mythical quality to the founding of modern Yugoslavia. Even though there was some outside support, the Partisans defeated the Germans as well as their internal rivals, leaving the country in the hands of a native Communist movement.

Transition to Socialism

Although the West had supported Tito, his first loyalty was to the Soviet Union. The model for his new socialist state was a Russian one. Beginning in 1945, he set up a standard "socialist" state on authoritarian, centralized lines. Factories and other businesses (but not land held by peasants) were confiscated, and ownership was vested in the state. Tight control was established by the party; planning on the Soviet model was instituted as rapidly as possible.

Tito's moves towards independence, especially his tentative explorations of the possibility of a Balkan federation, aroused hostility in Moscow. The increasingly paranoid Stalin viewed any sign of a second center of power in the Communist world as heresy to be extirpated. As a result, in 1948, Yugoslavia was ousted from the association of Communist parties, the Cominform. The economic ties that had formed with the Soviet Union and other socialist states were broken. The country was now on its own, except for a small amount of aid from the West.

Between 1950 and 1954, the overall organization of the country was changed from the Soviet model to a scheme that fit Tito's ideological system more closely. Ownership of factories and businesses was transferred from the state to the collective of workers affiliated with each operation. The movement towards collectivizing agriculture was suspended, although farmers were still encouraged to participate in producers' cooperatives. The Communist party, in a move towards democratization that is perceived as having great symbolic value, changed its name to the League of Communists and announced that its role was to be one of guidance rather than autocratic dictation. In actuality, the hierarchy of the party maintained control. But in many ways Yugoslavia came closer to a democratic form of social organization than any other Communist country.

During the fifties and early sixties, a continual process of experimentation produced a complex of new social forms. By means of taxes and credit systems farmers were urged to create cooperative schemes. Local governments based on rotating bodies of elected representatives began to grapple with the problems of housing, transportation, public order, and health. The economy slowly shifted from one of centralized planning to a kind of communal control. Lines of authority, which had been structured around downward movement of commands in a hierarchy, were restructured. Workers' councils assumed actual control as well as formal ownership.

All was not perfect. Even though the society was by far the most open of any of the Eastern European socialist states, class distinctions emerged rapidly. These were visible as early as the beginning of the fifties, when Tito's second-in-command, Milovan Djilas, broke with his fellow Partisans. Djilas accused them of setting up a stratified community in which a new class of party functionaries played the role of the owners and managers in the old society. As we shall see later in this discussion, this is still a pressing problem. Conflict between the advanced and backward sections of the country continued. The national government tried to equalize the various areas by concentrating investments in the southeast. But Croats and Slovenes felt exploited by this attempt at equalization; they also believed that the backwardness of the Macedonians and Serbs made investment in these regions unproductive.

Nevertheless, by the mid-sixties the country had made great progress. For a community devastated by war (one million dead out of a population of fourteen million), so backward that the per capita income had been eighty dollars a year, the changes were remarkable. A flourishing industry and agriculture had been built. Thousands of miles of roads had been laid down. Towns had been completely reconstructed in accord with modern approaches to urban planning. Yugoslavia, independent of both West and East, was a leader in the Third World. The country's pride in accomplishment was certainly justified.

The Reforms of 1965 and Their Consequences

The social and economic system that gradually evolved out of Yugoslavia's attempt to create a democratic socialism was not without problems. There was a built-in tendency towards low productivity in industry. The social order was committed to human concerns and a relaxation of the pressures from secret police and party. Although this improved the psychological quality of life, there were few rewards for working hard. No one was ever fired or seriously disciplined. Workers' councils mandated increases in wages without forcing compensatory improvements in output. The results were rising prices, consistent deficits in the international balance of trade, and a danger of national bankruptcy. It became clear to all that something had to be done to make efficiency and productivity central goals. The Soviet pattern, which used a combination of individual incentives to workers, planning at the top, and rigid discipline, was unacceptable.

In a bold move unprecedented among the socialist states, Yugoslavia effected a radical change in its economic system in 1965. All producing organizations were cut loose from central planning and set free to achieve maximum profit or to risk loss. Workers' councils were given the right to dispose of income above the level of expenses; they were also informed that they would not be rescued if the company's losses were so great that they could not convince the banks to extend credit. Suddenly all stood to gain from efficiency, to lose from lack of productivity.

The result was a massive shift in economic and social practices.

A million workers were declared redundant by their companies and released. Fortunately, this event coincided with a period when the West was suffering from a severe shortage of labor. Most of the newly unemployed were able to migrate to West Germany, Sweden, Holland, or Austria. The money they sent back to their families helped to stimulate the Yugoslavian economy and reverse the unfavorable balance of trade.

At present the country is still operating under the new system. The initial boom shows no signs of abating; traffic jams continue as floods of foreign tourists visit the beaches and mountains. Those who have jobs are buying automobiles, taking vacations in August, eating well. But the inflation is more severe than in almost any other country in Europe, except perhaps Italy. Unemployment is a serious problem, since many expatriate workers have had to return as the worldwide depression of the seventies erased their jobs. It would take an economic Nostradamus to predict the outcome.

The Organization of Yugoslav Life

The Public Domain and Private Enterprise. There are three kinds of economic activity. The first is carried out by government and consists of the usual public services. The second and largest sector consists of communally owned industry and trade directed by worker self-management. The third sector is privately owned business and agriculture.

The country is organized into republics and autonomous regions (Slovenia, Croatia, Serbia, etc.). These, in turn, are divided into communes, which form the local governmental apparatus in both urban and rural areas. As is usual in Europe, the national government controls education, but most other public services are handled at the level of the commune.

Most communally owned enterprises are autonomous; the workers' councils that direct them are elected. The councils hire managers to provide technical leadership. When a person is hired by a company, he or she automatically becomes a voting member of the organization, eligible to participate in the election of the workers' council and to share in profits.

The third segment of the economy, private enterprise, is rigidly controlled. Business for profit is considered to be a necessary evil and tolerated for the benefits it brings. But no individual entrepreneur may hire more than five employees. The level of taxation on private business is very high, as it is for farmers who are not members of co-operatives. Still there are many thousands of small businesses; their presence means that Yugoslavs can have access to restaurants, barber shops, shoemakers, TV and auto repairmen—amenities not available up to now in the other socialist countries.

Worker Self-Government. To a student of novel social forms, the most interesting aspect of Yugoslav life is the attempt at worker self-government. The philosophical basis for workers' councils has been explicitly stated by governmental leaders as well as by social scientists. It is that authority in a socialist state ought not to come from the top; it should reside in the people who actually do the work. If the Marxist ideal of a stateless society is ever to be realized, forms of social control must be evolved that permit spontaneous and free participation by all in the direction of society. There is no place in a true socialist state for the arrogance of power; a revolution that merely replaces an old bureaucracy with a new one is a travesty. To Yugoslav social theorists, official statements about the ownership of the means of production are meaningless unless the *control* of production is in the hands of the producers.

The system initiated in 1965 permits progress towards Marx's ideal of a community of self-governing associations because it separates decisions based on values from technical decisions. The latter must be based on information and technical expertise. They obviously must be in the hands of trained managers and technicians. But wherever considerations of values arise, the technical staff must answer to the workers' councils. Thus, a decision to replace machinery is partly technical, but it also involves the assessment of the relative worth of new machinery against other expenditures. An informed workers' council, ideally, should decide whether the company needs the new machinery more than child-care facilities for working mothers, housing, or centers for recreation. All of these must be balanced against the temptation to use surplus funds to increase wages.

The mechanism of the market, by providing profits and losses, indicates the success or failure of technical decisions and also offers incentives for efficiency without the potential for exploitation inherent in private ownership of the means of production. The market operates through the rise and fall of prices in a competitive system; prices are affected by the supply of money (the more money is available, the more people can bid up the prices of desirable goods). They are also affected by demand for consumer and capital goods and by productivity (i.e., goods in short supply become more expensive).

The community as a whole shapes the direction of society through tax structures and through the manipulation by banks of credit for expansion or for support during periods of temporary loss. Lastly, the community draws on the economy for something the Yugoslavs prize highly, which they call the *social product*. This consists of expenditures on health, education, public order, art, national defense—costs not controlled by the free market.

How Does the System Operate? The ideals described by a noted Yugoslav writer, Branko Horvat or by the papers presented at the national congress of self-managers sound magnificent. But the realization of these ideals is not without its problems. I shall begin by describing some of the operations of workers' councils and then go on to the broader issues of social planning and policy raised by the new system.

Membership in workers' councils is usually rotated; virtually everyone is expected to take a turn. Some people enjoy the participation in discussions of the organization's operations; others find them a waste of time. In one study by a Yugoslav psychologist, members of workers' councils were asked how much influence they felt they had over policy. Not surprisingly, managerial and technical workers reported a higher level of control than production or service workers. Many of the latter felt that their participation was purely for show. The relation between councils and managers is a perpetual headache. Managers are much more influential than their legal status suggests. Since they have access to information, and tend to be fluent and articulate, they often overwhelm the less informed among the council's members. Even more important, the managers have contacts with the all important banks and often can bring to bear informal influences from the party and from government.

One of the most vivid studies of the interaction of workers' councils and managers was reported by Ichak Adizes, a Yugoslav-speaking Israeli. He carried out an investigation of the activities of two organizations that manufacture textiles. One of these had a young, energetic, technically outstanding manager. In this company the workers' council was a passive group; it met briefly, listened to reports, and then acted as a rubber stamp. Authority clearly flowed downward. Planning was quick, but the plans were often adhered to rigidly since the prestige of the manager was involved in them, and the exchange of information and free exercise of judgment that are ideal in a governing body did not take place. One result was an impasse with a group of workers, which led to a strike. The other company had a very active workers' council and an older, less-trained manager. The meetings of the council were rowdy, dominated by vocal production and service workers. Authority was clearly horizontally diffused. But the intense involvement of the workers—especially the senior, skilled craftsmen—in the second company was in marked contrast to the passive character of the working force in the first.

In some ways the differences between these two companies are analogous to the differences in communication patterns between wheel and circle in the laboratory study described in Chapter 8. And the consequences are similar. The wheel is quick to operate, dependent on the central person, effective in handling routine. The circle is slow, provides satisfaction to the members, permits creative solutions.

Adizes describes several instances of major decisions in a number of other companies. In one, a textiles firm shifted from the use of natural fibers to the use of synthetics. The shift was initiated by the managers in response to the demands of the export market; there was much evidence that new kinds of synthetic materials would sell well. The other was a change in which each machine was tended by fewer workers, thus permitting the addition of new shifts so that the same number of workers and machines could produce more goods. In both instances, the change occurred only when a general feeling permeated the company that "it is time to do something." The feeling arose after a great deal of discussion and much input of information by technical people. Before the change could be made, a general consensus had to be established. As I have indicated, the first company was characterized by orderly meetings in which people listened. Their conservatism was overcome from above and, after much pressure, change was implemented. Long-range plans were adopted more quickly in the first company than the second. However, Adizes reports that the worker members of the council in the second company showed an extraordinary concern and knowledge in economic matters. New plans could be initiated from below. Although there was much conflict and jockeying for position among the various units in the company, the end result was a strong and stable organization. The two companies represent opposite extremes on the polarity between the flexibility and speed of centralized authority and the depth of commitment of a democratic, horizontal social structure.

How do these two kinds of organization fare under the new system? Unhappily, the strengths of each are needed, but the weaknesses of each may be profoundly handicapping. The reform in 1965 stressed a number of goals. First was the downgrading of production for its own sake; companies had to sell what they made. The second was an emphasis on efficiency, sales, profit. The third was the necessity for eliminating surplus workers, which created a conflict between social values and efficiency. Next was the shift from the certain world of centralized planning to the uncertainties of a market economy. This meant that both workers and managers had to become sophisticated in economic and technological matters. The outcomes of their decisions directly affected their pocketbooks.

One result of the change was that the position of the hired manager has become even more difficult than it had been before. He must continuously walk a tightrope between assertion of authority and persuasion. If he does not assert himself, he may have to stand by helplessly while decisions are taken that he knows will have disastrous outcomes. If he asserts himself too much, he may be fired. And some managers have been fired, especially if their policies have led to strikes.

The necessity for technical change and adjustment makes the centralized control characteristic of Adizes's first company desirable. But the hard decisions that must be taken require the second company's kind of communal involvement. One of the most perceptive observers of Yugoslavia is an American writer, David Tornquist, whose *Look East, Look West* is a beautiful example of nontechnical social science. Writing about strikes in a recent article in the journal, *Working Papers* (see references), he points out that the peculiar character of Yugoslav socialism is illustrated nicely by the ambivalent attitude of its leaders towards strikes. Officially, walkouts are illegal, or at least are not specifically legitimized by legislation. But they are condoned. They tend to take the form of quick job actions, rarely lasting more than a few hours or a day or two. In almost every instance, the company yields to the strikers' demands. There seems to be a general recognition that the very occurrence of strikes points to the inability of the formal mechanism of workers' councils to deal with grievances in every instance. When workers are too impatient to wait for the interminable discussions that are required for most decisions, or when one group of workers feels that it has been treated unfairly, the result is a walkout. That strikers are not dealt with harshly and summarily is a reflection of the open character of Yugoslav society. That workers feel the need to strike at all argues the inadequacy of self-management. Of course, strikes are probably more likely in centralized than horizontal organizations. But the efficient operations characteristic of centralized organizations are often necessary. If Yugoslavia is to adapt to the strains caused by inflation, increased unemployment, international tension, and internal conflict among its component groups, both the quick response of the centralized structure and the deep involvement of the horizontal structure will be needed. Resolution of the differences between these seemingly incompatible structures may be necessary for the success of the Yugoslav social experiment.

Further complicating the situation is the failure to move towards a genuinely classless society. Horizontal structure does require a feeling on everyone's part of a stake in the community and of equality both in treatment and in opportunity. Yet the gap between prosperous and poor has widened rather than narrowed during the sixties and seventies. Students in institutions of higher education are almost all sons and daughters of professionals, governmental or party functionaries, or managers. An index figure reflecting standard of living is almost ten times as high for Slovenia, the most prosperous region, as for the backward areas of Macedonia and the Kosmet. A potentially hostile Soviet Union, anxious to wipe out heresy, waits to pick up the pieces if there should be internal trouble. Unemployment is growing. It will take all the talent and ingenuity at the community's command to handle the emergency.

Evaluation

Unit Size and Scale of Operation. The representative democracy of communes, workers' councils, and farm cooperatives provides something approaching a human scale. Unfortunately, the country as a whole is still committed to the growth of large enterprises in the industrial, if not the agricultural, sector. Many corporations are national in scope. I have read of instances in which the workers' council of a branch of a national corporation has proposed actions satisfactory to the people it represents, only to be overruled by the council for the corporation as a whole. The latter must, of necessity, be remote from the workplace. Similarly, local institutions are often overruled by national government in the name of communal unity; this is especially true where there is any suspicion of separatism. It remains to be seen whether the country can continue to operate by means of group participation in units of a limited size.

Modes of Control. Is Yugoslavia a free society? The political and ethnic dissidents in jail would hardly say so. But an outsider should hesitate before criticizing a country for repression when the forces of destruction are so tenuously balanced against those of survival. The Yugoslav ideology envisions a social structure as close to a pure democracy as can be achieved in an industrial society. There are no political parties per se; the ruling Communist group calls itself a league rather than a party. There are, as we have seen, many elements of democratic institutions. Yet the reality of present-day Yugoslavia is that it remains an autocracy in which freedom operates on the sufferance of one man, Marshal Tito, and can be extended or withdrawn as he sees benefits or dangers.

At the moment, there is little freedom of dissent. The University of Belgrade, nominally as autonomous as all other organizations, was forced by governmental and party pressure to suspend from their jobs six world renowned professors of philosophy because they had engaged in social criticism. Discussions of strikes and other social disorders are less open than they were five years ago. Movements towards autonomy in Croatia have been vigorously suppressed. Whether the atmosphere will shift towards greater freedom if the current state of emergency is relieved is problematic. But there have been times when discussion was more free than it is now, when philosophy, art, and social science could express individual positions. One can hope that this atmosphere will return.

Responsiveness. Any group that could react as swiftly and completely to social danger as Yugoslavia did in the crises of 1948 and 1965 must be considered highly responsive. However, there are serious limitations to the current potential for responsiveness. The press is hardly free. Nor are the arts. The universities seem to be much less open for free discussion than they were some time ago. This means that the community cannot always gather the information necessary for response to danger.

Technology. Yugoslavia has passed through the first stages of an industrial revolution in the years since World War II. She accomplished the massive accumulation of capital necessary for this with relatively little suffering to her people. There is a marked contrast with the horrors of industrialization in nineteenth-century England described by Marx and Engels and vividly portrayed in Dickens's novels. The other socialist states, Russia in the 1930s for example, have had to carry out violent repressions in order to exact the savings necessary for industrialization from their populations. Yugoslavia escaped this necessity partly because of foreign investment, partly because of the earnings of emigrants and the spending of tourists, and partly because a frugal population was willing to save. Some of the alienation that Ellul describes as an inevitable accompaniment to industrialization was avoided by the involvement of individual workers through worker self-management. But the fact that capital accumulation has been fairly easy up to this point does not save the country from the necessity for continuing along this path, since the expectations of the population are for an ever rising standard of living.

Unfortunately, Yugoslavia has not been able to live lightly on the land. The air pollution in her cities is so great that they are barely habitable. Ten years ago one family in one hundred owned an automobile; today it is one in seven. The traffic jams on the roads provide visible evidence of this change. Belgrade and Zagreb are surrounded by miles of highrise housing with severely limited amenities. There are many huge factory complexes. True, some of the new towns are well planned. But a world looking beyond industrial civilization for alternate ways of organizing life would find little to study in Yugoslavia.

A Final Comment

It is hard to evaluate the Yugoslav trial of democratic socialism. The successes and the failures are influenced by the local circumstances, the tensions among the constituent peoples, the pressure of Russia on one side and of emigrés committed to the old regime on the other. Many observers develop a great feeling of attachment to this fascinating country. Partly it is due to the richness of the folk art, the beauty of the country, and the liveliness of the people. But in large part it is based on a feeling that Yugoslavia is the world in miniature. Like the rest of the planet, it has to fight a heritage that threatens at every moment to make it fly apart. The history of brutality and oppression, the hostility among peoples who speak the same tongue but have long memories of religious and political warfare, the differences between poor and prosperous regions, the pressure of limited resources on a growing population are all analogous to the forces that make the future of the whole race seem dim. But the creativity, the energy and resourcefulness make one hope, not only for Yugoslavia, but for all of us.

China: The Ultimate in Social Control

The Han peoples, whom we call Chinese, have had a continuous history of occupation in their extensive domains in Asia for many thousands of years. For most of this time, the vast majority of Chinese lived as peasants, cultivating land owned by a small group of landlords and managing a bare existence. Their lives were little affected by the comings and goings of rulers as one dynasty succeeded another. Far more important than changes in government were the frequent disasters caused by flood or drought.

In the cities, an advanced culture arose; the art and technology were far beyond those in most other areas in the world. The administration of the great empire was in the hands of a meritocracy, a class of scholars chosen by competitive examination. Almost all Chinese were tightly bound into extended families. The authority of elders in the family, landlords and merchants, government officials, and, at the end of the chain, the emperor, was based on a quasi-religious consensus derived from the works of Confucius.

Although China was ruled by foreign dynasties, the Mongols and the Manchus, for much of the past thousand years, the social system remained remarkably stable. In the nineteenth and early twentieth centuries, however, under foreign pressure first from Europeans and later from the Westernized Japanese, the orderly structure of Chinese society began to disintegrate. The history of China in the first half of the twentieth century is darkened by man-made as well as natural disasters; the exploitation by Europe and the United States was matched by the brutalities of the Japanese occupation. Shortly before World War I, the empire was overthrown. The republic that followed soon splintered into regions dominated by warlords, many of whom were little more than brigands. During the twenties, two national movements arose, one conservative, the other Communist. After the two came into conflict, Western support was given to Chiang Kai-shek, the leader of the conservative forces. A native Communist movement, taking Marx and Lenin as totemic figures, was able to foster a spirit that was both revolutionary and nationalist. The movement, in contrast to the one in the Soviet Union, was based in the peasantry rather than in the industrial workers of the cities. Despite the aid the conservatives received from the United States during and after World War II, the ability of Chiang Kai-shek and his party to unite the country was destroyed by corruption and inefficiency. In the end, Mao Tse-tung and the Communist party triumphed because of the weakness of their opponents as well as the inner strength of their own movement. By 1949, the entire country was in Communist hands.

For the purposes of this discussion, several stages in the next twenty years are worth describing. The first stage of the new Communist era was marked by nationalization of industry and commerce and confiscation of large landholdings. The old class of landlords, merchants, and bankers was wiped out, in large part quite literally. Mass trials were held before huge crowds of people; shouted death sentences were carried out immediately by firing squads. In the beginning, the Soviet Union provided aid in the form of machinery, expertise, and loans. During the latter part of the fifties, however, Soviet support was gradually withdrawn, and by the early sixties China and the Soviet Union were bitter enemies. The development of the new China had to proceed with virtually no assistance from abroad. At first, the Soviet model was accepted, and attempts were made to collectivize agriculture. The focus of the country's efforts was on industrialization on a large scale. The break with Moscow led to a shift towards agricultural development through communal forms.

The late fifties saw two major developments. The first was a brief period of free discussion when Mao announced that his policy was to "let a hundred flowers bloom." This resulted in such an outpouring of sentiment negative towards the policies of the regime that free expression was rapidly ended by severe repression. Mao also initiated a radical departure from the Soviet model in his "Great Leap Forward." This program was based on the need for intensive and rapid expansion of productive facilities without external aid; the goal was to be accomplished by intensive development of small-scale industry. For example, steel was to be made in tiny backyard furnaces with charcoal as fuel. The concept was admirable, but the technology was not sufficiently developed; the "experiment" of the Great Leap Forward was quietly abandoned.

The next major upheaval occurred in the mid-sixties with the "Cultural Revolution." This began with an attack on traditional art forms, especially the highly stylized Peking Opera. It soon spread to include violent destruction of much that was old as an expression of hostility towards the past. Schools at every level closed, and hordes of young people, formed into quasi-military groups, the Red Guards, traveled over the country by train at government expense, exhorting the people to revolutionary zeal. Virtually all the leaders in the party, in industry, in the schools, and in government were subjected to harassment; elderly men who had given their lives to the Communist cause were put on trial, beaten, even killed. For a time it almost seemed as if all organized social activity had come to a halt.

A few of the old leaders managed to survive the disorder. Foremost among these was Mao's oldest associate, the premier and foreign minister, Chou En-lai. Under his direction, and with the cooperation of the Red Army, the country gradually settled down. One by one, the schools reopened, many under new direction. Technicians and managers gradually resumed control of industry and trade. The wandering Red Guards with their sixteen-year-old leaders were returned to their homes. Many were banished to rural areas.

A major reason for the upheaval had been Mao's fear that China would go the way of the Soviet Union and end as a society in which a new class of party functionaries, industrial managers, and intellectuals dominated the masses. The Cultural Revolution certainly slowed such a trend. Most intellectuals and officials were forced to undergo extensive "reeducation" that included long periods of manual labor. The necessity for periodic return to farm and workbench was made a part of the normal life pattern of all professional and technical workers. Great stress was placed on the dignity of labor. Furthermore, a trend towards greater compensation for intellectual than manual labor was reversed. And within the factories, the use of monetary rewards to spur output was abolished. Even though the excesses of the Cultural Revolution were ended, these trends survived into the early seventies.

The mid-seventies have seen a slow return to the practices of the period before the Cultural Revolution. Incentives began to be used in industry. Many of the old leaders were rehabilitated. An opening to the West was encouraged, and ties with the United States, broken during the Korean War, were reestablished. However, with the death of Chou En-lai and Mao Tse Tung, it now seems uncertain whether these trends will continue or whether there will be a return to the puritanical atmosphere of the mid-sixties. Nothing in China today can be seen with any clarity from the outside. There are long periods of apparent quiet followed by massive upheavals, such as the disorders that marked the mourning of Chou's death. As we go to press, the "conservatives" have the upper hand in China. Chairman Mao's widow, who was ascendent for a brief period after his death, has fallen from power, along with her three associates (the "Gang of Four"). The "radicals" are being purged, as scientific work and scholarship are slowly regaining momentum. Incentive pay is being discussed. But there is no assurance that another convulsive change is not in the offing.

The Social Organization of the People's Republic of China

The formal organization of the country is a pyramid at whose top is a state council. As Figure 13.1 shows, the pyramid rests on an enormous number of small groups in which each citizen finds his or her niche. These work teams and neighborhood groups are on a scale that permits some acquaintance among all the members. The structure fits the ideal described in Chapter 11; it provides face-to-face groups in which everyone can enjoy a sense of identity and of participation. Much of the work of the country revolves around these groups. The work teams in the agricultural communes not only live

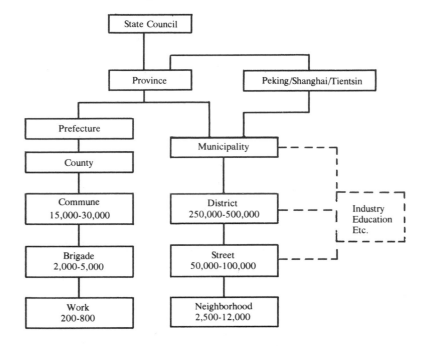

Fig. 13:1. Political subdivision in China.
Reproduced by permission of the Society for Applied Anthropology
from *Human Organization,* Vol. 3,3, 1975.

together in the same village but also are responsible for tilling a particular area. Of course, they also participate in large projects such as
the construction of roads or irrigation works with other work teams
from their brigade or commune. But it is the commune that provides
the economic direction, the resources in seed, fertilizer, and machinery, and the educational and medical facilities needed by the
workers on the farms. Much of the medical care is provided by "bare-
foot doctors," paramedical practitioners who work alongside their
patients and live in the villages.

The neighborhood units in the cities control subsistence activities such as maintenance of housing, provision of child care for
preschool children of working mothers, and development of activities

for the retired. A large number of small-scale industrial establishments are located in the neighborhoods so that many people, especially women, can work in close proximity to their homes. Large factories are similarly organized into small work units; overall their administrative structures also supply workers' needs for housing, child care, recreation, and health.

The pyramidal social organization permits rapid mobilization of the community to meet emergencies and also provides a system for tight control. Direction comes from the top; although there is a great deal of discussion, it consists primarily of vigorous self-searching to expose any reservations about the current directives of the party line. The small size and high level of cohesiveness of the groups at the bottom of the pyramid create a social atmosphere in which deviation is extremely difficult. As in Schachter's research in the laboratory (see Chapter 8), the cohesiveness of the group permits enormous pressure to be exerted on anyone who wishes to dissent. The rewards for conformity are considerable, both in the sense of community with the group and in the possibility of preferment. The punishment for dissent is equally great. The deviant is faced by a continual barrage of exhortation, with a threat of ostracism, loss of livelihood, and banishment in the background. The system is, however, available for use by forces of change. It could be mobilized by the majestic leader Mao for a Great Leap Forward or a Cultural Revolution as easily as for the maintenance of the status quo.

Child Rearing in China

The institutions devoted to the upbringing of the young are designed to produce the ideal member of a communal society. Visitors to Chinese schools at all levels have remarked on the apparently effortless achievement of perfect discipline. The emphasis is on control rather than creativity. Individuality is taboo; conformity is highly valued. Every moment of the school child's life is pervaded with ritual. There is no questioning, no discussion, no freedom for the imagination to wander. Much of the control is carried out by the group of children, with the teacher as a gentle guide. Observers stress the quiet warmth, cheerfulness, and loving character of the social atmosphere. Children are shaped, in good Skinnerian fashion, by reward rather than punishment.

As the Chinese child progresses through school, the emphasis is increasingly placed on his or her ability to participate fully and easily in the work of the group rather than on individual accomplishment. Middle-school education always includes a fairly considerable component of work in factories or fields. The curriculum may include foreign languages, basic science, and mathematics. But at every step, the stress is placed on application to the problems of life rather than on art or learning for its own sake.

Relatively few Chinese young people are permitted to go on to higher education. Periodically, all the Chinese who graduate from middle school during a single year are removed from their families and, without exception, sent to the frontiers of the country for lifetime work in farming communes. This has led to considerable friction; the educated newcomers find it hard to adjust to country living, and their families are disturbed at having children exiled to areas thousands of miles away. But the needs of the community are paramount. For all middle-school graduates, a period of work in farm or factory is required. Those who go on to higher education are chosen, not by competitive examination, but by their fellow workers. It is probable that intellectual ability plays a part in the choice, but political purity and ability to win the acceptance of fellow workers are paramount.

Chinese universities are just beginning to recover from the disturbances of the Cultural Revolution. During that period the universities ceased to function. They are now opening again, but traditional scholarship is frowned upon. Work in classrooms, libraries, and laboratories cannot be separated from the outside world; the Chinese university is no ivory tower. Both students and faculty take time for productive labor. The ideal is the use of education to solve the problems faced by the mass of people. And the ordinary worker must always be regarded as a higher authority than the book or the professor.

The Economy

China has a completely managed economy with few or no elements of a free market. She has been able, through the exercise of centralized control, to turn herself in one generation from a backward, feudal, half-starved state into a modern, industrialized community that has apparently solved the problem of providing an acceptable standard of subsistence to a huge population. Centralized controls have been used to keep the prices of food, clothing, and housing almost completely stable; alone among the countries of the world, China has not suffered inflation.

Controlled prices in a period of expanding demand usually lead to black markets, as those with money try to get a disproportionate share of goods. In China's egalitarian society, this could not happen. Periodically, as I have indicated, some of China's leaders have tried to move the country towards the use of monetary incentives to increase production. But this "capitalist road" has almost always been rejected by resurgent forces dedicated to pure Marxist-Leninist ideology. Still, there is some evidence that the withdrawal of incentives *has* led to a slackening of effort. And at times, the lure of consumer goods has seemed to beckon even the most committed of idealists. China today has a public policy that requires that social goals be made the central aspiration of every citizen's life; whether a whole country can be stimulated to ever increasing effort without individual reward remains to be seen.

Evaluation

Size of Unit. The Chinese have fully accepted the thesis that a small operating unit in which all of the members interact personally is essential to the conduct of society. The record of the past twenty years argues that they have been successful in building on such units and maintaining a tightly organized, modern industrial society. But the very size of the units makes it easy for them to be coercive; there is no place for an individual in China to hide.

Modes of Control. Both in overt discipline and in the demand for proper thought, China is a totally authoritarian community. In the polarity between the needs for social control and for individual freedom (see Chapter 11), the People's Republic places itself entirely on the side of social control. Human needs for security are abundantly fulfilled. But when people thirst for exploration, new stimulation, and creation, China must be devastatingly inadequate. The evidence that the total concentration on order has its price may be found in the sudden explosions of rage that have characterized recent Chinese history. The outbreaks of the Cultural Revolution, the recent events surrounding the funeral of Chou, and the disgrace of his successor suggest that repressed violence may be a serious problem for a totally controlled society. There are reports from refugees that the young people who rampaged through the cities during the Cultural Revolution are not passively accepting their banishment to the countryside. Of course, these reports should be discounted, since they originate in groups who have rejected the socialist creed and have fled over the borders. One can only wait for future developments to find out whether the Chinese model is a good one for human society.

Responsiveness. The Chinese society is not responsive to signs of danger. For one thing, the closed nature of the society results in blocks to the flow of information that make it difficult for most people to know what is going on. For another, Chinese leaders are so trapped in their rhetoric that they are unable to react to stress with any degree of flexibility. Another handicap has been the preoccupation with the past. In Chinese documents, one reads again and again about the heroic events of the twenties and thirties. The early years of virtually all children are spent with old people, who tend to dwell on the miseries of their lot under the landlords and merchants. While most groups develop a mythology dealing with the origins of their societies, the leaders of Communist China seem to have focused on their past with overwhelming intensity. This cannot help but limit their ability to react with openness to the future.

Technology. Traditional Chinese agriculture was incredibly skillful in utilizing all possible resources. Human and animal wastes were used as fertilizer (night soil); intensive mulching helped preserve moisture and organic content in the soil. Contemporary China builds on this ancient peasant wisdom, but adds modern techniques in dam building and drainage to prevent the regular disasters of flood and drought. The rivers have, in large part, been tamed. Small-scale machinery is brought to the villages. The Chinese press is full of reports on the ingenuity with which modest resources and superhuman labor are used to solve problems. A story which symbolizes this combination of ingenuity and energy is told all over China. The hero is the old man who moved a mountain. Everyone said that the mountain made it impossible to do what had to be done; the old man led his people to master their fate by doing what had been considered impossible. Virtually with their bare hands, they moved the mountain.

If the small-scale technology of the agricultural sector were the entire picture, China would be more advanced than almost every other country in developing techniques for survival in the postindustrial world. But unfortunately, industry in China, although it has components on a small scale, has also concentrated on the standard factory complexes—enormous, inefficient, and polluting—that are found in the rest of the planet. And the resources of fossil fuel are being exploited with as little frugality in China as elsewhere.

Final Comment

When one hears of the masses of cheerful, well-fed, busy people, the streets filled with bicycles, the absence of flies and dirt, the remarkable orderliness, China does seem to be utopia realized. But to balance this picture, one reads the violent tirades denouncing Schubert and Beethoven as bourgeois menaces. One hears of young people forced to leave their families for a lifetime in the far corners of the country. Again, medical care is universally available, and there is no trace of the Western two-class system that provides competent care to the wealthy, indifferent care to the poor. But the rigid constraints of dogma may make it difficult for the basic sciences on which medical advances depend to flourish. And always in the background are violent upheavals, the failure to provide for free examination of alternatives, the secrecy—all the inadequacies of a closed society that make it a poor prospect for survival in a dangerous world.

Is it possible that the rest of the planet could take the best of the Chinese model and reject the weaknesses? Can one have the social commitment, the orderliness, the egalitarian spirit without the constraints on freedom and the suspicion towards thought? This may, indeed, be the most important question to face the human race.

On Your Own

1. It is hard to find good, generally available materials on the societies described in this chapter. Several of the countries publish magazines in English that present the image they would like to show the world. *Sweden Today* and the *Peking Monthly Review* do not make exciting reading; the latter especially is incredibly doctrinaire. But they do give the flavor. A journal that frequently publishes critical analyses of social experiments is *Working Papers For a New Society,* published by the Cambridge Policy Studies Institute, Cambridge, Mass. If its left-wing position seems extreme, that can be

countered with William Buckley's *National Review,* which deals with many of the same issues from a conservative point of view.

2. The four critical areas used in this chapter—unit size, modes of control, responsiveness, and approach to technology—offer a useful approach for the analysis of many societies, even those that are not markedly experimental. Can you put together enough information about another country in Western Europe—The Netherlands, for example—to apply the criteria to an evaluation of its success? Or Cuba? Can you apply the criteria to an analysis of the proposals offered by your favorite political party in the United States? Or its opposition? Presumably each party platform should have something to say about the important problems described in each area.

Postlude

We are all familiar with the litany of impending disaster recited by experts in ecology—such scientists as Paul Ehrlich or Barry Commoner. They tell us that the population of the earth will approach six billion by the turn of the century. The ability to provide a decent standard of living for these billions will decrease to the danger point as our sources of fossil fuel vanish, as we pave over arable land, as we increasingly pour our treasure into unproductive armaments. Meanwhile, we pin our hopes on nuclear energy. We store the wastes from reactors in leaking containers; the bequest we are leaving our descendants requires that they guard these lethal by-products of our profligacy almost to the end of time. We pour new substances into the air, water, and soil without waiting to find out whether they are compatible with life. Meanwhile the social fabric loosens, the random violence in our cities is matched by the purposeful violence of assassination and guerrilla warfare in Ireland, Lebanon, and Argentina. Every day a new horror awaits us as we open the newspaper or watch the screen. This morning it was the news that PCB, a plastic that is used to make electrical insulation and that has been identified as a cause of cancer as well as other illnesses, has turned up in mothers' milk. And Taiwan is illegitimately building a plant to salvage weapons-grade nuclear material from the atomic power plant we gave her. She joins the Brazilians, the South Koreans, the Israelis, the Indians in approaching the day when she can make the bomb. It is all so awful that we find it hard to take it all seriously.

293

And yet the problems will not go away. Millions will be born each year in the poor countries south of the equator. Chemicals will continue to be concentrated in the fish, the birds, the crops, eventually in our own bodies. The petroleum burnt each day is irreplaceable. The armaments pile up; someone will surely be tempted to use them. The murderous hostilities flare up in one place after another.

People are working on technical solutions to the problems of the environment, searching for ways of obtaining energy from sun and wind. Groups like the New Alchemists of Falmouth, Massachusetts, and Prince Edward Island are trying to construct balanced, ecologically sound systems for fish. culture and gardening, using windmills, solar heat, and waterpower as sources of energy. The fight against environmental pollution seems a rearguard action, but today no one can release a carcinogen unchallenged. Agricultural scientists search for biologically sound methods of combating weeds, insects, and rodents so as to avoid the supposedly miraculous chemicals that have turned out to be something less than a blessing. The emissaries of the Population Council work for the adoption of contraceptive techniques in povery-stricken countries. Highly sophisticated procedures for monitoring indicators of trouble are being worked out. Groups like the Club of Rome have evolved computer simulations that permit alternate paths for society to be tested and their outcomes predicted. Man's ingenuity seems boundless. If technical solutions were adequate we would have little to fear.

But technical solutions are useless unless people are willing to apply them fully and without hesitation. From Chapter 5 on, we have seen evidence that psychological and social barriers stand in the way of such application. Actually, we know enough now to solve most of the critical problems facing the earth's population. But the solutions require changes in ourselves that we are not prepared to make. We would have to moderate our appetites, give up the absolute thinking that makes for unsolvable conflict among peoples differing in religion or political creed, learn how to free our creativity, accept new kinds of responsibilities towards each other. The tasks before us, then, are really not technical at all. They are psychological and social.

The premise of this book has been that the study of the nature of the human race as a species, of motives, of the impact of culture, and class and social groups on behavior would permit steps to be taken in finding the solutions to the social problems that face our planet. Most of the attempts at new social forms presented in the last two chapters were developed without the help of formal social science. But we were able to use the tools of the social sciences to evaluate them. The history of humanity's attempt to understand itself through the use of the methods of science is just beginning. There are few answers; but we are beginning to define some of the questions. The quick glance at this process that I have offered in this book has been prepared to convince the reader that the social sciences do offer some promise for solutions that will enable humanity to carry out technical solutions to its problems. It may very well be a race with disaster. Let us hope that there will be time.

References

Chapter 1. The Nature of Social Sciences

Bandura, Albert. Social-learning theory of identification processes. In *Handbook of socialization research and theory,* ed. David A. Goslin. Chicago: Rand McNally, 1969.

Bandura, Albert, and Walter, Richard H. *Social learning and personality development.* New York: Henry Holt & Co., 1963.

Bronowski, J. *Science and human values.* Rev. ed. New York: Harper, 1965. (Paperback)

Dahl, Robert A. *Who governs.* New Haven, Conn.: Yale University Press, 1961.

Lasswell, Harold P. *Psychopathology and politics.* New York: Viking Press, 1960.

Malinowski, Bronislow. *Sex and repression in savage society.* London: Routledge and Kegan Paul, 1927.

Odum, Eugene P. *Ecology.* New York: Henry Holt & Co., 1963. (Paperback)

O'Neill, Eugene. *Mourning Becomes Electra.* In *Plays of Eugene O'Neill.* New York: Random House, 1955.

Warner, W. Lloyd, and Lunt, Paul S. *The social life of a modern community.* New Haven, Conn.: Yale University Press, 1941.

Chapter 2. On Scientific Method

Allport, G. W. The historical background of modern social psychology. In *The Handbook of Social Psychology,* ed. G. Lindzey and E. Aronson, vol. 1, 2nd ed. Reading, Mass.: Addison-Wesley, 1968.

Beals, R. L., and Hoijer, H. *An introduction to anthropology.* 3rd ed. New York: Macmillan Co., 1965.

298 / A CITIZEN'S GUIDE TO THE SOCIAL SCIENCES

Boulding, K. E. *The meaning of the twentieth century: The great transition.* New York: Harper, 1964.
Braithwaite, R. B. *Scientific explanation. A study of the function of theory, probability, and law in science.* New York: Harper, 1953.
Bronowski, J. *Science and human values.* Rev. ed. New York: Harper, 1965.
Cohen, M. R., and Nagel, E. *An introduction to logic and scientific method.* New York: Harcourt Brace, 1934.
Coulson, W. R., and Rogers, C. R., eds. *Man and the science of man.* Columbus, Ohio: Charles E. Merrill, 1968.
De Grazia, A. *Politics and government. Political behavior,* rev. ed., vol. 1. New York: Collier, 1962.
Gouldner, A. W. *The coming crisis of western sociology.* New York: Basic Books, 1970.
Krech, D.; Crutchfield, R. S.; and Balachey, E. L. *Individual in society: A textbook of social psychology.* Hightstown, N.J.: McGraw-Hill, 1962.
Kuhn, Thomas S. *The structure of scientific revolutions.* Chicago: University of Chicago Press, 1962.
Lundberg, G. A.; and Schrag, C. C.; Larsen, O. A.; and Catton, W. R., Jr. *Sociology.* 4th ed. New York: Harper, 1968.
Madge, J. *The origins of scientific sociology.* New York: Free Press, 1962.
Wann, T. W., ed. *Behaviorism and phenomenology: Contrasting bases for modern psychology.* Chicago: University of Chicago Press, 1964.
Ward, Barbara, and Dubos, Rene. *Only one faith.* New York: Norton, 1972.
Watson, W. H. *On understanding physics.* New York: Harper, 1959.

Chapter 3. Biology and Behavior

Ardrey, R. *The territorial imperative.* New York: Atheneum, 1966.
Barnett, S. A. *Instinct and intelligence: Behavior of animals and man.* Englewood Cliffs, N.J.: Prentice-Hall, 1967.
————. On the hazards of analogies. *Man and aggression,* ed. M. F. A. Montagu, p. 18-26. New York: Oxford University Press, 1968.
Critchley, M. The evolution of man's capacity for language. In *Evolution after Darwin, The Evolution of Man,* Vol. 2, ed. S. Tax, pp. 289-308. The evolution of man, Vol. 2. Chicago: University of Chicago Press, 1960.
Eibl-Eibesfeldt, I. *Ethology: The biology of behavior.* New York: Holt, Rinehart & Winston, 1970.
Ewer, R. F. *Ethology of mammals.* London: Logos Press, 1968.
Gorer, G. Man has no "killer" instinct. In *Man and aggression,* ed. M. F. A. Montagu, pp. 27-36. New York: Oxford University Press, 1968.
Hallowell, A. I. Self, society, and culture in phylogenetic perspective. In *Evolution after Darwin, The Evolution of Man,* Vol. 2, ed. S. Tax, pp. 309-72. Chicago: University of Chicago Press, 1960.

Jones, F. R. H. *Fish migration.* London: Edward Arnold, 1968.
Kuo, Zing-Yang. *The dynamics of behavior development.* New York: Random House, 1967.
Lorenz, K. *On aggression.* New York: Harcourt, Brace & World, 1963.
―――. *Evolution and modification of Behavior.* Chicago: University of Chicago Press, 1965.
Montagu, M.F.A. The new litany of "innate depravity," or original sin revisited. In *Man and aggression,* ed. M. F. A. Montagu, pp. 3-17. New York: Oxford University Press, 1968.
―――, ed. *Man and aggression.* New York: Oxford University Press, 1968.
Morris, D. *The human zoo.* New York: McGraw-Hill, 1969.
Pfeiffer, J. E. *The emergence of man.* New York: Harper and Row, 1969.
Schneirla, T. C. Instinct and aggression. In *Man and aggression,* ed. M. F. A. Montagu, pp. 59-64. New York: Oxford University Press, 1968.
Scott, J. P. That old-time aggression. In *Man and aggression,* ed. M. F. A. Montagu, pp. 51-58. New York: Oxford University Press, 1968.
Stevenson, H. W.; Hess, E. H.; and Rheingold, H. L., eds. *Early behavior: Comparative and developmental approaches.* New York: Wiley, 1967.
Tax, S., ed. *Evolution after Darwin, The Evolution of Man,* Vol. 2. Chicago: University of Chicago Press, 1960.
Wilson, Edward O. *Sociobiology, the new synthesis.* Cambridge, Mass.: Harvard University Press, 1975.

Chapter 4. Motives

Atkinson, J. W. *Motives in fantasy, action, and society.* Princeton, N.J.: D. Van Nostrand Co., 1958.
―――. *An introduction to motivation.* Princeton, N.J.: D. Van Nostrand Co., 1964.
Freud, S. *The basic writings of Sigmund Freud.* New York: Modern Library, 1938.
Goldman, R.; Jaffa, M.; and Schachter, S. Yom Kippur, Air France, dormitory food, and the eating behavior of obese and normal persons. *Journal of Personality and Social Psychology,* 1968, 10:117-23.
Gurin, P.; Gurin, G.; Lao, R. C.; and Beattie, M. Internal-external control in the motivational dynamics of Negro youth. *The Journal of Social Issues,* 1969, 25:29-53.
Hall, C. S. *A primer of Freudian psychology.* New York: New American Library, 1954.
McClelland, D. C., ed. *Studies in motivation.* New York: Appleton-Century-Crofts, 1955.
McClelland, D. C.; Atkinson, J. W.; Clark, R. W.; and Lowell, E. L. *The achievement motive.* New York: Appleton-Century-Crofts, 1953.
Nisbett, R. E. Taste, deprivation, and weight determinants of eating behavior. *Journal of Personality and Social Psychology,* 1968, 10:107-16.

Rotter, J. B. Generalized expectancies for internal versus external control of reinforcement. *Psychological Monographs,* 1966, 80:1-28.

Schachter, S. Obesity and eating. *Science,* 1965, 150:971-79.

Schachter, S.; Goldman, R.; and Gordon, A. Effects of fear, food deprivation, and obesity on eating. *Journal of Personality and Social Psychology,* 1968, 10:91-97.

Schachter, S., and Gross, L. P. Manipulated time and eating behavior. *Journal of Personality and Social Psychology,* 1968, 10:98-102.

Chapter 5. Culture and Behavior

Banton, M., ed. *The relevance of models for social anthropology.* London: Tavistock Publications, 1965.

Barnouw, V. *Culture and personality.* The Dorsey Series in Anthropology and Sociology, ed. R. M. Williams, Jr. Homewood, Ill.: Dorsey Press, 1963.

Bennett, J. W., and Wolff, K. H. Toward communication between sociology and anthropology. In *Current anthropology,* pp. 329-51. ed. W. L. Thomas, Jr., A supplement to *Anthropology Today.* Chicago: University of Chicago Press, 1956.

Brown, R. *Words and things.* New York: Free Press, 1958.

———. *Social psychology.* New York: Free Press, 1965.

Cohen, Y. A. Culture as adaptation. In *Man in adaptation: The cultural present,* ed. Y. A. Cohen, pp. 40-60. Chicago: Aldine Publishing Company, 1968.

Cohen, Y. A., ed. *Man in adaptation: The cultural present.* Chicago: Aldine Publishing Company, 1968.

Eggan, F. Social anthropology and the method of controlled comparison. In *Cultural and social anthropology. Selected readings,* ed. P. B. Hammond, pp. 465-80. New York: Macmillan Co., 1964.

Firth, R. *Elements of social organization.* Josiah Mason Lectures delivered at the University of Birmingham, England. Boston: Beacon Press, 1951.

———. Function. In *Current anthropology,* ed. W. L. Thomas, Jr., pp. 237-58. A supplement to *Anthropology Today.* Chicago: University of Chicago Press, 1956.

———. *Social change in Tikopia: Re-study of a Polynesian community after a generation.* London: George Allen & Unwin, 1959.

Fromm, E. Psychoanalytic characterology and its application to the understanding of culture. In *Culture and personality,* eds. S. S. Sargent and M. W. Smith, Reprint. New York: Bobbs-Merrill, 1949.

Geertz, C. The impact of the concept of culture on the concept of man. In *Man in adaptation. The cultural present,* ed. Y. A. Cohen, pp. 16-29. Chicago: Aldine Publishing Company, 1968.

Goldschmidt, W. Anthropology and the modern world. In *Cultural and social anthropology: Selected readings,* ed. P. B. Hammond, pp.

480-88. New York: Macmillan Co., 1964.

Goodenough, W. H. *Cooperation in change.* New York: Russell Sage Foundation, 1963.

————. Rethinking "status" and "role": Toward a general model of the cultural organization of social relationships. In *The relevance of models for social anthropology,* ed. M. Banton, pp. 1-24. London: Tavistock Publications, 1965.

Hall, E. T. *The silent language.* Greenwich, Conn.: Fawcett Publications, 1959.

Hallowell, A. I. Culture and personality. In P. B. Hammond (ed.) *Cultural and social anthropology: Selected readings,* pp. 451-64. New York: Macmillan Co., 1964.

Hammond, P. B., ed. *Cultural and social anthropology: Selected readings.* New York: Macmillan Co., 1964.

Herskovits, M. J. For the historical approach in anthropology: A critical case. In *Cultural and social anthropology. Selected readings,* ed. P. B. Hammond, pp. 436-43. New York: Macmillan Co., 1964.

Honigmann, J. J. *Personality in culture.* New York: Harper & Row, 1967.

Howells, W. W. Universality and variation in human nature. In *Current Anthropology,* ed. W. L. Thomas, Jr., pp. 227-36. A supplement to *Anthropology Today.* Chicago: University of Chicago Press, 1956.

Kluckhohn, C.; Murray, H. A.; and Schneider, D. M. *Personality in nature, society, and culture.* 2nd ed. New York: Alfred A. Knopf, 1954.

Koppers, W. Diffusion: Transmission and acceptance. In *Current Anthropology,* ed. W. L. Thomas, Jr., pp. 169-81. A supplement to *Anthropology Today.* Chicago: University of Chicago Press, 1956.

Kroeber, A. L. What culture is. In *Man in adaptation. The cultural present,* ed. Y. A. Cohen, pp. 13-16. Chicago: Aldine Publishing Company, 1968.

Levi-Strauss, C. *The savage mind.* Chicago: University of Chicago Press, 1966.

Lindzey, G., and Aronson, E., eds. *The handbook of social psychology.* 2nd ed. The individual in a social context, vol. 3. Reading, Mass.: Addison-Wesley, 1969.

Lloyd, P. C. *Africa in social change.* Baltimore: Penguin Books, 1967.

Mead, M. *New lives for old. Cultural transformation—Manus, 1928-1953.* New York: William Morrow, Mentor Books, 1956.

Miller, G. A., and McNeill, D. Psycholinguistics. In *The handbook of social psychology,* ed. G. Lindzey and E. Aronson, pp. 666-794. The individual in a social context, 2nd ed., vol. 3. Reading, Mass.: Addison-Wesley, 1969.

Montesquieu, Charles Louis de Secondat. Persian and Chinese letters transl. by Davidson, J., Washington and London: Universal Classics Library, 1901.

Murdock, G. P. *Social structure.* New York: Macmillan Co., 1960.

————. Changing emphases in the study of social structure. In *Cultural and social anthropology: Selected readings,* ed. A. B. Hammond, pp. 444-50. New York: Macmillan Co., 1964.

McClelland, D. C. *The achieving society.* New York: D. Van Nostrand, 1961.

Redfield, R. *The primitive world and its transformations.* Ithaca, N.Y.: Cornell University Press, 1953.

Steward, J. H. The concept and method of cultural ecology. In *Cultural and social anthropology. Selected readings,* ed. P. B. Hammond, pp. 427-36. New York: Macmillan Co., 1964.

Tajfel, H. Social and cultural factors in perception. In *The handbook of social psychology,* ed. G. Lindzey and E. Aronson, pp. 315-94. The individual in a social context, 2nd ed., vol. 3. Reading, Mass.: Addison-Wesley, 1969.

Tax, S. The integration of anthropology. In *Current anthropology,* ed. pp. 313-28. W. L. Thomas, Jr. A supplement to *Anthropology Today.* Chicago: University of Chicago Press, 1956.

Tax, S.; Eiseley, L. C.; Rouse, I.; and Voegelin, C. F., eds. *An appraisal of anthropology today.* Chicago: University of Chicago Press, 1953.

Thomas, Jr., W. L., ed. *Current anthropology.* A supplement to *Anthropology Today.* Chicago: University of Chicago Press, 1956.

von Mering, O., and Kasdan, L., eds. *Anthropology and the behavioral and health sciences.* Pittsburgh: University of Pittsburgh Press, 1970.

Wallace, A. F. C. *Culture and personality.* 2nd ed. New York: Random House, 1970.

White, L. A. The evolution of culture. In *Cultural and social anthropology: Selected readings,* ed. P. B. Hammond, pp. 406-26. New York: Macmillan Co., 1964.

Wharf, B. L. *Language, thought, and reality: Selected writings of Benjamin Lee Wharf.* Ed. J. B. Carroll. Cambridge, Mass.: M. I. T. Press, 1956.

Zigler, E., and Child, I. L. Socialization. In *The handbook of social psychology,* ed. G. Lindzey and E. Aronson, pp. 450-589. The individual in a social context, 2nd ed., Vol. 3. Reading, Mass.: Addison-Wesley, 1969.

Chapter 6. The Anatomy of Society

Barber, B. *Social stratification: A comparative analysis of structure and process.* New York: Harcourt, Brace & World, 1957.

Bendix, R., and Lipset, S. M., eds. *Class, status, and power.* 2nd ed. New York: Free Press, 1966.

Bronfenbrenner, U. Socialization and social class through time and space. In *Basic studies in social psychology,* ed. H. Proshansky and B. Seidenberg. New York: Holt, Rinehart & Winston, 1965.

Brown, R. *Social psychology.* New York: Free Press, 1965.

Campbell, A.; Converse, P. E.; Miller, W. E.; and Stokes, D. E. *The American voter.* New York: Wiley, 1960.

————. *Elections and the political order.* New York: Wiley, 1966.

Centers, R. *The psychology of social classes. A study of class consciousness.* Princeton, N.J.: Princeton University Press, 1949.

Coleman, R. P., and Neugarten, B. L. *Social status in the city.* San Francisco: Jossey-Bass, 1971.

Dahrendorf, R. *Class and class conflict in industrial society.* Stanford, Calif.: Stanford University Press, 1959.

————. Marx's theory of class. In *Readings on social statification,* ed. M. M. Tumin. Englewood Cliffs, N.J.: Prentice-Hall, 1970.

Davis, A., Gardner, B. B., and Gardner, M. R. The class system of the white caste. In *Basic studies in social psychology,* ed. H. Proshansky and B. Seidenberg. New York: Holt, Rinehart & Winston, 1965.

Davis, K., and Moore, W. E. Some principles of stratification. In *Readings on social stratification,* ed. M. M. Tumin. Englewood Cliffs, N.J.: Prentice-Hall, 1970.

Djilas, M. *The new class.* New York: Frederick A. Praeger, 1957.

Goldthorpe, J. H.; Lockwood, D.; Bechhofer, F.; and Platt, J. *The affluent worker in the class structure.* Cambridge Studies in Sociology, vol. 3. London: Cambridge University Press, 1969.

Gordon, M. M. *Social class in American sociology.* Durham, N.C.: Duke University Press, 1958.

Hodges, J. M., Jr. *Social stratification: Class in America.* Cambridge, Mass.: Schenkman, 1964.

Hollingshead, A. B., and Redlich, F. C. *Social class and mental illness.* New York: Wiley, 1957.

————. Social stratification and psychiatric disorders. In *Basic studies in social psychology,* ed. H. Proshansky and B. Seidenberg. New York: Holt, Rinehart & Winston, 1965.

Kohn, M. L. *Class and conformity: A study in values.* Homewood, Ill.: Dorsey Press, 1969.

Lasswell, T. E. Variable meanings of social class. In *Readings on social stratification,* ed. M. M. Tumin. Englewood Cliffs, N.J.: Prentice-Hall, 1970.

Lazarsfeld, P. F., Berelson, B. and Gaudet, H. *The people's choice.* New York: Columbia University Press, 1948.

Lenski, G. E. *Power and privilege: A theory of social stratification.* New York: McGraw-Hill, 1966.

Myers, J. K., and Roberts, B. H. *Family and class dynamics in mental illness.* New York: Wiley, 1959.

Stein, M. R. *The eclipse of community: An interpretation of American studies.* Princeton, N.J.: Princeton University Press, 1960.

Tumin, M. M. *Social stratification: The forms and functions of inequality.* Englewood Cliffs, N.J.: Prentice-Hall, 1967.

————. Some principles of stratification: A critical analysis. In *Readings on social stratification,* ed. M. M. Tumin, Englewood Cliffs, N.J.: Prentice-Hall, 1970.

Chapter 7. Social Interaction

Argyle, M. *Social interaction.* Chicago: Aldine Publishing Co., 1969.

Cattell, Raymond. *Scientific analysis of personality.* Baltimore: Penguin, 1965.

Dunphy, Dexter C. *The primary group: A handbook for analysis and field research.* New York: Appleton-Century-Crofts, 1972.

Goffman, E. *The presentation of self in everyday life.* Garden City, N.Y.: Doubleday, 1959.

————. *Encounters: Two studies in the sociology of interaction.* Indianapolis, Ind.: Bobbs-Merrill, 1961.

————. *Behavior in public places: Notes on the social organization of gatherings.* New York: Free Press of Glencoe, 1963.

————. *Strategic interaction.* Philadelphia: University of Pennsylvania Press, 1969.

Jones, E. E., and Gerard, H. B. *Foundations of social psychology.* New York: Wiley, 1967.

Kelley, H. H. The process of causal attribution. *American Psychologist,* 1973, 28:107-28.

Mischel, Walter, *Introduction to personality.* New York: Holt, 1971.

————. Toward a cognitive social learning reconceptualization of personality. *Psychological Review,* 1973, 80:252-83.

Secord, P. F., and Backman, C. W. *Social psychology.* New York: McGraw-Hill, 1960.

Thibaut, J. W., and Riecken, J. W. Some determinants and consequences of the perception of social causality. *Journal of Personality,* 1955, 29:113-33.

Chapter 8. The Study of Groups

Banton, M., ed. *The relevance of models for social anthropology.* London: Tavistock Publications, 1963.

Etzioni, A. *The active society: A theory of societal and political processes.* New York: Free Press, 1968.

Golembiewski, R. T. *The small group: An analysis of research concepts and operations.* Chicago: University of Chicago Press, 1962.

Hare, P. A. *Handbook of small group research.* New York: Free Press of Glencoe, 1962.

Hare, P. A., Borgatta, E. F., and Bales, R. F., eds. *Small groups: Studies in social interaction.* New York: Alfred A. Knopf, 1965.

Homans, G. C. *Social behavior: Its elementary forms.* New York: Harcourt, Brace & World, 1961.

Horowitz, I. L., and Strong, M. S. eds. *Sociological realities: A guide to the study of society.* New York: Harper & Row, 1971.

Hyman, H. H., and Singer, E. *Readings in reference group theory and research.* New York: Free Press, 1968.

Lewin, K. *Resolving social conflicts.* New York: Harper, 1948.

Likert, R. *New patterns of management.* New York: McGraw-Hill, 1961.
Manis, J. G., and Meltzer, B. N. *Symbolic interaction: A reader in social psychology.* Boston: Allyn and Bacon, 1967.
Merton, R. K. *Social theory and social structure.* New York: Free Press, 1968.
Mills, T. M. *The sociology of small groups.* Englewood Cliffs, N.J., Prentice-Hall, 1967.
Olmstead, M. S. *The small group.* New York: Random House, 1959.
Roby, T. B. *Small group performance.* Chicago: Rand McNally & Co., 1968.
Zander, A. *Motives and goals in groups.* New York: Academic Press, 1971.

Chapter 9. The Elements of a Functioning Community

Agger, R. E., Goldrich, D., and Swanson, B. E. *The rulers and the ruled.* New York: Wiley, 1964.
Dahl, R. A. *Pluralist democracy in the United States.* Chicago: Rand McNally & Co., 1967.
Golembiewski, R. T., Welsh, W. A., and Crotty, W. J. *A methodological primer for political scientists.* Chicago: Rand McNally & Co., 1969.
Lindblom, C. E. *The intelligence of democracy.* New York: Free Press, 1965.
————. *The policy-making process.* Englewood Cliffs, N.J.: Prentice-Hall, 1968.
Miller, D. W., and Starr, M. K. *The structure of human decisions.* Englewood Cliffs, N.J.: Prentice-Hall, 1967.
Mills, C. Wright. *Power politics and people.* New York: Oxford University Press, 1963.
Parsons, M. B., ed. *Perspectives in the study of politics.* Chicago: Rand McNally & Co., 1968.
Pennock, J. R., and Smith, D. G. *Political science.* New York: Macmillan Co., 1964.
Simon, Herbert A. *The new science of management decisions.* New York: Harper & Row, 1960.

Chapter 10. The Interstate Highway System

Buel, R. A. *Dead end: The automobile in mass transportation.* Baltimore: Penguin Books, 1972.
Dahl, R. A. *Pluralist democracy in the United States.* Chicago: Rand McNally & Co., 1967.
Friedlaender, A. F. *The interstate highway system.* Amsterdam: North-Holland Co., 1965.
Healy, K. T. *The economics of transportation in America.* New York: Ronald Press, 1940.
Kantorovich, L. V. *The best use of economic resources.* Cambridge, Mass.: Harvard University Press, 1965.

Lansing, J. B. *Transportation and economic policy.* New York: Free Press, 1966.

Leavitt, H. *Superhighway-superhoax.* Garden City, N.J.: Doubleday, 1970.

Locklin, P. D. *Economics of transportation.* Homewood, Ill: Richard D. Irwin, 1966.

Luna, C. *The UTU handbook of transportation in America.* New York: Popular Library, 1971.

Masannant, G. S., ed. *Basic issues in American public policy.* Boston: Holbrook Press, 1970.

Chapter 11. Criteria for a Good Society

Benello, C. G., and Roussoupoulos, D. eds. *The case for participatory democracy.* New York: Grossman Publishers, 1971.

Buckley, William F. *The jeweler's eye.* New York: Putnam, 1968.

Commoner, B. *The closing circle: Nature, man, and technology.* New York: Bantam Books, 1968.

Dahl, R. A. *After the revolution.* New Haven, Conn.: Yale University Press, 1970.

Doxiadis, C. Ekistics: The science of human settlements. *Science,* 1970, 170:393-404.

Eells, R., and Walton, C. eds. *Man in the city of the future.* New York: Macmillan Co., 1968.

Ellul, J. *The technological society.* New York: Random House, 1967.

Goodman, P. *Growing up absurd.* New York: Random House, 1962.

Hardin, G. The tragedy of the commons. *Science,* 1968, 162:1243-48.

Helfrich, H. W., Jr., ed. *The environmental crisis.* New Haven, Conn.: Yale University Press, 1970.

Neill, A. S. *Summerhill: A radical approach to child rearing.* New York: Hart Publishing, 1960.

Skinner, B. F. *Beyond freedom and dignity.* New York: Knopf, 1971.

Surtz, E. *The praise of pleasure.* Cambridge, Mass.: Harvard University Press, 1957.

Walsh, C. *From utopia to nightmare.* New York: Harper & Row, 1962.

Chapter 12. Utopias

Bailey, J. O. *Pilgrims through space and time.* New York: Argus Books, 1947.

Bellamy, Edward. *Looking backward.* Boston: Houghton Mifflin, 1888.

Boguslaw, R. *The new utopians.* Englewood Cliffs, N.J.: Prentice-Hall, 1965.

Butler, S. *Erewhon.* New York: Penguin, 1976.

Chianese, R., ed. *Peaceable kingdom: An anthology of utopian writings.* New York: Harcourt Brace Jovanovich, 1971.

Gallagher, L. *More's* Utopia *and its critics.* Chicago: Scott, Foresman, 1964.

Haworth, L. *The good city.* Bloomington: Indiana University Press, 1963.
Huxley, A. *Brave new world.* New York: Harpers, 1932.
Mannheim, K. *Ideology and utopia.* New York: Harcourt, Brace and Co., 1936.
Manuel, F. *Utopias and utopian thought.* Boston: Houghton Mifflin Co., 1966.
Marcuse, H. The end of utopia. In *Five lectures.* Boston: Beacon Press, 1970.
More, T. *Utopia.* New York: Dutton, 1975.
Morley, H., ed. *Ideal commonwealths:* New York: George Routledge, 1886.
Morris, W. *News from nowhere.* Baltimore: Penguin Books, 1962.
Morton, A. L. *The English utopia.* London: Lawrence & Wishart, 1952.
Mumford, L. *The story of utopias.* New York: Peter Smith, 1941.
Nelson, W., ed. *Twentieth-century interpretations of utopia.* Englewood Cliffs, N.J.: Prentice-Hall, 1968.
Orwell, G. *1984.* New York: Harcourt Brace, 1949.
Plato. *The Republic.* New York: Basic Books, 1968.
Sarason, S. B. *The creation of settings and the future societies.* San Francisco: Josey-Bass, 1972.
Skinner, B. F. *Walden II.* New York: Macmillan Co., 1948.
———. *Beyond freedom and dignity.* New York: Alfred A. Knopf, 1971.
Vonnegut, K. *Player piano.* New York: Delacorte, 1971.
Walsh, C. *From utopia to nightmare.* New York: Harper & Row, 1962.
Webber, E. *Escape to utopia.* New York: Hastings House, 1959.
Weiss, M. *A lively corpse.* Cranbury, N.J.: A. S. Barnes & Co., 1969.
Wells, H. G. *A modern utopia.* Lincoln: University of Nebraska Press, 1967.
Zamiatin, Eugene I. *We.* Transl. by Gregory Zilboorg. New York: Dutton, 1959.

Chapter 13. Some Attempts at New Social Forms

Adizes, I. *Industrial democracy, Yugoslav style.* New York: Free Press, 1971.
Bettelheim, B. *The children of the dream.* London: Macmillan & Co., 1969.
Bourdet, C. Yugoslavia: Experiments with liberty. *Nation,* September 1971, pp. 234-38.
Bronfenbrenner, U., and Mahoney, M. A. *Influences on human development.* 2nd ed. Hinsdale, Ill.: Dryden Press, 1975.
Butterfield, F. Reporter's notebook: A visit to Canton illumines only the surface of Chinese politics. *New York Times,* 16 May 1976.
Convening and preparatory committee of the second congress of self-managers of Yugoslavia. Summaries of analytical texts prepared for the congress. Belgrade: 1971.
Elon, A. *The Israelis: Founders and sons.* New York: Holt, Rinehart, and Winston, 1971.

Fan, K. H., and Fan, K. T. *From the other side of the river: A self-portrait of China today.* New York: Doubleday, Anchor Books, 1975.

Fein, L. J. *Israel: Politics and people.* Boston: Little, Brown, 1967.

Fleisher, F. *The new Sweden: The challenge of a disciplined democracy.* New York: David McKay, 1967.

Furubotn, E. G., and Pejovich, S. A. Tax policy and investment decisions of the Yugoslav firm. *National Tax Journal,* 1970, 23:335-348.

———. The formation and distribution of net product and the behavior of the Yugoslav firm. *Yearbook of East-European Economics,* vol. 3, 1972:265-288.

———. Property rights and economic theory: A survey of recent literature. *The Journal of Economic Literature,* 1972, 10:1137-1162.

———. Property rights, economic decentralization, and the evolution of the Yugoslav firm, 1965-1972. *The Journal of Law and Economics,* 1973, 16:275-302.

Gerskovic, L. *Social and economic system in Yugoslavia.* Belgrade: Publishing House Jugoslavia, 1960.

Horvat, B. *Essay on Yugoslav society.* White Plains, N.Y.: International Arts and Sciences Press, 1969.

Hunnius, G. The Yugoslav system of decentralization and self-management. In *The Case for Participatory Democracy,* ed. C. George Benello and Dimitrios Roussopoulos, pp. 140-177. New York: Grossman Publishers, 1971.

Jenkins, D. *Sweden and the price of progress.* New York: Coward-McCann, 1968.

Källberg, S. *Off the middle way: Report from a Swedish village.* New York: Pantheon, 1972.

Kanovsky, E. *The economy of the Israeli kibbutz.* Cambridge, Mass.: Harvard University Press, 1966.

Kessen, W. *Childhood in China.* New Haven, Conn.: Yale University Press, 1975.

Lindbeck, J. M. *China: Management of a revolutionary society.* Seattle: University of Washington Press, 1971.

London, M., and London, I. D. China's lost generation: The fate of the Red Guards since 1968. *Saturday Review-World,* 30 November 1974, pp. 12-19.

Myrdal, J. The reshaping of Chinese society. *Bulletin of the Atomic Scientists,* June 1966, pp. 76-79.

Neuberger, E. *The Yugoslav visible hand system: Why is it no more?* International Development Research Center, Working Papers, no. 3, April 1971.

Neuberger, E., and James, E. *The Yugoslav self-managed enterprise: A systematic approach.* International Development Research Center, Working Papers, no. 4, May 1971.

New, P. K., and New, M. L. The links between health and the political structure of new China. *Human Organization,* 1975, 34:237-51.

Oksenberg, M. *China's developmental experience.* New York: The Academy of Political Science, Columbia University, 1973.

Pejovich, S. *The market-planned economy of Yugoslavia.* Minneapolis: University of Minnesota Press, 1966.

Popovic, M. D. *Yugoslavia: The new class in crisis.* Syracuse, N.Y.: Syracuse University Press, 1968.

Samuelsson, K. *From great power to welfare state.* London: Allen & Unwin, 1968.

Shouval, R.; Kav Venaki, S.; Bronfenbrenner, U.; Devereux, E. C.; and Kiely, E. Anomalous reactions to social pressure of Israeli and Soviet children raised in family versus collective settings. *Journal of Personality and Social Psychology,* 1975, 32:447-89.

Snow, E. China's communes, success or failure? *The New Republic,* 26 June 1971, pp. 19-23.

Soinit, A. Wear and tear in the commune. *The Nation.* 26 April 1971, pp. 524-527.

Spiro, M. E. *Children of the kibbutz.* Cambridge, Mass.: Harvard University Press, 1975.

Stern, S. The kibbutz: Not by ideology alone. *New York Times Magazine,* 6 May 1973, pp. 36-37.

Suyin, H. Reflections on social change. *Bulletin of the Atomic Scientists,* June 1966, pp. 80-83.

Tornquist, D. *Look east, look west: The socialist adventure in Yugoslavia.* New York: Macmillan Co., 1966.

———. Strikes in Yugoslavia. *Working Papers for a New Society,* 1975, 3:50-61.

Willen, P. Introduction to *Anatomy of a Moral,* by Milovan Djilas, ed. Abraham Rothberger. New York: Praeger, 1959.

The Yugoslav commune. *Unesco—International Social Science Journal,* 1961, 13:3 pp. 379-474.

Andelman, D. A. UN studying simple energy sources for the rural poor of Southeast Asia. *New York Times,* 21 October 1975.

Back, K. W. *Beyond words.* New York: Russell Sage Foundation, 1972.

Blumberg, P. *Industrial democracy: The sociology of participation.* New York: Schocken, 1974.

Campbell, A.; Converse, P. E.; and Rodgers, W. L. *The quality of American life: Perception, evaluations, and satisfactions.* New York: Russell Sage Foundation, 1976.

Cass, E. L., and Zimmer, F. G. *Man and work in society.* New York: Van Nostrand Reinhold Co., 1975.

Chianese, R. L. *Peaceable kingdoms: An anthology of utopian writings.* New York: Harcourt Brace Jovanovich, 1971.

Etzkowitz, H. *Is America possible?* St. Paul, Minn.: West Publishing Co., 1974.

Fuller, R. B. *Operating manual for spaceship earth.* New York: Pocket Books, 1970.

Galbraith, J. K. *Economics and the public purpose.* Boston: Houghton Mifflin, 1973.
Herrick, N. Q. Activities to enrich work in other developed countries. Paper read at 138th meeting, American Association for the Advancement of Science, 27 December 1971, at the U.S. Department of Labor, Washington, D.C.
Journal of the New Alchemists. Woods Hole, Mass.: New Alchemy Institute, 1974.
Levi, L., and Andersson, L. *Psychosocial stress: Population, environment, and quality of life.* New York: Spectrum Publications, 1975.
Mesarovic, M., and Pestel, E. *Mankind at the turning point.* The Second Report to The Club of Rome. New York: E. F. Dutton & Co., Reader's Digest Press, 1974.
Miller, G. T. *Replenish the earth: A primer in human ecology.* Belmont, Calif.: Wadsworth Publishing Co., 1972.
———. *Living in the environment: Concepts, problems, and alternatives.* Belmont, Calif.: Wadsworth Publishing Co., 1975.
Moos, R. H., and Insel, P. M. *Issues in social ecology: Human milieus.* Palo Alto, Calif.: National Press Books, 1974.
Myrdal, G. *Against the stream: Critical essays on economics.* New York: Pantheon Books, 1972.
Rangan, K. Gas unit using cow dung gaining on India's farms. *New York Times,* 21 October 1975.
Richter, P. E. *Utopias: Social ideals and communal experiments.* Boston: Holbrook Press, 1971.
Roberts, R. E. *The new communes: Coming together in America.* Englewood Cliffs, N.J.: Prentice-Hall, 1971.
Sheldon, E. B., and Parke, R. Social indicators. *Science,* 1975, 188: 693-99.
Skinner, B. F. *The design of cultures.* Andover, Mass.: A Warner Modular Publication, 1973. Daedalus, Summer-reprint ed.
Strumpel, B. *Economic means for human needs: Social indicators of well-being and discontent.* Ann Arbor: Survey Research Center, Institute for Social Research, The University of Michigan, 1976.
Tannenbaum, A. S. *Control in organizations.* New York: McGraw-Hill, 1968.

Index

311